THE COLOR OF SOUND

The Color of Sound

Race, Religion, and Music in Brazil

John Burdick

NEW YORK UNIVERSITY PRESS
New York and London

NEW YORK UNIVERSITY PRESS
New York and London
www.nyupress.org

References to Internet websites (URLs) were accurate at the time of writing.
Neither the author nor New York University Press is responsible for URLs
that may have expired or changed since the manuscript was prepared.

LIBRARY OF CONGRESS CATALOGING-IN-PUBLICATION DATA
Burdick, John, 1959-
The color of sound : race, religion, and music in Brazil / John Burdick.
p. cm.
Includes bibliographical references and index.
ISBN 978-0-8147-0922-1 (cl : alk. paper) — ISBN 978-0-8147-0923-8 (p : alk. paper) — ISBN
978-0-8147-0924-5 (e-book) — ISBN 978-0-8147-2313-5 (e-book)
1. Gospel music—Brazil—History and criticism. 2. Blacks—Brazil—Music. 3. Blacks—
Brazil—Religion. 4. Evangelicalism—Brazil. I. Title.
ML3187.B85 2011
782.25'40981—dc23   2012027273

New York University Press books are printed on acid-free paper,
and their binding materials are chosen for strength and durability.
We strive to use environmentally responsible suppliers and materials
to the greatest extent possible in publishing our books.

Manufactured in the United States of America

c 10 9 8 7 6 5 4 3 2 1
p 10 9 8 7 6 5 4 3 2 1

CONTENTS

In 1996, I spent a year in Brazil researching the delicate interrelations between religious belief and racial identity among people who identified as Christians. While engaged in that project, I came across a small, budding movement of evangelical Protestants based in São Paulo who were inspired by their theology to struggle against racial injustice and to build a proud black identity. What I found intriguing about this movement— its participants were at the time just beginning to identify themselves as the *movimento negro evangélico*, or MNE—was that it was embedded in a religious context that most black movement organizations had dismissed as deeply hostile to their cause. The main sticking point, from the black movement's point of view, was evangelicals' attitude toward the Afro-Brazilian religions of candomblé and umbanda. I was keenly aware that evangelicals preached against these religions and that some denominations, such as the Igreja Universal do Reino de Deus, had been implicated in direct iconoclastic assaults on Afro-Brazilian temples. While I found such assaults repugnant, the example of the MNE persuaded me that evangelicals' rejection, on theological grounds, of Afro-Brazilian mediumship religion was not itself an insurmountable barrier to the development of strong antiracist and problack views.

Yet for years, whenever I spoke in public about the MNE, I found myself met with strong skepticism. Some colleagues implied that I had been hoodwinked, taken in by evangelical leaders who cared little about the struggle against racism and played the race card merely to garner souls and offerings for their churches. While my own experience suggested that the MNE was rather more complex than that—the depth and durability of the antiracist commitments of people like Hernani da Silva or Rolf da Souza showed that the MNE could not be explained away as simply another missionary stratagem—no one was trying to document that complexity. So in 2002 I decided to embark on an effort to discover what made the MNE tick ideologically, that is, how and why its participants were moved to fight collectively through some amalgam of theology and ethnoracial experience.

As I began the study, it struck me that what I needed to do was to find a dimension of the everyday cultural lifeworld of evangelicals which had different effects on identity. My eventual decision to focus on music was not an easy one. For a few years, I avoided looking systematically at music at all. As someone who had spent years thinking about social practices that matter in people's everyday lives—what I regarded as tough, sinewy things such as labor, religion, kinship, politics—the idea that music might be, on its own, an important social force seemed dubious to me. Anyone who has sat through a musical performance is aware of the peculiar evanescence of music, its fleeting, temporary quality, making it seem a rather weak reed on which to hang things as weighty as political consciousness and social identity. Several things, however, ultimately convinced me that music would be a fruitful channel of investigation into the evangelicals' social world. First, I realized that while music might be experienced fleetingly by an audience, it was part of the very structure of life for serious musicians and artists. I became mindful, as well, that even if music were secondary in my own life, it was central to the lives of many evangelicals, for whom music was constant company both inside and outside church. And I became aware that even if I was not absolutely certain of the deep importance of music, this uncertainty was in no way shared by my informants. Anytime I began a conversation about music with an evangelical, I was treated to a rush of warm, deep, complex ideas, views, opinions, and claims. If music was not as weighty a factor in the lives of my informants as occupation, food, or employment, they had not received the memo.

If these considerations allayed my concerns, I still had one more hurdle. I am not a trained ethnomusicologist. Though I can read music and have made it my job for the past eight years to read ethnomusicology, I am in general innocent of the technical apparatuses that give ethnomusicology its gravitas. I am also not a practicing musician. It is daunting to pick up volumes written by ethnomusicologists and to learn from their prefaces about all the amateur (and semiprofessional) music-making they have done. I bring to this study not the insights of a ethnomusicologist but those of a social anthropologist who pays close attention to the valued cultural practices of the people I am striving to understand. My hope is that this point of view may allow me to bring freshness to the observation of the daily social practices implicated in musical scenes. Whether I have succeeded I leave to the reader to decide.

Naturally some readers will want to know why I, a white North American, am interested in the politics of blackness at all, let alone black politics in Brazil. To the extent that I can know my biases and motivations in this regard, here they are. I grew up as a Jew in the US Midwest in the 1960s, surrounded by evidence of the consequences of racism. In 1967, I saw tanks roll down Woodward Avenue in Detroit after the city exploded in race riots, and in 1971 I saw buses firebombed in my home city of Pontiac because they were going to be used to desegregate the public schools. My father ran (and lost) for school board that year on a platform of school desegregation, and every spring for many years, our family celebrated Passover by inviting members of local chapters of the NAACP and CORE to talk about the similarities between the struggles of Moses and Martin Luther King Jr. I also read Cleaver and Baldwin and Wright and Malcolm X and Haley and Hansberry and Morrison.

All of this laid down in my brain what some critics might call an "American" way of looking at race. But it also instilled in me something more important: an understanding that the devastation wrought by racism is often hidden deep within the human heart, and that the privileges that accrue to whiteness are commonly shrouded in layers of self-delusion and denial. These are the things I have seen for the past twenty-five years not only in the United States but in Brazil as well. I have been told more times than I can count that "race is different in Brazil than in the United States" and that I must not impose my own culture's racial paradigm (including the rule of hypodescent) where it does not belong. I assure the reader that I fully agree. Indeed, I have spent the better part of the past quarter century striving to understand the distinctive complexities of the Brazilian color and phenotypical system. I have written about the subjectivity of *morenas* and *mulatas*, which has no clear correlate in the United States. What I have not forgotten, however, is that Brazil, like the United States, participated for hundreds of years, and continues to participate, in a global system in which phenotypical similarity to the most socially powerful people in the world—Europeans and their descendants—is a channel to unearned authority and power. The Brazilian system may thus be very different from that of the United States, but it is also profoundly similar. Twenty-five years of listening to the testimony of Brazilians from all walks of life have convinced me that the pain of suffering indignities due to how one looks is as bad in Brazil as it is in the United States. And so is the blindness of white people. So those are my biases and motivations. I have striven over the years to be as aware of them as possible. Whether I have succeeded in this book I also leave to the reader to judge.

All research projects, even those not undertaken by a team, are inevitably deeply social. Gathering and reflecting on the material for this book has been among the most rewarding social experiences of my life. Since I began work on this project in the early 2000s, I have had the honor of learning from a large number of activists, pastors, scholars, politicians, and colleagues, in the United States and in Brazil. I will only name here those who have made a special or sustained contribution to this project. I would never have begun research on this topic without the stimulus and encouragement of Hernani da Silva and Rolf da Souza, whose work at the intersection of scholarship and activism continues to be an inspiration to me. Sérgio Melo, pastor of the Church of God in Christ (COGIC), offered support, advice, and *cafezinhos* for over five years. David Ramos, ex-pastor of Pedra Vida, was a source of insight into all matters racial and theological. I was also honored to be supported by Marco Davi (Igreja Batista), Pastor Josías (Brasil Para Cristo), Pastor Joilson (Mintre), Pastor João Adel (Pão da Vida), Daniela Zeidan (Pão da Vida), and Luiz de Jesus (Pão da Vida). On the hip hop scene, Pregador Luo and Cristina Borge (Tina) provided guidance way beyond the call of duty. Others on the scene who provided help long after their interviews were over include Adimilson (Gênesis), Will (Disparo Fatal), Professor Pablo, Pastor Anderson, Fábio, Preto Jay, DJ Alpiste, Pretto, Vilmar Junior, the brothers of Família Jesus Cristo (FJC), and Gabriel da Fé. On the black gospel scene, I received extraordinary support from Sérgio Saas, Ferrisbeck, Silveira, Isabêh, Débora, and Priscilla. On the samba gospel scene, many thanks to Jairo and the members of Deus Crioulos. Legislative deputy Claudete Alves went out of her way to help me understand the political implications of evangelicalism. Halley Margon provided comfort, good cheer, and a place to sleep whenever I made it to Rio de Janeiro.

Over the years, this work has been enriched through the criticism and feedback of numerous scholars. In Brazil, the project benefited from input by Batista, Marcia Pinheiro, Vagner Gonçalves, Sérgio Guimarães, Yvonne Maggie, Olivia Da Cunha, Marcia Contins, and the many master's students at the Universidade de São Paulo who shared with me copious libations and conversations about the *paulista* music scene. In the United States, this project has been enriched by the thoughtful criticisms of Carol Babiracki, Kia Caldwell, John Collins, Kwame Dixon, Jan French, Sydney Hutchinson,

Corey Lafevers, Jeffrey Lesser, Derek Pardue, Keisha Khan Perry, Patricia Pinho, Karen Rosemblatt, Stephen Selka, David Smilde, Christen Smith, and Peter Wade. I have benefited over the years from the more general collegial support of Kwame Dixon, Stephen Parks, Deborah Pellow, Tom Perreault, and Robert A. Rubinstein. Any merit the work possesses is due mainly to the good sense of all these people; any flaws are due to my failure to heed that good sense. The field research for this project was supported by a Fulbright-Hays Faculty Research Abroad Grant #3532366.

A special thanks to my mother, Dolores Burdick, for serving as first proofreader and editor of the book manuscript. My father, Harvey Burdick, continues to inspire me to more challenging projects. Over the years this one has been a source of both joy and stress. For helping me to feel the joy and deal with the stress, I thank Judy, Ben, Molly, and Fred.

Introduction

Something 'Bout the Name of Jesus: Racial Meanings and Brazilian Evangelical Musical Scenes

The Way It Is

I am in the home of Angélica, a gospel singer in her late twenties. It is late afternoon, and the light in her living room is dying, but neither of us is able to get up to turn on the overhead light, because we are in the vortex of a musical whirlpool, swept in circles by the recorded voice of Rance Allen. Angélica closes her eyes as Allen's silvery baritone belts,

> There's something 'bout the name of Jesus
> It is the sweetest name I know

Angélica's eyebrows rise and knit, as if she is asking a painful question. Allen's voice on the CD continues, shifting from silver to gravel:

> Oh, how I love the name Jesus

> Oh, how I love the name Jesus
> It is the sweetest name I know

We listen, our eyes shut, and soon the song is over. "I play this all the time," Angélica finally says, coming up for air. "I don't know why. I can't understand the words. But when this voice is here with me, I feel the presence of God." She presses the old, big CD player's replay button, and the music swells again. She turns it down a bit so we can talk, and the voice continues to envelop us.

Angélica's house is located in the neighborhood of Capão Redondo, one of the many gritty, multiclass districts that lie in the sprawling southern zone of metropolitan São Paulo. It was only recently, after a messy divorce, that Angélica returned to this house, the place she grew up, to live with her mother and younger brother. I have known her for a couple of months, having visited her in church, to listen to her church's well-reputed R&B band, but mainly to hear her sing. Her voice, people say, is anointed by the Holy Spirit. All I know is that her singing raises the hair on the back of my neck.

Angélica's brother is at school, and her mother is running errands. It is a peaceful time of day, time to tell the story of how she fell in love with music. As she does so, Rance Allen's voice sounds in the background like a church organ, giving her words the feel of a prayer. She tells me how she felt the call at the age of seven to sing in church and how afterward an old lady had come to her. "You have the gift," the lady said. "The Lord is using you."

"How did the old lady's remark make you feel?" I ask. She looks away. Rance Allen's vocal cords are pounding full tilt.

"Angélica, we don't have to talk about this if you don't want to."

She shakes her head slowly.

"No, I want to talk about it. Put this in your book. You see, those ladies, they praised my voice. And I went home that day, and my father, he did not praise me. He criticized me. He said I should never get up there again, that no one wanted to hear a little *neguinha* [little black girl] make noise, that I should be quiet in church."

Then we are quiet.

Angélica's complexion is light, but other traits of hers indicate African ancestry. Her hair forms a crinkled halo close around her forehead and ears; her lips are full, her nose broad, her nostrils flared. Although she called herself *morena* while growing up, she now proudly calls herself *negra*.[1] The reason for the change in terminology? "The singing," she said. "When I saw what God was doing to me, filling me with the Holy Spirit, anointing me, I took pride in that. That gave me the courage to call myself *negra*."

That was in an earlier conversation. Today, memories of troubled years are coming back to her.

Finally I say something. "Your father said you shouldn't sing because you were a *neguinha*?"

She nods. "Yes. I was the ugly one. My father, a beautiful *branquelo* [big white guy], was ashamed of how I looked, always asked my mother, how did I turn out to be a *neguinha*, did she sleep with someone? They would fight; she had always been faithful. My mother is even lighter than I am. You have seen her, you know. . . . My father treated me like a slave. My sister always got to go study in her room after dinner, but not me. I had to do the dishes."[2]

Rance Allen's voice is swelling to a crescendo.

"But why, Angélica?"

She looks at me. Allen's voice comes crashing down.

"Because she was lighter than me. I was the ugly one. I had bad hair. My features were ugly. And I didn't understand. I would walk around the house with a little pocket mirror. I kept it with me. And when no one was looking, I would take it out, at the age of seven, eight, nine. I would take it out and look at it. And I would cry, looking and asking, 'Why, God, why have you made me so ugly? Why did you give me this skin, this hair? Why didn't you make me look like my sister?' I wanted so badly to be beautiful. But I was ugly, so I did the dishes, while my beautiful sister got to study. That is the way it is."[3]

A year before my conversation with Angélica, I had gotten to know Django, a dark-skinned *negro* in his forties, also in São Paulo, who had worked as a bank clerk for fifteen years and was a leading pastor at a Brasil Para Cristo church. One evening, seated in his brick house on an asphalt street in Tiradentes, a lower-middle-class neighborhood at the foot of a favela, he recounted to me moments that had been seared into his memory. As we sat in his living room, the television tuned to a soap opera, his two teenage daughters doing homework in the kitchen, his wife, Magali, preparing dinner, Django explained what had happened to him many years earlier.

"Her family was not happy, I can tell you, about her marrying a *negão* like me. So I would go over to her house—"

"My father couldn't stand it!" Magali called from the kitchen. "He wanted me to marry a nice white guy."

Django knitted his brow, pursed his lips. "Right," he said, "that's how it was. Never approved of me. I was too black [*preto*]. I didn't come from that pedigree. I remember I would go over there, to her house, and the looks I got from her father. And one time he had called me . . . well."

Magali entered the room. "My love, he didn't mean it. You know that. He was just joking." She looked at me. "One day he called Django a *macaco* [monkey]."

"That was unacceptable, Magali. You know that. You know that."

On another day Django spoke to me about his job. "See, I have been there at that bank for fifteen years. Fifteen! I know I do a good job, a very good job. In fifteen years, there has not been a *centavo* out of place. A lot of the other young ones, these girls, come and go—they don't have any loyalty to the place—but I do. They know that." He glanced at his hands. "So there are other tellers, younger than me, girls even. And they get advanced to head teller. Not me. And what is the difference? What is the only thing they have that I do not?" He bent over and grasped his glass of coffee. "Drink your coffee!" he commanded.

I begin with these two stories because they draw us into Brazil's heart of darkness: its deep, complex mistreatment of people with Afro-descended phenotypes. These stories remind us that discrimination on the basis of phenotype continues to infect the everyday lives of Brazilians, inside and out of families, leaving dull, aching wounds. Their stories remind us that in Brazil, for people with visibly African features, the experience of differential treatment creates scars that never entirely heal. As Angélica said, that's the way it is.

A Century of Struggle

Such is the dull ache, or sharp pain, that has kept the fight against antiblack racism in Brazil[4] going for over a century. Between 1888, the year Brazilian slavery was abolished, and the 1920s, Afro-Brazilians' effort to survive physically and psychically in Brazilian society expressed itself in a range of struggles, from anti-immigrant organizing and demands for an end to racial discrimination in education to the racially conscious press in São Paulo and the Frente Negra Brasileira (the Brazilian Black Front; Andrews 1991; Butler 1998; Hanchard 1994). Antiracist activism became more difficult in the 1930s, when Brazil's national ideology turned increasingly exceptionalist, asserting that the country's long history of miscegenation had made its people characterologically incapable of racism (Skidmore 1993; Dávila 2003). The 1940s and '50s saw efforts to challenge this ideology, including Abdias do Nascimento's Teatro Experimental do Negro (Black Experimental Theater), but a military coup in 1964 drastically limited all contestatory politics (Hanchard 1994). With political problack activism shut down, Afro-Brazilians who wished to express their racial pride turned to seemingly depoliticized cultural activities. Thus, in the early 1970s, the Black Rio dance movement expressed black pride among young people in Rio and São Paulo, and the Instituto de Pesquisas da Cultura Negra (the Institute for Research on Black Culture) organized symposia about African religions and musical traditions (Alberto 2009; Dunn 2001; Moore 1989; Pereira and Alberti 2007). When the dictatorship loosened its grip in the late 1970s, black political organizing revived in the form of the Movimento Negro Unificado (the Unified Black Movement) (Covin 2006), and after the dictatorship ended in 1985, there arose an expansive network of groups dedicated to combating racism and building a positive black identity (Damasceno and Santos 1988; Domingues 2007). Between 1985 and 1995, the agendas of these groups included challenging the myth of racial democracy, valorizing Afro-Brazilian culture, and ending racial discrimination in the labor market (Gomes 2011). During this period, the Brazilian government agreed to a variety of symbolic steps such as making into a national holiday the anniversary of the death of Zumbi, a leader of runaway slaves in the seventeenth century;[5] but when it came to addressing racial discrimination in the job market, it sat on its hands.

The year 1996 ushered in a new era. That year, President Fernando Henrique Cardoso, a sociologist who had studied racism, announced that Brazil was a racist society. Then, during the late 1990s, with the opening of the Brazilian economy to world markets, the desire to attract new investment, the aspiration to increase the nation's prestige on the world stage, the growth of the black middle class, and the increasing influence of international standards of human rights, Cardoso's call for steps to increase racial equality fell increasingly on sympathetic ears (Htun 2005). The tipping point came in 2001, when Brazil took part in the United Nations conference on racism in Durban, South Africa (Bairros 2002; Carneiro 2002). After that, the Brazilian government moved swiftly to institute policies designed to combat racial inequality. In 2003, with the arrival in power of the Partido dos Trabalhadores (Workers Party), these policies came to include support for

affirmative action at public universities, a public school curriculum that
included the history of Afro-Brazilians, the creation of a national ministry
dedicated to combating racism, and support for the passage of the Statute
for Racial Equality (Domingues 2007). Brazilians of African descent are
currently positioned to claim greater justice, opportunity, and equality than
ever before (Reiter and Mitchell 2009). Today, thousands of Brazilian high
school teachers are getting trained to teach about Brazil's African heritage
(Valente 2005). Affirmative action policies have begun to change the racial
composition of student bodies at universities across the nation (Cicalo
2012). The presence of Afro-Brazilians on television, in magazines, and in
advertising is slowly, haltingly on the rise (Santos 2011). National museums
of Afro-Brazilian culture have been founded, and Africanness in Brazil is an
important magnet for international tourism (Sansone 2003; Collins 2005;
Sansi 2009; Pinho 2010).

Despite such progress, the harsh reality is that the more African one's
phenotype, the more marginalized one is in education, the job market, and
health care (Bailey 2009; Reiter and Mitchell 2009; Reiter 2008; Telles 2004;
Caldwell 2007; Lovell 2006). At the national level, the percentage of people
identifying themselves as nonwhite who are functionally illiterate remains
nearly twice that of *brancos* (whites).[6] Nationwide, *brancos* average over two
years more schooling than do nonwhites. In Brazil's southeastern region,
only 27% of nonwhites have any education beyond high school, compared to
nearly 60% of *brancos* (IBGE 2006, 255).[7] Both male and female Brazilians of
African descent continue overall to be poorer than whites, earning on average *half* the income of *brancos*.[8] *Pretas* (black women) die of cerebrovascular
diseases twice as frequently[9] and in childbirth seven times more frequently[10]
than do *brancas* (white women). *Pretas* suffer from higher hypertension than
do *brancas*, and nonwhite women who report having experiences of racial
discrimination have a 50% higher rate of hypertension than do women without such experiences (Chor 2005, 1592).

São Paulo echoes these national figures. Here, nonwhites earn between
20% to 40% less than do *brancos* with the same amount of education (Lovell
2006, 70, 77, 80)[11] and are about twice more likely than *brancos* to fall below
the poverty line.[12] Black women in São Paulo are about twice more likely
than *brancas* to be domestic servants and half as likely to be clerical workers, professionals, or administrators. In addition, Afro-Brazilian men's and
women's physical and mental health are poor when compared with that of

whites. While the mortality rate from AIDS in the early 2000s in São Paulo was 5% for *brancas*, it was 11% for *pretas* (Cruz 2004; Batista 2002). *Pretas* in São Paulo have higher rates of depression than do *brancas* (Bento 2005; Lopes 2005) and are three times more likely to die than white women due to mental problems (Cruz 2004; Kalckmann et al. 2007; Loureiro and Rozenfeld 2005; Lopes 2005; Batista and Kalckmann 2005). A contributing factor to these contrasts is very likely differential treatment by color in health clinics and hospitals. In a study of 240 people in São Paulo, 60% of the *preto* respondents claimed that they had encountered inferior treatment in these settings because of their phenotype, and they reported comments by medical staff such as "*negras* are stronger and more resistant to pain" and "*negros* don't get sick" (Kalckmann et al. 2007; Leal and Lopes 2005).

One should also note that new governmental policies that support Afro-Brazilian interests are not set in stone. Affirmative action and the national statute against racism have generated multiple judicial challenges and are currently being seriously tested in the courts of political and public opinion (Heringer and Ferreira 2009; M. Gomes 2009). As recently as March 2011, a public hearing was held in Federal Court to decide the constitutionality of quotas at the federal level.[13] Such legal challenges will no doubt continue (Cicalo 2012, 178; Bevilaqua 2005; Goss 2009; Daniels 2006; Martins, Medeiros, and Nascimento 2004). The issue of racial inequality thus promises to be a source of contention in Brazil for a long time to come. It is clearly too early to declare victory in the war against racism in Brazil.

The Importance of *Evangélicos*

Given the political importance of the issue of race in Brazil, there is a pressing need to understand what *evangélicos* (Protestants) think about it. But first, a few words as to what I mean by *evangélicos*. In Brazil, the word has been used since the late 1980s as a generic term to cover all Protestant denominations. Among these, I draw four main distinctions. First there are the *históricos*, or historical churches, which include the historical Baptists, Lutherans, Methodists, Anglicans, and Presbyterians. These churches, founded in Brazil in the nineteenth century, mainly by non-Portuguese immigrants, are characterized by their rational reading of the Bible and deemphasis on the gifts of the Holy Spirit. For most of the twentieth century, these denominations have been based in the middle and upper classes. Historical denominations such as the Methodists and Presbyterians have sustained major presses and centers of higher learning. Much of the liberal and progressive Protestant elite is based in these churches. The second main division is the classic Pentecostals, which include the Assembléia de Deus (Assemblies of God), the Congregação Cristã do Brasil (Christian Congregation of Brazil), the Igreja Quadrangular (Foursquare Gospel Church), Brasil Para Cristo (Brazil for Christ), Casa da Benção (House of Blessing), and Deus é Amor (God Is Love). These churches, founded in Brazil between 1910 and 1962, are characterized by the enthusiastic embrace of the gifts the Holy Spirit, particularly of glossolalia, prophecy, laying on of hands, discernment of spirits, and prayer healing. These churches were rooted until the 1980s mainly in the poor and working classes, but have in the past thirty years broadened their appeal to the middle and upper classes as well. While the political views of Pentecostals vary, their pastors have adopted official positions that range from complete hostility to this-worldly politics, to centrism, to conservatism, though a growing contingent of Pentecostals have started to lean to the left (Freston 2008). Pentecostals were the fastest growing sector of the Protestant arena until the 1980s, and their style of ritual and music and the emphasis on the gifts of the Holy Spirit have influenced the historical churches, leading to the formation of "renovated" historical denominations. The third main distinction is the so-called neo-Pentecostal churches, including the Igreja Universal do Reino de Deus, the Igreja Internacional de Graça de Deus, Renascer em Cristo, Igreja Nova Vida, and many more. These churches formed starting in the late 1970s. They rely far more than their cousin Pentecostals on mass media, to create large, impersonal congregations, and use large spaces such as stadia and cinemas to attract large unaffiliated audiences for the delivery of mass spiritual services, such as exorcism. These churches appeal across class lines and invest in outreach to youth, the use of worldly music, and the theology of this-worldly prosperity. Neo-Pentecostals tend to issue politically conservative public statements, though their participants represent the full range of the political spectrum. Finally, there are two main millennial Protestant churches: the Seventh-Day Adventists and the Jehovah's Witnesses. These have grown considerably over the past fifty years and appeal across most class lines. For this book, I interviewed informants from all four divisions, though most of them were drawn from the Pentecostals, neo-Pentecostals, and Adventists.

According to Brazil's national census, the percentage of Brazilians who identify themselves as members of a Protestant denomination grew from 9% in 1991 to 15.4% in 2000, and more recent data indicate that this growth is continuing. In 2007, Datafolha, the national research institute, surveyed forty-five thousand people nationwide and found that *evangélicos* constituted 22% of the total,[14] and in 2010, Datafolha estimated that this percentage had grown to 25%.[15] At this rate, one assessment of the number of *evangélicos* in Brazil by 2011 has placed it at over fifty million; and by 2020, some observers forecast that over half of Brazil's populations will be *evangélicos*.[16] Whether or not one believes these projections, there is no denying the importance of *evangélicos* in Brazilian society. They are present in every nook and cranny of Brazilian life, from media to higher education, from electoral politics to public marches, from street-corner proselytizing to being one's next-door neighbors (Freston 2004, 2008; Fonseca 2008; Birman 2006; Pinheiro 2004; Oosterbaan 2008).[17] And it must be emphasized that *evangélicos* take their faith very seriously. They attend church regularly, try to live according to their understanding of the Bible, seek to spread the gospel, and are active in their congregations. It must be noted that people of African descent are over-represented among *evangélicos*, particularly among the Pentecostal rank and file: in 2000, 14.2% of all people who identified themselves as *preto* or *negro* were members of Pentecostal churches, compared with 11% of all *pardos*[18] and 9% of all *brancos* (Pierucci 2006).

The implication of all the foregoing should be clear: any effort to under-stand and bring about change in Brazilian attitudes and practices about race cannot afford to ignore the *evangélicos*. Yet systematic research on what Brazil's *evangélicos* have to say about blackness, black identity, race, and racism is still embryonic. What we know is that when asked point-blank whether racial inequality exists in Brazil, *evangélicos* say that it does, that it should not, and that the Brazilian government ought to play some role in reducing it (Selka 2005, 2007). To this extent, evangelicals are similar to the majority of Brazilians (Bailey 2009). They do not, however, tend to see a special role for their churches in advancing these goals; indeed, they generally dislike the idea of their churches encouraging public discussion of black issues and rights (Novaes 1985; Freston 1998; Corten and Marshall-Fratani 2001; Pedde 2002; Prandi 2004; Carvalho 2006; Pierucci 2006; Reinhardt 2007). "It is not for the church," explained Mario, a pastor of an Assembly of God church in São Paulo, "to work on these things, to encourage or ask people to talk about such things. There is racism in Brazil, yes, but this thing about debating it and saying, 'Let's talk about it!' and getting involved in the movement against it—that is not a job of the church. Our job is salvation, not talking about *negros*."[19]

This lack of enthusiasm for ethnoracial activism has several roots. First is *evangélicos'* perennial reluctance to mix religion with politics, a realm they regard as inherently corrupt. "We cannot get too distracted with debates about this-worldly things," said Francisco, of Deus é Amor. "Our mission is to save souls, not to adopt a cause, even a worthy one like the black cause. If you adopt these causes, you always get your hands dirty." Second, *evangélicos'* insistence on the universal equality of believers leads them to claim that inside their churches they have already achieved racial equality. "Listen," explained pastor Martin of Brasil Para Cristo, "believers in Christ are *already* equal! If the rest of the fallen world wants to become more equal, they should convert to Jesus!" Third, from *evangélicos'* perspective, the only identity that ultimately matters is the grand worldwide brother- and sisterhood of the redeemed in Christ; thus, feeling too enamored of any this-worldly identity is surely a sign of spiritual immaturity. "If you want to fight for *uma identidade*," said Joilson, of the Igreja Batista Renovada in Capão Redondo, "then fight for being a Christian! These other identities don't redeem you. They don't save you." Lastly, devout Christians reject as the devil's playground all mediumship religions such as Afro-Brazilian candomblé. Hence, black movements' celebration of these religions as key to authentic black identity gives *evangélicos* pause. "We Christians," said Arturo, of the Igreja Universal do Reino de Deus, "cannot participate in a movement that says we must embrace these religions."

There is no denying that the views I have just described interfere with *evangélicos* committing themselves to championing black pride. Yet it would be a mistake to conclude that their stance toward antiracist struggle is the same everywhere or set in stone. In nooks and crannies across the evangelical landscape, one finds scattered, fledgling ideas that run counter to the religion's general aversion to ethnoracial struggle. Recent research reveals pockets of *evangélicos* who are eager to talk about black pride, racism in their churches, the role of Africans in the Bible, and affirmative action (Dawson 2008; Burdick 1999; Collins 2004; Aquino 2007). *Evangélicos* who want to think about these things can now exchange ideas via social networking sites such as Facebook and Orkut, over e-mail lists, or on the websites of "*cristãos negros.*"[20] Some have started to adopt the causes of antiracism and black self-esteem (Selka 2005), and a few have begun to participate directly in secular black movement organizations.[21] Some have even formed face-to-face evangelical problack movement groups (Burdick 2005; Pinheiro 2009; Branchini and Kronbauer 2011). The existence of such groups raises a core question. To what extent may *evangélicos* develop black pride from within the ideological matrix of evangelical Christianity? What practices and beliefs embedded in evangelical culture might nourish a proud black identity? Where in an ideological desert so hostile to ethnoracial identity might such an identity find oases?

Looking for Oases

I mulled over these questions in May 2002, during a series of conversations with Hernani da Silva, a leader of the fledgling black evangelical movement and longstanding member of the Pentecostal Brasil Para Cristo church. Hernani had started a black Christian website in 1999 and had accumulated several dozen virtual and real allies, but he needed more. Where to find them? How to turn this little network into a broader movement? I was committed to developing a project that could help him do this. I had for some time conceptualized my role as an anthropologist as codesigner of investigations that might help reveal hidden allies and constituencies, clusters of people who shared political activists' attitudes without clearly articulating them, either among themselves or in public. I had offered to come that spring and start conceiving an ethnographic project with Hernani that I would undertake over the next few years in order to help him expand his movement (Hale 2006; Burdick 1995; Speed 2006).

We talked late several nights in a row, wrestling with questions of strategy: where were the audiences of *evangélicos* who might be sympathetic toward the movement's message? Where were the people who might have an affinity with the notion that love of Jesus and love of black identity were mutually reinforcing? "We need something more focused too, something targeted," he said to me. But who should the targets be? (Snow and Benford 1988; Snow et al. 1986).

One evening, we had a breakthrough. Hernani was telling me about a recent meeting he had organized of black Christian theologians and activists in São Paulo and mentioned offhandedly that as part of the event he had invited several musical groups to perform. Only one had shown up, and it was one of the usual suspects, the Black Resistance Choir, made up of congregants of several historical churches. Hernani told me that the groups based in Pentecostal and neo-Pentecostal churches were very hard nuts to crack. "They just don't want to participate in anything like this," he said.

Music! Of course! It had been staring me in the face, but I had not seen it. My visits to Brazilian churches for nearly twenty years had taught me that music was utterly central to the ritual and emotional lives of *evangélicos*. I had listened for two decades to stories of religious conversion in which the key moment of change was prompted by a hymn. I knew that in any three-hour church service, all three hours were filled with some kind of music. I had heard congregants hum religious arias in the street, on the bus, on the job, in their kitchens. I had spoken with ministers bursting with pride about their musicians, bands, and choirs (cf. Corbitt 1998; Harris 1992; Chitando 2002). By studying music, I knew I would be opening an important window onto *evangélicos'* worldview.

What other groups had he invited? I asked.

"All rappers," Hernani replied. "Gospel rappers. If any groups are going to be sympathetic to our message, it's going to be them. They are confrontational, they have that connection to black culture. But I keep inviting, inviting, and they don't come. I don't get it."

"Gospel rappers? You mean kids rapping about their love of the Lord?"

He nodded.

"Are there a lot of them?"

"Hundreds, maybe thousands. There are lots and lots of gospel rappers. It is very big among young people in the *periferia*."

"Perfect!"

Hernani laughed. "John, you're not listening. It isn't perfect. I have been inviting them, and they don't want to come."

"Yes, yes," I said, "I get that. But it must just be in the nature of the outreach. We have to figure out how to invite them so they come. Once they are here, that is a natural audience."

Hernani was unconvinced.

The next day, we took a walk near Hernani's house, in the neighborhood of Guaianazes, in the farthest reach of São Paulo's eastern periphery. We talked about gospel rappers, and I was feeling animated. Then, turning a corner, we suddenly came face-to-face with a billboard announcing a megaconcert at a local Assembléia de Deus, with the words "Come to the 5th annual Black Gospel extravaganza! Come and hear the greatest acts!" The billboard graphic was of five black singers in suits. I asked Hernani what we were looking at. "Oh, that. You aren't going to find any black consciousness there. They just use music to fish for souls. They have no interest in the black cause. They know the music is appealing. They sing to missionize. Trust me, you won't find any interest in black pride there [*você não vai achar conciência negra lá*]. If we want to find consciousness, we'll need to stick to the gospel rappers."

Now I was looking at not one but two musical genres that might, in ways that were still obscure to me, be loci of evangelical problack sentiment. Surely, I thought, an arena of Brazilian evangelical culture that highlighted blackness was worth a closer look. What did blackness mean for the *evangélicos* who played black gospel music? Was Hernani right that we would find no black consciousness there? Was he right that we would find it instead among gospel rappers?

In the following days, I began to focus more on what the research project would look like. What gospel rap and black gospel had in common was that they both belonged to a broader domain, that of the evangelical version of *música negra* (black music), that encompassed a wide range of genres, all laying claim to participating in the multiple traditions of the African diaspora in the Western Hemisphere. There were, I learned, evangelical versions of all these genres and their hybrids: samba, samba-reggae, reggae, American funk, R&B, soul, blues, gospel, black gospel, and rap. But they were not all equally popular. Given limits of time and my desire to be useful to the black evangelical movement, I wanted to stay focused on the genres that had the largest audiences. "No question," Hernani said, "gospel rap and black gospel. If anything, black gospel is the biggest of all. The biggest. They pack in people in auditoriums and churches, much more than gospel rap." Later, I started to think that I had also to include gospel samba. Samba was, after all, the national music of Brazil. But how popular was it? "I think there are only a handful of gospel samba groups," Hernani said. "Far fewer, for sure, than the rappers and black gospel groups." But samba was deeply Brazilian, and I needed to include it in any comparison with US-originated genres. By the end of the week, I had decided to undertake a three-way comparison, of gospel rap, black gospel, and gospel samba.

As I contemplated these plans, and talked about them with Hernani, the nature of my questions began to shift. Initially I had seen myself as on a hunt for "black consciousness" in an effort to unveil hidden allies for Hernani's movement. But as I pondered the three-way comparison, my thinking evolved. Why limit the project just to finding allies? Equally useful would be to understand the ideological resistances to blackness as well. Should I not try to portray as sympathetically as possible different meanings of blackness, even if some were not about pride? Might there not be a convergence between the activist and academic agendas by framing the project as seeking to paint as realistic a portrait as possible of the role different kinds of music played in the formation of different kinds of blackness? (cf. Jackson 2005).

The more I learned, the more I came to understand how rich the arena of evangelical *música negra* was, how thousands of Christian artists throughout São Paulo played religiously themed soul, funk, gospel, R&B, gospel blues, rap, and samba. São Paulo was home to more than thirty black gospel choirs, over one hundred Christian R&B bands, dozens of gospel samba groups, and over two hundred Christian rap groups; and I had chosen the three scenes that might articulate the issue of black identity in different ways. How did making music in different scenes influence the music makers' sense of blackness?

Studying Music in São Paulo's *Periferia*

Over two years, between 2003 to 2005, I studied the influence of music on *paulista* evangelicals' attitudes about blackness. During this time, I carried out nine months of fieldwork in ten different neighborhoods in São Paulo's *periferia*. This vast territory, home to some ten million people, lies like an enormous tattered blanket over the hills and plains of the northern, southern, western, and eastern zones of this huge metropolis. The territory includes middle-class, lower-middle-class, working-class, and very poor areas. I spent most of my time in areas known locally as *asfalto* (lower-middle and working class) and favela (working-class and poor). Since so much of what appears in this book originates in the everyday experience of these environments, it is important for the reader to get a feel for them. Let us therefore visit São Paulo's *periferia*.

Taking a bus through the *periferia*, we are surrounded by the smell of diesel, interrupted occasionally by the aroma of fresh sweet rolls. We hurtle past a blur of three- and four-story red-brown brick buildings with white plaster

The periferia of São Paulo

façades, gray concrete pillars, blue and red metal garage doors, and black iron verandas covered by dark green vines. At every intersection hang banners advertising festivals or businesses or electoral campaigns or gospel or *forró* or samba or hip hop dances ("Women enter for free!"). On every white, cracked plaster wall are spray-painted calls to support local political candidates. Over pitted asphalt, we pass Fiat sedans, VW bugs, and flatbed Chevy trucks with "Deus Seja Louvado" (God Be Praised) on rear mudflaps and the Lord's Prayer on bumpers. We pass pharmacies, toy stores, shops with shiny silver pots, crowded Internet cafés, video rentals, butcher shops, cell-phone outlets, construction material suppliers, supermarkets, car repair shops, and an endless parade of those most social of places, churches and beauty salons. Many of these buildings are adorned by brilliant hand-painted murals: a handyman brandishes an oversized wrench; dark red sofas and chairs surrounded by an orange aura; and everywhere sunrises, sunsets, moons, and clouds, adding the natural and the fantastic to a harsh concrete landscape.

Getting off the bus and walking away from the asphalt, into the favela, we find ourselves in an alleyway ten feet across, surrounded by walls four stories high, topped with shards of broken bottles, the blue sky above but a sliver, crisscrossed by electric ganglia. As we walk, an old man dangling plastic bags greets us as "*irmãos.*" We pass by metal gates, small churches that hold twenty congregants, overhanging walls on either side, roofs graced with gray water reservoirs, and white satellite dishes. Middle-aged women sit on stoops, smoking. In a corner bar, two young men in sunglasses sit shirtless at a yellow plastic table, elbows spread, before four tall, empty bottles of beer. Someone has placed a television in front of his house, and a cluster of people are standing, chatting, watching the soccer game. Young men walk by in hooded jackets with basketball insignia, knitted ski caps, Bermuda shorts below the knee, and sandals; and young women in tight-fitting jeans revealing the tops of hips. Everywhere we hear mothers calling for children, motorcycles whining, dogs yelping, the thud of feet meeting soccer balls, and the thump, thump, thump of radios—from each house a different music: *forró* from this one, *sertanejo* from that, funk and samba from this, reggae-samba from that, axé from this, gospel from that, and everywhere, rap, rap, rap.

In order to study black gospel music, gospel rap, and gospel samba in these places, I attended musical performances several times each week. On any given day, it was possible to attend a performance of some group in a church, hall, home, or street. I thus came to know the work of nearly thirty black gospel artists (soloists, duos, trios, quartets, choirs, and bands), fifty gospel rap artists (soloists, duos, and groups), and half a dozen gospel samba groups. I witnessed rehearsals, backstage gatherings, and everyday transits. Among black gospel groups, I accompanied the comings and goings of Raiz Coral, Link-4, and Banda Azusa; among gospel rappers, I hung out with Pretto, Sexto Sello, Rimas Proféticas, Profetas do Apocalipse, and Pregador Luo; and among gospel sambistas, I became involved in Deus Crioulos. I sat, hours on end, in garages and churches and basements and living rooms, as artists practiced, rehearsed, I climbed into and bounced around in minivans surrounded by cables and speakers, hung out back- and off-stage, gossiping, kibbitzing, and shadowboxing, and stood elbow to elbow with fans, bobbing, clapping, stretching, and pointing. I participated in workshops, classes, seminars, and trainings, led by directors, conductors, coaches, and teachers. And I became a regular visitor to several churches with particularly energetic musical groups: Pedra Viva in the neighborhood of Vila Mariana, Deus em Cristo-Azusa in Vila Matilde, Mintre in Guarulhos, Assembléia de Deus Kadoshi in Bom Retiro, Brasil Para Cristo in Freguesia do Ó, and Pão da

Vida in Morumbi. In all of these, I recorded digital audio files, videotaped, and took copious notes.

In addition, I gathered posters, announcements, websites, published interviews, and feature stories. And I scoured lyrics. I found that to get at racial identity, evangelical lyrics were an opaque resource, since they almost always treated of the universal themes of salvation and redemption but rarely of blackness. It was only when I paid attention to other discursive contexts—explanatory comments made during rehearsals, lectures during music workshops, informal interpretations shared informally among artists, study groups, verbal introductions to performances, onstage commentaries between musical numbers, media interviews, liner notes, and artists' offhand comments—that I began to encounter ideas about blackness, black identity, and racism. I thus join other cultural analysts of music who recognize that much of a scene's discourse takes place not in lyrical composition but in other discursive contexts (Bennett 2004; Frith 1996b).

Early on, I decided to interview artists rather than audiences. To examine the relationship between a specific musical scene and particular constellations of ideas, beliefs, and identities, it is of course desirable to conduct audience studies, as some ethnomusicologists have done (e.g., Brooker and Jermyn 2002). Yet for many audience members—inveterate fans aside—listening to music is an evanescent activity. While lines of influence exist between that activity and identity, they tend to be crowded out by other factors. Dedicated musicians, in contrast, devote large parts of each day to thinking about music. If I wanted to see the linkages between musical activity and ethnoracial consciousness, these connections would be most evident among people in whose lives music plays a pivotal role. Thus, by the time I had completed the study, I had conducted in-depth interviews, ranging from one to three hours, with thirty black gospel artists, thirty-five gospel rappers, and twenty gospel sambistas.

I limited my interviews to individuals who, when asked "Qual é a sua cor ou a sua raça?" (What is your color or race?), responded, "Sou negro" (I'm negro) or "Sou preto" (I'm black). My focus on such people does not mean that I regard as unimportant the experiences of people who call themselves by other terms, such as branco (white), moreno (brown), or mestiço (mixed). The focus on pretos and negros was motivated by my desire to achieve ethnographic depth. Like other recent writers on ethnoracial consciousness in Brazil, I understand that ser negro (to be black) does not correspond to a single identity but to a range of sentiments and ideas, from casual signifiers to deep-seated political beliefs (cf. Bailey 2009; Sansone 2003; Roth-Gordon 2008; André 2008; Pravaz 2008). Among evangelical Protestants, I wish to capture the range of what being *negro* or *preto* means to those who use the term. Keeping my sample limited to self-identified *negros* and *pretos* allows me to examine how meanings of blackness vary and how involvement in different musical scenes contributes to this variation.

Theorizing Music and Collective Identity

I focus in this book on three distinct musical *scenes*. I understand a musical scene to be an identifiable bundle of durable music-making practices and discourses, including routines of participation and performance; lyrical thematic emphases; distinct sonic patterns; routinely deployed musical instruments; typical training practices; how, when, and where rehearsals take place; how musicians balance individual with group performance; what parts of their bodies get skilled to produce desired sounds; and what preexisting social relations and networks get mobilized into the formation of the scene's music-making groups (Bennett and Peterson 2004; Turino 2008; Murphy 2006; Kaemmer 1993). My focus in this volume is on the practices and discourses of musicians and performers. I was drawn to musicians because of the centrality of music in their lives and thus the possibility that their lives might be windows onto the connections between music and identity. I take *identity* to refer to a set of beliefs held by a person that focus on the idea that he or she possesses values, experiences, or essences that are salient and central in his or her life and are durable over time. Values, experiences, or essences of the person him- or herself, without reference to others, are the person's *individual identity*; values, experiences, or essences held in common with some larger group of people are the person's *collective identity*. It is the salience, centrality, and durability of these values, experiences, or essences that render them definitive of the person's identity (Brubaker 2004; Mohanty 1997; Stone-Mediatore 2003, 149; Moya 2006, 46).

In this book, I examine how specific practices of music-making help generate collective identities. To do this, I build on the view that music-making practices are not simply reflections of preexisting identities but are catalysts of new ideas and practices of selfhood (Frith 1996a, 1996b; Wade 2000, 2002; Reagon 2001; Bell 1999; Phelan 2008; McGann 2004). As anthropologist

Peter Wade writes, "Music is not just an expression of identity; rather it helps to form and constitute that identity. . . . Music—listened to, danced to, performed, talked and written about—is part of the process of [identity] formation and change" (2002, 22). Or, as musicologist Naomi Cumming has argued, practices of musical training and performance shape not only musicians' identities as performers but their broader, extramusical identities as well (2000, 13ff.).

The challenge is to describe the specific ways that musical practices form, shape, and constitute these identities. First, we need to ask how and why music serves as a medium for people to think of themselves as sites of continuity over time. Here the writing of musicologist Tia DeNora is instructive. She draws our attention to the capacity of music to evoke strong, visceral, even visual memories and thus to assure listeners of their own continuity (2000, 64ff.). As she puts it, "music simultaneously helps to recapture or construct a sense of the capacity within which one once acted (one's aesthetic agency); in so doing, it helps dramatize to self a set of heightened life experiences. Through this vicarious review of past experience, this stock-taking of 'who one is' or 'where, interpersonally, one has been,' one registers one's self to one's self as an object of self-knowledge, in the aesthetic construction that is memory" (ibid., 65).

But what about the social, collective side of this? How does music get us to think of ourselves as bearers of collective identity? One clue is that, while DeNora is interested in how music strengthens individual identity, her description of this process is eminently social: for her, as we listen to music to strengthen our own identities, we do this not as atomized individuals but through participating in the circulation and sharing of ideas with others. As people consider, reflect, and talk about music together, they learn shared ways of thinking about their own lives. To understand this process, I build on philosopher Elizabeth Grosz's (1994) notion that place, body, and time are key ingredients in the constitution of identities and on Aaron Fox's observation that musical practices swirl around the "themes of emplacement, embodiment, [and] the organization of temporal experience" (2004, 21). My core theoretical argument in this book is that in order to understand the role of music in the formation of collective identities, we must attend to how musical practices and discourses articulate and generate ideas and feelings about *history*, *place*, and *the body*. While these are certainly not the only dimensions of human experience pertinent to the development of group belonging, they are sufficiently broad in scope and appear with sufficient frequency as themes in music that they merit examination as key forces in the formation of collective identity. This book examines how historical narratives become claims about what in a group stays the same, places become sites of enduring collective attachment, and bodies become sites of enduring "natural" and "cultural" qualities of "peoples."

Temporal narrative. Music can stimulate feelings of collective identity by announcing and disseminating—in lyrics, training, rehearsal, commentary, informal conversation—a shared, emotionally charged narrative of a group's origin, ancestry, glory, rights, endurance, suffering, resistance, and interaction with other groups. When Australian Aborigines sing about their kin group's mystical pasts, they point to the origin of each group's current land claims; while singing, they experience an overflow of feelings of group loyalty (Magowan 1997, 135ff.). When praise singers among the Kalasha of Pakistan sing of the glorious achievements of their ancestors, they experience, they say, a strengthened common bond (Parkes 1997, 172). Paul Gilroy points to the "special fascination with history and the significance of its recovery by those who have been expelled from the official dramas of civilization," a fascination that infuses much of identity-construction work of black music in the Western Hemisphere (1991, 98). A host of practices are central to the scene of reggae music, including reading works of historical nonfiction and speaking to each other of past African civilizations and the history of slavery, and these are key ingredients in the deepening of Afrocentric black identity (Daynes 2005, 26). Ideas about the collective past are also available in ways that are not verbal: thus, Armenian singers say that the timbre of their voices—a dark, gravelly tone acquired through years of training—"sounds Armenian" because it preserves the cry of agony that originated in the Armenian genocide at the start of the twentieth century (Eidsheim 2006, 6).

In this book, I emphasize a certain kind of narrative: stories told by musicians about the founding and unfolding of the musical scenes of which they are practitioners. I argue that a key way musicians create and reinforce their own identification with a larger ethnic group, nation, or "race" is by learning and recounting narratives about the history of their art. Such recounting is embedded in musical cultures throughout the hemisphere. Ingrid Monson has argued that knowledge of the details of jazz history—in particular, knowing and talking about its involvement over the years in international flows of people and ideas—is central to black jazz artists' idea of themselves as "black

cosmopolitans." As she put it, "When jazz musicians learn traditional reper-
tory, quote a particular musician's solo, play a tune with a particular groove,
or imitate a particular player's sound, they reveal themselves to be very aware
of musical history" (1996, 97). Similarly, when Brazilian musicians in the
early twentieth century spoke of their art's rootedness in a layered historical encounter between Amerindian, European, and African peoples and cultures, they reinforced their own sense of music as the carrier of their national
"soul" (Reily 1994, 81–82). Taking my cue from such examples, I pay attention to the narratives artists tell about the history of their music and to the
way these narratives relate to the solidification of a sense of black identity.

  Place. Music possesses a stunning capacity to evoke textured memories of and feels for *places* (Stokes 1997; Whiteley, Bennett, and Hawkins
2005; Peddie 2006; Layshon, Matless, and Revill 1998; Saldanha 2002).
Listeners readily recount the experience of being returned in their imaginations by particular passages of music to specific settings and locations
(Finnegan 1989; DeNora 2000; Sancar 2003). "The musical event," writes
Stokes, "from collective dances to the act of putting a cassette or CD into
a machine, evokes and organizes collective memories and present experiences of place with an intensity, power, and simplicity unmatched by any
other social activity" (1997, 3). This relationship between music and place
may have to do with music's peculiar phenomenological capacity to "fill"
space, like a liquid taking on a container's shape. Music "floods" places as
liquids do and, by surrounding the occupants of these places, unites occu-
pant and place. "Music fills and structures space within us and around us,"
writes Sara Cohen, "inside and outside. Hence, much like our concept of
place, music can appear to envelop us" (1995, 444). The places evoked for
us by music are charged with social meanings, such as a home, a street, a
cemetery, a family's farmland, the site of a birth or a wedding or a burial, a
church, a battlefield, a government building. "Places," writes Cohen, "reify
or symbolize social relationships" (ibid., 438). Thus, when music symbolizes
a place, it evokes feelings of relatedness to the group for which that place
is socially significant (Blacking 1995, 39). As Kevin Dawe and Andy Bennett have argued, "a shared connection with a locally created musical style
becomes a metaphor for community, a means through which people articulate their sense of togetherness through a particular juxtaposition of music,
identity and place" (2001, 4). But note: the places evoked by music do not
need to be immediate or real: they can be abstract, distant, fantasized, and

mediated by intervening images, such as movies. Anyone who has watched a music video, seen a film with a score, or listened to lyrics describing a place he or she has never seen knows that imagination takes over where personal experience leaves off. This point is particularly important for diasporic populations (Bennett and Peterson 2004; Bowen 1997). Therefore, in this book, I attend to how artists think about and relate through their music to particular places, and I argue that ideas and practices that connect their music to places—such as neighborhoods, churches, the nation, the transnation—shape their attitudes and ideas about black identity.

Body. Finally, there can be no doubt that music is experienced both in production and reception through the body. As Aaron Fox (2004), John Blacking (1987), Tia DeNora (2000), Richard Middleton (2006), and Simon Frith (1996b) have all insisted, producing and listening to music are occasions for heightened physical experiences, from intense pain to extreme pleasure; from deep, heavy breathing to rapid shortness of breath; from highly accelerated to slowed heart rate; from hot sweat to coolness on the skin; from limb-aching exhaustion to viscera-energizing arousal; from warmth to tingling; from throbbing to goose bumps; and more (DeNora 2000, 99; Gilbert and Pearson 1999, 44–51). The intensity of such bodily experience prompts reflection on why some bodies seem to be more open, receptive, or attuned than others to such experiences. Music is, as Susan McClary suggests, "a medium that participates in social formation by influencing the ways we perceive our feelings, our bodies, our desires, our very subjectivities" (1994, 211). In cultural contexts with readily available racializing discourses, such reflection frequently leads to patterned talk that attributes particular musical aptitudes and affinities to particular "races" (Frith 1996b, 131; Wong 2000, 67). It is important to underline that while such talk claims that particular "races" "naturally" possess particular music-related aptitudes, it also frequently claims that these aptitudes were caused by "culture" or "history." Sometimes all these causal claims (of nature, culture, and history) are combined in complex hybrids—hence the utility of the broader term *ethnorace*.

Two kinds of ethnoracial discourse about music that focus on bodily aptitudes are especially common: those about bodily *rhythm and movement* and those about *voice.* Examples of the former are legion. "My mom was born in Cuba," writes a young Cuban American, "and she has pure Latin American blood. When she hears some of her native music, she just can't control herself" (Aparicio 2000, 103). Thus, too, the racializing assumption about rhythm underlying Eric Clapton's declaration, "I'm no longer trying to play anything but like a white man. The time is overdue when people should play like they are and what color they are" (qtd. in Adelt 2007, 62). Or consider Deborah Wong's interlocutor when she reports on listening, along with an African American musician, to a tape of jazz musicians that included Asian American musicians: "He wasn't listening blind," she writes. "He knew that the musicians were ethnically diverse but mostly Asian American. . . . At one point . . . he observed that the musicianship was technically good but 'stiff'—that the musicians consistently maintained a rather close metronomic sense of the beat that 'revealed' them as not African American. He even stopped the tape at one point to demonstrate how an African American musician might realize a particular phrase with a looser, more fluid sense of rhythm" (2000, 71).[22]

The other primary way that ideas about the body intersect with music is through *voice*. Thinking about the human voice is often accompanied by ethnoracializing claims, partly because, as Frith has argued, "the voice seems particularly expressive of the body; it gives the listener access to it without mediation." He continues: "The voice is a sound produced physically, by the movement of muscles and breath in the chest and throat and mouth; to listen to a voice is to listen to a physical event, to the sound of a body" (1996b, 191) This is no doubt partly why people so often claim to be able to "hear" race or ethnicity (Eidsheim 2009, 2011, forthcoming). A familiar ethnoracializing notion is that European voices are "cool," "rational," "cerebral," "smooth," "controlled," "unemotional," and otherwise somehow "bodiless," "conceal[ing] their own means of physical production" (Frith 1996b, 191). Voices "south of the equator," in contrast, are all too often conceptualized as "thick" with corporeality: "hot," "warm," "emotional," "ragged," "throaty," "free," and, in a convergence between musical and racial language, "dark." One US voice teacher, commenting about the "Latin American voice," stated, "I think [Latin Americans] naturally have that connection. . . . They're connected to their bodies and their guts, and they make music from their hearts. . . . That's how their music sounds. It's very gut" (Eidsheim 2006, 5).

These examples suggest some of the political complexities I will be navigating in this book. While views about the racial naturalness of rhythm are commonly complicit with racist politics, Ronald Radano has argued that ideas about body rhythm can also serve as a positive political resource for people of African descent. "Rhythm," he writes, "has typically been inscribed as something beyond the grasp of whites; accordingly, it offers

performers and insiders a powerful tool for inventing an exalted racialized space" (Radano 2003, 1–2). Robin Sheriff (1999) and Natasha Pravaz
(2003) have argued that racialized discourses about rhythm in Brazil have
been deployed by Afro-Brazilians as sources of pride. The politics of vocal
ethnoracialization cut in different ways. In the mouths of white Europeans,
allusions to "dark" voices may be exoticizing, imperialist nostalgia and fan-
tasy; but as Radano suggests, for black singers, finding "blackness" in their
voices is frequently a matter of pride. When African American opera singer
Reri Grist says she recognizes "blackness" in a voice as a distinct sound—
"throatier, a sound placed lower with a very low larynx, a sound that can
be . . . warm and rich and with a very open throat" (qtd. in Eidsheim 2006,
11)—is she using, as Radano might insist, "a powerful tool for inventing an
exalted racialized space" (qtd. in Wong 2000, 72)?

The Book's Chapters

By focusing on how ideas of history, place, and the body are embedded in
musical practices and discourses, this book investigates how those practices
and discourses cultivate different modes of black identity among evangelical
black musicians in Brazil.

   Chapter 1 provides a historical and ethnographic overview of the three
music scenes which are the book's main foci. I treat each scene in turn, trac-
ing its emergence and describing its main current performative practices.
Gospel rap appeared in the early 1990s with the conversion to Protestantism of influential rappers. Gospel samba arose in the 1990s as well, as several
neo-Pentecostal churches sought to bring their missionary message into the
belly of the beast during Carnaval. Black gospel began in the 1960s, in the
efforts of Brazilian church singers to bring North American Negro spirituals
into their midst, and took off in the 1990s with the arrival of videos of North
American black churches. For each type of music, through an ethnographic
account of an exemplary performance, I seek to convey each genre's appeal.
I end the chapter by describing several key ideas shared by artists across the
three genres: the religious value of music, its role in spiritual life and evangelization, and the meaning of spiritual anointing in music. These ideas infuse
gospel musicians with remarkable intensity.

   I turn my attention in chapter 2 to the ethnoracial ideas and practices of gospel rap. I find, first, a preoccupation among rappers with the

periferia. This is a place marked by class deprivation and ethnoracial diversity. Despite claims by the black consciousness movement that the *periferia* is homogeneously *negro*, gospel rappers know that this is not the case: they identify with a place defined not by race or color but by poverty. Meanwhile, their intense interest in the present, their general mistrust of things North American, and their disinterest in justifying themselves to their churches lead them to have little enthusiasm for black musical history. Finally, gospel rappers have an ambivalent relationship to the essentialized black body. In Brazilian rap, a spoken form, there is little emphasis on the melodious, decibel-packing voice. At the same time, the gospel rap scene emphasizes flow and rhythm, which in Brazil have been racialized, though not with the same depth and consistency as they have in the United States. Indeed, because of the ideology of miscegenation, the view is widespread in Brazil that a racial predilection for rhythm has been distributed widely throughout Brazil's population, making it possible, in this view, for most Brazilians to rap effectively. Hence, I argue black gospel rappers, though identifying themselves as *negros* and Brazilian, place greater emphasis on their class and on their transnational commonalities with all who are poor and oppressed than on their racial identity.

Chapter 3 focuses on the ethnoracial meanings of gospel samba. This scene's self-identified *negro* musicians place little emphasis on ethnic blackness. To explain this, I show that gospel samba is closely associated in the imagination of its artists with the imaginary place of the Brazilian nation: the "Brazil" that has been constructed for the past eighty years as a *mestiço* (racially mixed) nation has found its way into the heart of gospel sambista identity. As for how gospel sambistas narrate history, the story they tell echoes the national myth of "race mixture," a story not of conflict or domination but of exchange, creativity, pleasure, and cordiality, with a correspondingly weak interest in Afro-Brazilian heroism. More complex is gospel samba's relationship to the body and its attendant ethnoracializations. On the one hand, the gospel samba scene has no need for a highly developed, spectacular, timbre-marked voice. This is a scene of melody and beat, not vocal skill; consequently, there is little room for the development of thinking about the "raced" voice. On the other hand, ethnoracialized ideas about rhythm remain present in gospel samba but coexist alongside rejection of mixed-sex dancing. The scene has marginalized such dancing and thus has reduced the influence of the rhythmic ethnoracialized body. Together, these cultural forces mean that in gospel samba, evangelical Christianity's general lack of enthusiasm for ethnoracial boundary marking has maximum room for play. The identity that emerges from the gospel samba scene is less a bounded blackness and more a nationalist mixedness.

In chapter 4, I show how three main features of the melody- and voicecentric scene of black gospel contribute to the formation of a strong, self-aware, and politically committed *negro* identity. One feature is that the place which occupies the imaginations of black gospel artists is that of the North American black church. To be trained as a black gospel artist means watching videos and DVDs of black churches, thus coming to cherish as the key symbolic location of one's chosen musical scene a place that is unquestionably, homogeneously, black. Self-construction as a Brazilian black gospel singer thus includes celebration of an institution that is profoundly different from what exists in Brazil, where the very idea of a homogeneously black church is taboo. The second feature is that, because black gospel artists ardently desire to be accepted and embraced by their churches, they expend copious amounts of energy on mastering the details of North American black musical history, thereby teaching them that their musical scene has long been at the forefront of the struggle for racial equality. Finally, the extreme physical demands of black gospel singing place front and center the racialized, essentialized black voice, thinking about which fills black gospel artists' days and nights. The outcome of these three features is that for black gospel artists, black identity is a strong, sinewy priority.

Chapter 5 considers how the identities cultivated within each of the musical scenes influence musicians' attitudes toward struggles for racial justice, including *negro* leadership, the formation of a primarily *negro* church, the development of *negro* theology, the articulation of racial issues inside the church, the encouragement of churches to act in solidarity with the secular black movements, support for policy initiatives such as affirmative action, involvement in educational programs for *negro* youth, and support for local *negro*-owned businesses. Gospel samba artists have a weak record of supporting any of the causes just mentioned; rather, their mode of reaching out to the world remains fixed on religious evangelization. Gospel rappers, in contrast, have become involved in a variety of racial justice projects but, significantly, do not a take a leadership role in promoting them. Their identities as poor and young motivate them to lead projects intended to help the poor; when it comes to race-based initiatives, they participate primarily in secondary roles. At the end of the day, it turns out that it is the melody-based black gospel artists, catalyzed by their strong black identities, who are best represented as leaders of racial justice projects.

I conclude by reviewing the book's chief findings, then arguing that these raise questions of broader significance. First, I argue that the fact that black gospel music sustains a richly textured oppositional ethnoracial conscious- ness should provoke us to ask how much more sympathy toward black iden- tity might be buried just beneath the surface elsewhere in the evangelical landscape. Second, I suggest that the fact that blackness has markedly differ- ent meanings for musicians of the three scenes indicates the need to examine the *multiple* meanings of blackness in the African diaspora, as well as the need for more investigations into the meanings of whiteness and mixedness. Third, I point out that the usefulness of the categories of history, place, and body to ferret out the underlying ethnoracial meanings of different musi- cal scenes suggests the value of applying them to other musical scenes and arenas of expressive culture, to unearth ethnoracial meanings. Finally, I dis- cuss how and why the fact that expressive culture sometimes supports and sometimes dilutes ethnoracial identities among evangelicals may contribute to the improvement of strategy by black evangelical movement activists. The study thus seeks to realize its mission as action research, by showing how a nuanced analysis of society may make not only good scholarship but good social action as well.

1

We Are the Modern Levites

Three Gospel Music Scenes

In order for us to begin our journey toward the deep, buried ethnoracial meanings of three scenes of gospel music, we need to
begin slowly and gently, by witnessing them from the outside. In
later chapters, we will encounter these scenes from the inside out;
but for now, let us encounter them as shapes seen from an external vantage point—as people clustering together on- and off-stage,
singing and playing their hearts out for all the world to see and
hear. For now, let us be spectators and watch how these scenes
came into being and how their artists look and sound when they
perform. At the end of the chapter, we will take our first tentative
step inside their world and begin to touch the deeper significance
of what they do and who they are.

Gospel Rap in São Paulo
A Brief History of Gospel Rap in São Paulo

Paulista rap (i.e., rap from São Paulo) has lived through four main periods,
each distinguished by a different lyrical theme. From 1983 to 1987, *paulista*
rap was primarily ludic and recreational, with no political agenda. From 1988
to 1994, it became heavily politicized, with *negritude* strongly emphasized.
From 1995 to 2000, these themes became less central, the theme of *periferia*
took center stage, and gospel rap became a major tendency on the scene.
Since 2000, *paulista* rap has grown more diverse, with many new styles
and no clear thematic core, while the growth of gospel rap has continued
unabated, influencing the lyrics of everyone else.

In the late 1960s, when Friday afternoon arrived, young men armed with
vinyl records, a turntable, a pair of speakers, and an extension cord would
assemble makeshift sound systems on streets across São Paulo's vast working-
class neighborhoods. These were the original *equipes de som*—sound teams.

By the start of the 1970s, teams such as Chic Show (Macedo 2003, 12) and Black Mad were organizing bigger and better parties, playing recorded soul and Motown, US funk, and, increasingly, Brazilian singers such as Tim Maia, Jorge Ben, Toni Tornado, and Cassiano (Macedo 2003, 10; Assef 2003). The parties became a movement under the military regime's very nose, a movement whose energy came not from a political impulse but from a black attitude expressed in posture, dress, gesture, and taste (Alberto 2009). Dancegoers let their hair grow into black power Afros; idolized Curtis Mayfield and Isaac Hayes; wore bell-bottoms, V-necked shirts, and platform shoes; and repeated James Brown's motto "say it loud, I'm black and I'm proud" and Jorge Ben's "negro é lindo." In the late 1970s, the parties settled into clubs and became paying affairs. By the end of the decade, the main distinction was between *bailes soul* (soul dances) for younger people and *bailes nostalgia* (nostalgia dances) for an older crowd. The former, organized by Chic Show, took over the Palmeiras sport club; the latter found homes in Clube Homs and Casa de Portugal (Felix 2000). Indoor dances required a certain polish. "Everyone had to dress up," recalled Dexter, now a major Christian rap artist. "We all had to put on our best clothes: fine shoes, silk shirts with designer labels, black hair cuts that were really finely cut and expensive."

Not surprisingly, this brand of polish was not for everyone. The first break-dance crews were made up of kids who could not get into the clubs. They were led by Nelson Triunfo, a poor Northeasterner, who migrated to São Paulo in 1976. Rebelling against the atmosphere of the clubs, he formed Black Soul Brothers in 1982 (Rocha, Domenich, and Casseano 2001) and set up shop near the Praça da República. In 1983, Triunfo won a nationally televised break-dance contest. Interest grew in 1984 with the arrival in Brazil of the US films *Breakin'* and *Beat Street* and Triunfo's contract with the country's largest TV station to perform to the opening credits of the nationally televised soap opera *Partido Alto*. In 1985, São Paulo's breakers moved to the São Bento subway station, which looked like settings from the US breakdance movies. The first serious Brazilian break-dance crews developed there, such as Street Warriors, Back Spin, Nação Zulu, and Crazy Crew. "We would stand around exchanging ideas," recalled DJ Alpiste. "We would exchange tapes and vinyl records. We would talk about the new record that just came out." Until then, Brazilians listened to markedly unpolitical rap. Favorites included American artists MC Cooley C, Whodini, Kurtis Blow, Malcolm McLaren, and Kool Moe Dee; the Brazilians included Black Juniors, Pepeu, and Thaíde. These were all "party" rappers who rhymed not about politics but about physical attractiveness, partying, drinking, hanging out, and romance. "It was a style," recounted DJ Alpiste. "We were fascinated by it. It had nothing to do with any kind of denunciation. It was not political. It was a continuation of the dance parties. It was a cool way to get people to dance. People would sing along with 'Tagarela, tagarela!'"

Then, starting in 1986, as Vilmar put it, "there started to be more of a connection with the political side of things." The end of military censorship in 1985, the acceleration of preparations for the centennial of the abolition of slavery, the growing influence of the black movement, and the mobilization around the writing of the new federal constitution thrust the issue of race squarely into the public eye. Influenced by these developments, a faction at the São Bento subway station began to focus explicitly on black identity and political commentary. Mano Brown, later to become the single most famous rapper in Brazil, recalled,

> The ones who were at São Bento, because we saw that a lot of white kids had started to gravitate to us, and everyone who was there were starting to accept that, but I didn't accept that. I started thinking that there needed to be more blacks in the movement, the movement was a black one, so there had to be blacks, and there weren't that many. Ice Blue and I, we always had this vision: we have to have a place that is just for us, and Roosevelt plaza, because that was where the favela began, began there. We weren't doing hip hop so much, there we were doing rap. We didn't dance, we just rapped. (DJ TR 2007, 156)

A racially militant attitude flourished in Roosevelt Plaza. Freed from the dance-party scene and attending black movement meetings in the vicinity, the Roosevelt Plaza rappers formed the first Brazilian posse (a collection of rap groups) Sindicato Negro (Black Union) in late 1988.

Several forces solidified *paulista* rap's emphasis on black politics during this period. First was the influence of Sindicato Negro. Members of the Sindicato traveled throughout the city to help found new posses. When, for example, youths in the neighborhood of Tiradentes wanted to start a posse in 1990, they invited a delegation from the Sindicato to come talk with them. From the delegation, they learned (according to one of the founders of Tiradentes' posse) that "blacks should marry blacks and whites should marry whites." Second was the arrival on the Brazilian market of the North American rap group Public Enemy, with its message of racial liberation, as well as of movies such as *Boyz in the Hood*, *New Jack City*, and Spike Lee's *Malcolm X*. These influences made themselves felt in *paulista* rap lyrics. The early 1990s saw the release of Racionais MCs' record *Choose Your Path*, on which Mano Brown's gravelly voice declared,

> Read, study, learn
> Before hidden racist fools with atrophied brains
> Finish you off
> This is not a recent strategy of theirs
> It's been going on four hundred years
> Maybe someday you'll be proud
> Choose your path
> Be a true black, pure and educated
> Or remain one more limited black

All my informants agreed that by the early 1990s, as Luo said, "things were really divided. You had blacks in the rap movement who would have nothing to do with whites. There were lots of groups—DMN, Posse Mente Zulu, and the Racionais,[1] who started to raise that banner. It was very strong." By the early 1990s, "to be taken seriously you had to talk about Zumbi of Palmares," said Preto Jay, now lead vocalist for the gospel rap group Sexto Sello (Sixth Seal). He described what he wrote lyrics about at that time: "Nelson Mandela, Martin Luther King, the history of blacks, trying to bring knowledge to my people."

By the second half of the decade, however, *paulista* rap shifted from its focus on ethnoracial themes toward an interest in the *periferia*. The shift can be seen, for example, in changing group names. Atualidade Negra (Black Reality) had been formed in 1990; in 1995 it changed its name to Causa e efeito (Cause and Effect). "By then we were dealing with more than just black issues," said Alex, MC of the group. "Because in '92 or '93, many groups had '*negro*' in their title. Everyone was militant on the question of racial prejudice. But by '96, you saw names of groups that were different. People's minds started opening up to the larger social question. We wanted to talk about all the poor who lived in the periphery, not just blacks." By 1997, in Mano Brown's own music, gone was race-first oratory; in fact, the words *negro* and *preto* were hardly present at all. Instead, virtually every track in Racionais MCs' recording of that year defended the people of the *periferia*, whose color remained unmarked.[2]

A factor in the deracialization of Brazilian rap ideology was that by the mid-1990s, dozens of nongovernmental organizations (NGOs) and São Paulo's municipal government were recruiting rappers to assist in local *projetos sociais* (social projects), focusing on health, AIDS, hunger, recreation, sport, and marketable-skills building for poor youths.[3] Another factor was that the posse had begun to outlive its usefulness. For roughly five years, from 1989 to 1994, *paulista* rappers' world revolved around posses, collaborative associations between rap groups based in each of the four main zones of the city. On any given weekend, rap groups spent time away from their neighborhood homes, in order to rehearse and perform in places organized and sponsored by posses. But by the second half of the '90s, amateur rap groups were staying closer to home. NGOs and the government were offering rappers deals to perform in their own neighborhoods. In addition, as CD players became cheaper, rappers no longer depended on posses for good sound systems and recording equipment. These changes affected the content of rhymes. "In the posse," Ton explained, "they told us to read things, the history of slavery, Malcolm X. But in my backyard, we didn't read anything: there was no 'cultural' side to rap; we just rapped on what we saw. We didn't want to rap about what they told us in posses; we wanted to say what we saw happening in our own neighborhood."

By the late 1990s, then, as rappers came to focus their attention on their immediate environments, the theme of race, although still present, became less central than the class- and place-based theme of *periferia*. By the end of the decade, according to the anthropologist Derek Pardue, blackness had been "pushed aside within the general hip hop imagination" (2008, 113).[4] It was in the latter half of the 1990s, too, that the first rap groups began to appear that were dedicated to spreading the message of Jesus Christ. The first rapper to do so was DJ Alpiste. A sound man by trade, he converted to evangelicalism in 1994 and went to work for the evangelical soul band Kadoshi in 1995. He wrote his first gospel rap that year—"Ser ou não ser"—which appeared on a Kadoshi album; he went on to make his first commercial record in 1997, which sold over thirty thousand copies. Between 1998 and 2005, Alpiste released a CD every two years and inspired dozens of other young Christian artists. In 1998, for example, a young man named Luciano formed a group named Apocalipse 16 and made a record which became one of the best-selling rap albums in the country. Luciano took on the name Pregador Luo (Preacher Luo) and became the most popular gospel rapper in Brazil.

By the start of the new millennium, the field of gospel rap was becoming crowded, with a rapidly growing number of artists making a name for themselves through CDs, concerts, and radio play (cf. Baker-Fletcher 2003). Gospel rappers were influenced not only by religion but by the secular subculture of hip hop. Indeed, evangelical rap had the same social base and circulated in the same social world as secular rap. The more successful gospel rap groups included Ao Cubo, Provérbios X, Rap Sensation, Cirurgia Moral, O Pregador, Profesor Pablo, Lito Ataiala, Tina, E-Beille, Alvos da Lei, Alibi, Resgatados do Inferno, Alternativa C, X-Barão, Juízo Final, Discípulos do Rei, Sexto Sello, Gênesis, and Relato Bíblico. A vibrant grass-roots movement of gospel rappers expanded, relying on outdoor festivals, churches, and contests. Sometimes a small amateur group would save some cash, get access to a recording studio, produce a CD, and put it into the hands of friends and family. After about 2003, some created CDs from their own computers, aided by new, easily downloadable sound-mixing programs. By 2004–2005, there were more than a hundred such amateur gospel rap groups in metropolitan São Paulo, including Profetas do Apocalipse, Território D, Faces da Verdade, Pretto, Herdeiros, Alerto Vermelho, Mano da Fé, Saqueadores, Profetas do Apocalipse, ZN/AP, Guerreiros do Senhor, Gueto em Cristo, Família Jesus Cristo, Caçadores de Almas, and Porte Verbal. There were so many gospel rap groups that they came to influence secular rap artists. The themes of Christ, God, and salvation began to appear in the 2000s more than ever before among self-professed secular rappers. Even Mano Brown was by 2005 incorporating the language of Christ into his lyrics. "I don't think there is any question," said Nego Chic, a well-known secular rapper, "that it is contagious. My lyrics have shifted. I would say, we are surrounded by that. With all the gospel rap, the rest of us have become 'gospel rappers' too."

From gospel rappers' point of view, rap played a key role in their process of religious conversion. Listen to Ton:

> There are a lot of rappers out there who speak the name of the Lord. But talk is cheap—you have to take a close look at their conduct. Are they obedient to the Word? You know, you can rap about God and Jesus, but then these

Gospel rappers taking a stage by storm

guys go backstage, and they are drinking whiskey and smoking and committing adultery. . . . And they are out there in front talking of God?! Well,
there were many of us who saw that hypocrisy. And each one has his own
story to tell. But I noticed it about ten years ago. One after another of us,
we were converting to the Lord. And I was really worried at first because I
thought, "My Lord, I love rap so much. Does this mean I will have to give it
up?" And the Lord spoke to me and said, "No, Ton, use this art to spread my
good news." That is what he said. That was the Holy Spirit speaking to me. I
even thought for years that I would have to wear a suit and tie out there as I
rapped, but little by little I realized that God doesn't care about that. So now
you see a long list of these guys who had rapped as seculars, they converted,
and then others in their group followed, or they went out on their own. So I
think that is what happened, John—like me, lots of rappers just started converting, so we brought our faith into our rhymes.

Now these rappers see themselves as endowed with a divine mission. Listen
to Nathan:

I see all this as God's using us, absolutely. Because look, who is it that has the ear of today's young people, the poor kid who lives in the favela? Is it the government? No. Is it the media? No. Is it these churches? No, young kids think churches are really square and boring. They say, "Why should I go there? That is not interesting." They want to hear music. They want to move. They have energy. And God knows this, even if many of our pastors do not. So God has seen our work, and he is using us to spread the Word to these kids. I praise God for that. I see this as really the unfolding of a plan, that we are at the cutting-edge of a reaching out to a whole new generation. Without question. Every soul is precious. We go one by one. At the end of each show, I ask for those who have been touched by my words to raise their hand to Jesus, to come forth and stand up and come to the stage so we can pray over him. And God sees that we are converting many souls.

Gospel Rap in Performance

On a gusty Saturday afternoon, I travel by subway and bus from the center of São Paulo to Jardim São Jorge, a neighborhood of several thousand inhabitants nestled in the southern reaches of the urban periphery. I am going to attend a "Festival Rua Gospel," a day-long street concert, organized by a local Assembly of God church, that promises to bring together gospel rappers from across the southern zone. São Jorge, one of hundreds of "Jardins" (gardens) in the *periferia*, is a neighborhood divisible into the larger, better-off buildings and homes closest to the store-lined asphalt road named Peixoto de Melo Filho, and the *conjunto*, the crazy-quilt of hundreds of red-clay and gray-cement homes built by their owners, set back from the main street. The main street is packed with people circulating among a pharmacy, a supermarket, a bar, a hardware supplier, a car repair shop, a toy store, and a bank, each adorned with its own vibrantly blue or yellow or red hand-painted façade. I turn into the *conjunto*, following directions given to me by Pretto, an amateur rapper who just produced his own do-it-yourself CD. There I am flanked by houses two and three stories high, rising above narrow alleyways, some plastered, some not, with dirty white cement columns and windows without panes, topped by satellite dishes, clotheslines, TV antennae, water reservoirs, and electrical lines. On the roofs, boys are flying paper kites. In the narrow streets, I navigate around a sweetish-sour smell wafting up from the creek, pass amid shouts of children and barking

Gospel rappers with anthropologist

dogs, and feel in my heart and lungs the throbbing rap and samba drum-
beats pouring out of open windows. I stop an old woman with long hair and
ask her to direct me toward the gospel festival. She smiles and says, "It is so
wonderful that God is using this music to bring the young into the fold. Are
you a missionary?"

The drum machine grows louder, and I can make out the recorded voice
of Pregador Luo. I enter a dead-end street, with a growing crowd of young
men in sneakers and knee-length baggy pants and loose T-shirts and baseball caps, the women in jeans or knee- or calf-length skirts, hair flowing or
tied in back. A big hand-lettered banner tied to electric poles on either side
of the street announces, "Festival Rua Gospel: Jesus Quer Vida e Paz na Periferia" (Gospel Street Festival: Jesus Wants Life and Peace in the Periphery).
Under the banner, a twenty-foot flat-bed truck is a stage on which big, black,
square speakers lie stacked in two pyramids. The MC is on stage, microphone
in hand. "Brothers and sisters!" he shouts. "Gather round, gather round!" He
is wearing a black beret and a green T-shirt with the words "Jesus Te Ama"
(Jesus Loves You); his left hand alternates between palming his chest and

forming a middle- and forefinger *V*. "*Manos* [Brothers]! We have brought this to you today to say that Jesus is Lord. Amen? What you see there on this banner, that is what we want to say today! Life and peace in the *periferia*! We have come so that there can be life and peace in this place, in this community of Jardim São Jorge. Amen?"

A few more young men in warm-up jackets, baggy pants, and white sneakers wander into the street, standing in little circles, some with their backs to the truck. Someone arrives by motorcycle. The afternoon is growing warmer. The sound is good, and the clouds are evaporating.

"Now listen up," the MC continues. "How many mothers have given up in despair and do not know what has happened to their sons? That he might get killed any time of day? Many of the artists you'll hear today lived a life that was nearly destroyed by drugs and crime, but they found the truth. Amen? Show some love—to Fabinho and Roxo!!"

The rapping duo climbs onto the truck stage amid sincere applause, decked out in chains, loose warm-up pants, and leather jackets. They hold their mikes like weapons. "Look, *manos*," says Fabinho, "I am here to say that you need to treat your mothers with love and respect. Because no matter how messed up you are, she is always there to protect you, you know what I'm saying? For her, you are forever a hero."

Fabinho launches into a slow and simple rhyme, enunciating every word against the playback's heavy bass drum. A few heads start to bob. Both rappers move slowly, deliberately, across the surface of the truck bed. Fabinho leads the vocals; Roxo comes in to accent the syllables. "I miss you mother," Fabinho begins:

> How many times have I cried out for you at night, but you are not there?
> You are my queen, but I abandoned you. I walked out because I did not understand.
> But I want you to know today that you never left my heart.
> I know you have passed on. I know that we argued and fought.
> But Jesus knows that I really loved you.
> Mother, I am thinking of you now, and Jesus is giving me the strength to return to all the lessons you taught me growing up.

Now Roxo comes in with a faster, harder, syncopated rap:

Lord, I pray, do not let me forget her face. I need to remember it
    always.
Don't let it slip out of my mind.
Let her keep me strong to resist temptations and all things that destroy
    us.
Mother, I have a daughter now. She looks just like you. Now that I
    know better, I am going to raise her in the commandments and
    love of Jesus.

The crowd, heads bobbing, is getting bigger and more energetic. I move
around, chatting with people, asking where they are from; all are from the
immediate neighborhood. Some are already converts, but many are not: they
are locals attracted by the sound.

Now it is Pretto's turn to take the stage. This is the guy who invited me,
the reason I am here. I had met Pretto a few weeks earlier and have already
heard him speak of the major passions in his life: Jesus Christ, his family, and
hip hop. Thirty years old, a convert for ten, Pretto is given to reflective pauses
before answering questions. He earns a living by making deliveries for a large
downtown firm on a small motorcycle, fighting traffic and car fumes for nine
hours a day. He has been listening to rap since he was sixteen and writing
rhymes since he was twenty. "Rap is my life," he says. "It is the way to be
me—to be the person that God wants me to be." On the cover of his do-it-
yourself solo CD, he looks away; but on the inside cover he looks straight at
you, with large, long-lashed eyes. Friends say he resembles Tupac Shakur.

After greeting the crowd, now some two hundred strong, Pretto launches
into "Just One More." The battering-ram bass drum begins. He grips his
microphone and starts pacing, pouring out his rap in one hot continuous
syllabic stream. "Just one more, just one more," he cries.

Dead kid in the *periferia*, just one more kid from the neighborhood.
Here, one more body fallen on the ground, one more body under the
    traffic sign.
Next to the police, there moves a crowd, tumultuous, curious, trying to
    find out some information.
Ten minutes later, the mother appears, doesn't believe what she sees.
That is not why she carried her son for nine months.

How little she did suspect. It is reality, it is a fatality, it is the final path,
life devalued.
White or black, it doesn't matter, here in the *periferia*, everyone is fair
game.

Pretto raps more bullets, and he is sweating. "Here in the *periferia*," he told
me in our interview, "you say the wrong thing, you end up dead. Here the
kids I grew up with are either in prison or dead. This is my reality." The problem diagnosed, now comes the remedy: do what is right, know who your
true friends are, resist the promise of easy money, get educated, read, stay
away from drugs, entrust your soul to Jesus. "Brother," he preaches, "the only
way to value your life, the way to save yourself from this disaster, brother, I
tell you, the one who will free you is Jesus Christ."

I turn and look at the crowd. In one corner is a clutch of young men and
women, their eyes tightly closed, their palms raised to the sky. Elsewhere it
is a sea of bodies moving slowly and appreciatively to Pretto's cadences. Late
afternoon is falling, and there are still dozens of artists to come. In act after
act, rappers rhyme about the dangers of the *periferia* and the path out of danger through love of Jesus Christ. The verbal bullets of salvation will go on
being fired for seven hours to come. By the end of the night, maybe a thousand young people will have passed through this dead-end street. Only the
Lord will know for certain how many will be saved.

Samba Gospel
A Brief History of Samba Gospel

In the late 1980s, a radical idea irrupted in evangelical churches located in
the poor neighborhoods of Rio de Janeiro: a widening circle of youth groups
began to believe that samba—widely denounced by evangelicals as devil
music—might actually be a good way to spread the gospel. I recall from my
own experience (I was conducting research in Rio at the time) the idea getting raised in the weeks after Christmas 1987. Young believers enthusiasti-
cally championed the idea of gospel samba as a way of reaching out to the
spiritually endangered during the Carnaval season that was about to arrive.
The idea had been raised from time to time since the early 1970s but had
always been quashed by God-fearing believers who regarded samba—playground of drinking, dancing, and eroticism—as absolutely irredeemable. In

early 1988, the idea finally found some traction. Church youth groups made formal proposals; time was set aside on church committee meeting agendas; articles both for and against appeared in church newsletters. For the first time, it was thinkable that evangelicals might play the *cavaquinho*, the *tam-tam*, and the *tambor*, the classic instruments of Brazil's national music.

Why pastors opened up space for this discussion is not hard to fathom. Simply put, by the late 1980s, they were finally coming to terms with the need to address the tastes of restless, musically voracious youth (Cunha 2007). With the ending of government censorship in 1985, the opening of the Brazilian consumer market to international commodities, the young demographic bulge, and the falling price of music tapes, popular music, always a richly fertile field in Brazil, arguably became more verdant and flourishing than ever (Perrone and Dunn 2001; McCann 2004; Avelar, Dunn, and Paranhos 2011). Urbanization, television, and the growth of cheap US consumer imports all meant, by the late 1980s, more consumption of music by young Brazilians than ever before. A pastor said to me at the time, "If we don't have the music they want, they simply won't come." Still, the idea of gospel samba was more than most evangelicals could stomach, and it was, in the end, defeated by traditionalist Pentecostal churches such as the Assembly of God and Deus é Amor (God Is Love). In late January 1988, a minister of the Assembly of God explained the defeat. "John," he said, "does anyone really believe that in all that orgy of Carnaval, anyone will pay attention to what we say? And if we let our young people do this, will they resist that temptation?"

But if the idea died among the classic Pentecostals, it met a rather different fate among neo-Pentecostal churches such as Renascer em Cristo and Igreja Universal do Reino de Deus. In these, in early 1988, a surprising consensus quickly grew around the idea of a Christian samba *bloco* (music group). "Yes, this year there will be a Christian samba group," a deacon in the Universal Church told me at the time. Since the late 1970s, the neo-Pentecostals' view of themselves as battling to take over spaces occupied by the devil had been leading them to embrace electronic media, consumer desires, and an ever-broadening array of musical genres. Since the late 1970s, such churches had been playing rock and roll, *sertanejo* (Brazilian country; Dent 2009), *forró*, *música popular brasileira* (MPB; Dunn 2001), soul, R&B, and reggae; it thus was but a short step to include in their repertoire samba, that most dangerous of musics. As a minister of Renascer said to me in 1988, "The devil has no hiding place. He has no kingdom that Christ cannot vanquish. So it is with samba. What a blessing it will be when we have restored it to God's hands."

Thus, it came to pass that Marco Antônio Peixoto, a young minister of the Comunidade Evangélica Internacional da Zona Sul, a neo-Pentecostal church in Rio de Janeiro, formed the Bloco Mocidade Dependente de Deus—the "Music Group of Youth Who Depend on God"—in January 1988, providing the hundred-person *bloco* with uniforms, instruments, scores, and rehearsal space. Bloco Mocidade debuted in the Carnaval of February 1988, parading through the streets of Rio's elite southern zone, wowing passersby with the sight of Bible-toting evangelicals playing samba (though not dancing). Other neo-Pentecostal churches were not far behind. In 1991, Ezequiel Teixeira, pastor of Rio's enormous Projeto Vida Nova de Irajá, founded the *bloco* Cara de Leão (the Lion's Face), sending five thousand congregants onto the bustling Avenida Rio Branco at Carnaval time. Marching in tight unison, bedecked in green and white T-shirts, led by the church's youth groups, sexes separated, the *bloco* played a samba written especially for the occasion. As they progressed, a team of evangelists distributed flyers advertising the church; and at preplanned intervals, an evangelical street-theater group dramatized religious narratives in devil-and-skeleton costumes.[5] And at a break in the music, from atop a sound truck, a preacher thundered condemnation of Carnaval as a tool of the devil.[6]

Every year since 1991, this *bloco* has continued to march,[7] and by the late 1990s, Cara de Leão finally had imitators. In 1997, the Bom à Beça (Too Good) was formed in the city of Curitiba by twelve regional churches, to sing biblical sambas and parade through the streets. In the city of Salvador, the Igreja Batista Missionária da Independência formed the group Sal da Terra. In the context of this trend, since 2000, gospel samba groups have also appeared finally in São Paulo: it is likely that in greater São Paulo there are currently dozens of such groups, including Samba Gospel Brasil, Borel Brasil, Ide (Go Forth), Divina Unção (Divine Anointing), Valentes de Davi (Warriors of David), and Perseverança (Perseverance). One of the first such groups to form in greater São Paulo was Deus Crioulos (a pun that joins the meanings "God Created Them" and "God/Blacks"), founded in 2002 inside the Comunidade Carisma in the periurban city of Osasco. The motives of Jairo, the founder of Deus Crioulos, were similar to those of Ezequiel. "I was praying at home," he explained, "when I realized that I really needed to worship the Lord with samba. Because I wanted to attract people who have this prejudice against samba. There is unfortunately a culture that says samba is not good enough to serve God. And Deus Crioulos came to show that, on the contrary, it was possible to play samba and serve God. Our goal is to break down all taboos. I want people to feel free to sing a samba in church with a lyric that they already know."

Gospel Samba in Performance

On a drizzly Saturday morning in São Paulo, I am nursing a bitter *cafezinho* (espresso) at a *lanchonete* (snack bar) near the center of the city, and my cell phone rings. On the other end, Débora's voice is a flawless bell. "John! I won't take no for an answer! You simply must go with us." Débora is inviting me to an outdoor gospel music festival. I have attended gospel festivals before, and know they are always good for setting up interviews. With a little looking, one can find some such festival in the urban periphery virtually every weekend. These are electrically amplified affairs, centered on a stage mounted either at the end of a street or on one of the small rectangular plots of grass designated as parks by the municipal ministry of public lands. A *festa* is a program with between five and fifteen performers, the long ones turning into marathons lasting the better part of a day and evening, the audience swelling and shrinking in function of the hour, weather, and act.

I met Débora, a woman in her thirties, a few months ago when she was a visiting soloist at the Azusa church and had brought down the house with her high-voltage voice. I visited her tiny Pentecostal church, a place so steeped in the Holy Spirit that congregants danced and whooped and hollered for four straight hours. My visit made us fast friends, and Débora proceeded to assign herself the task of ensuring that I heard as much gospel music as she could stuff into my calendar. Every week, she now insists on shepherding me somewhere—to a tiny church buried in the favela Jardim Angélica, to a midsized church in the Jardim São Carlos, to a crooked side street in the northern zone near Guarulhos, to an open-air festival near Cidade Tiradentes—that I might listen, hear, open my heart, and be penetrated by God's Levites, those he has chosen to spread his news to the world on the wings of music.

Today's excursion is to a large public *praça* (square) in Capão Redondo, a neighborhood in the farthest-flung corner of the southern zone. When I finally arrive, bedraggled from an hour and a half of standing in a bus, I wait in the spot Débora has designated as our meeting point, my collar up against the chill, watching the cold mist glisten on the square's muddy oases of broad-bladed grass. Débora's voice rings out. "God love you! Didn't I tell you to bring an umbrella?" We laugh, exchange news, eat spicy hot dogs, and begin our trek through the thickening crowd. Hundreds, maybe thousands, are gathering. Crentes[8] outnumber non-crentes, and everyone seems under the age of thirty—young working-class women in jeans, knit turtlenecks, and denim jackets; young men in T-shirts with their favorite musicians' logos, heavy jackets, and knitted caps. As we jostle to be nearer the stage, the words on the blue banner over the stage grow more distinct: "Welcome to the Fifth Annual Gospel Fest of Capão Redondo."

Huge speakers pound out strains of lead singer Rogério singing black gospel with Templo Soul, and Débora and I bob in place. Other acts follow, and the crowd warms up. Then the master of ceremonies, a middle-aged, short man, takes the microphone, three young men arrange their instruments behind him, and another two men hang a large Brazilian flag at the back of the stage. "OK, brothers and sisters!" the emcee bellows. "I want to introduce a new act, one that has never before been heard on this stage. Guess what this group plays? Samba! Samba in the name of the Lord! So give it up for . . . Samba Gospel Brasil!" There are good-natured shouts of welcome. Débora shoots me a sideways glance, wrinkles her forehead, and extends her lower lip. "Gospel samba? My Lord, that is new!"

Seven lanky men in their twenties and thirties walk onstage and take their places behind the microphones. Steam rises all around them, but not by design; it appears as hot klieg lights evaporate the heavy moisture in the air. Each musician carries an instrument—a large, elongated drum; a squatter, smaller one; a handheld shaker; a tambourine; something that looks like a ukulele (the cavaquinho); and a big six-string guitar. The group wears loose, faded jeans, running shoes, polo and T-shirts on which the words "Unção Divina" (divine anointing) float over a chalice and a map of Brazil. The man carrying the cavaquinho is very dark-skinned, bearded, with a head of natural Afro hair; the one on the big drum is tall and also very dark; the others are all shades of brown, and two are lighter-skinned. "The peace of the Lord be with you!" declares one. "I am Jairo. We are Divina Unção. We want to thank you for this opportunity tonight." Over his shoulder, Jairo is draped with a Brazilian flag. "It has been three years since we started in the city of Iguapé, with this group that has been blessed by the Lord."

The crowd is becoming increasingly excited. They have heard a lot of different kinds of Christian music, but few have heard Christian samba. "Wow, samba. Can you believe it?" "No, man, listen. Let's listen." "Hallelujah!" Jairo unfurls the flag and lets it flutter. A cheer wells up from the audience. "My friends!" he cries. "God has used us for the honor and glory of the Lord, yes, through samba, this Brazilian rhythm! Brothers and sisters, I love my Brazil, and I love my samba. I love it, but I do not exalt it. I am not an idolater."

"No, thank the Lord!"

"We are here to exalt the name of Jesus."

Behind Jairo, the musician on the *cavaquinho* begins to pick, and the air fills with the crinkly sound that can only be produced by this tightly strung tiny guitar. This is the sound of samba, its unmistakable instrumental preamble announcing the arrival of drums. A wave of sweet, warm emotion washes over the crowd.

"Many out there say this is the rhythm of the devil," Jairo continues. "But let me ask you, dear brothers and sisters, does anything belong to the devil?"

"Noooo!!"

"No, of course not! Everything is in the hands of the Lord! The devil has no power! He tried to steal this rhythm, but we are taking it back. Only Jesus has the power, and in his hands, all rhythms touch your soul!"

"Amen! Glory be to Jesus!"

"It has not been easy! It took the elders of our church a long time to let us play. They did not trust this rhythm! They thought it was just music for bars! But we preached the Word, and finally they let us play. Some think sambistas run after women. But we run after the Lord! We pray, we have our wives, our fiancées. We are certain that this project is not in our hands but in the hands of our Lord Jesus Christ."

Jairo recounts, to the gentle picking of the *cavaquinho*, how he met a woman who had fallen away from church because every one she entered preached against fun. "'No, no,' I told her, 'go to our church's service, because believe it or not, there is going to be a samba group!' And the woman says to me, 'A samba group?!' And I say, 'Yeah, go see!' So the woman shows up and marvels at what she hears. Samba in the church! Surely God is great if he can save this rhythm from hell! The Lord said, 'Go forth and preach the word of God!' And that is what we are doing, brothers!"

The picking behind Jairo grows more insistent, and rain is falling in earnest now, keeping time with the *cavaquinho*. Jairo launches into a song the words to which come quickly to everyone's lips. It is a familiar hymn in regular time, with only the guitar and the drum, "Eu vejo a Glória" (I See the Glory), a hymn made famous by Fernanda Brum, now sung weekly in churches and on Christian radio and TV. Débora knows it by heart.

"Eu quero ver agora" (I want to see now), Jairo sings, then aims his mike at the crowd, who yell back, "o Teu poder!" (Your power!).

"A Tua glória . . ." (Your glory . . .).

And the crowd, ". . . inundando meu ser!" (. . . flooding my being!).

Jairo: "Vou levantar as mãos e vou receber / Vou louvando o Teu nome, porque sinto o Senhor me tocar" (I will raise my hands and I will receive / I praise your name, because I feel the Lord touch me).

Through this first stanza, the instrumentation remains the familiar unsyncopated 4/4 rhythms of guitar and drum of conventional gospel. The band is softening up the crowd, preparing it for the shock of hearing this hymn turn into samba. Stanza by stanza, the musicians deposit new sonic layers: first comes the *reco-reco*, the rattle in the lead singer's hand; then the *tamborim*, the small drum; then the *repinique*, surrounding us with the sound of tinny, plucked strings; finally the loud *surdo* drum, pushing the sound to penetrate our lower bodily halves. Jairo, cradled by these enveloping layers, dances in place. The crowd goes wild, singing along.

> Eu vejo a glória do Senhor hoje aqui (I see the glory of the Lord here now)
>
> A sua mão o seu poder sobre mim (Your hand and your power over me)
>
> Os céus abertos hoje eu vou contemplar (The open skies today I will ponder)
>
> O amor descer nesse lugar (How love descends to this place)

Hearing this hymn on *cavaquinho*, *tambor*, and *tam-tam* may not strike the non-Brazilian reader as all that remarkable; but for Brazilians, who have been taught to see these instruments as tools of the devil, it is a jolt, similar perhaps to witnessing someone play Frisbee in Notre Dame cathedral. "Can you believe it?" cries Débora, as she sambas. "We are listening to Christian samba! Can you believe it?"

Jairo's voice is raw, untrained, a little pitchy. Behind it is the perfectly smooth thrum of the drum, tambourine, and *reco-reco*. The voices of the others are brazenly out of sync and refuse to hold notes for very long. (All of this is typical of most good samba bands, which do not treat singing with the same gravity that they do instrumentals.) At the start of this number, some young people are swaying modestly, arms over their heads, in a wave. Then the crowd gives in. Young men and women dance in a row, side by side, or in circles, not with each other, bodies shifting back and forth inside small imaginary squares, knees bending and straightening. The women are a little more daring than the men, who shift on their feet, watching the women out of the corners of their eyes.

The song is reaching a climax. Just as Carnaval samba singers do, Jairo shouts a nonmusical version of the next line to be sung, then leads the crowd to the final stanza:

> Eu quero ver agora o Teu poder (I want to see now your power)
> A Tua glória inundando meu ser (Your glory flooding my being)
> Vou levantar as mãos e vou receber (I will raise up my hands and
>   receive)
> Vou louvando o Teu nome, porque sinto o Senhor me tocar (I will
>   praise your name, because I feel the Lord touch me)

Jairo brandishes the Brazilian flag one more time and gives it a solid sweep across the stage. As the group exits, the crowd thunders its demand for more, chanting "Samba! Samba!" until Divine Anointing appears and plays once more, satiating the audience's need to hear that most Brazilian of rhythms. "I will never forget this," says Débora, after they disappear a second time. I am astonished to see tears rolling down her cheeks.

Black Gospel Music in São Paulo
A Short History of Black Gospel Music in São Paulo

Seventh-Day Adventists have long had a love affair with Negro spirituals, whose references to the Promised Land echo their millennialism (Blackman 1996; Bradford 1996; Jerma Jackson 2004, 103ff.) In the years after World War II, Seventh-Day Adventist missionaries brought Negro spirituals to Brazil (Schünemann 2009). Sergio Saas, an Adventist, remembers hearing spirituals in his church when he was growing up. "Everyone loved them," he recalls, "because spirituals were full of good Bible language. . . . The church elders would never have considered admitting into the church heavier beats with drums; but the spirituals were fine." Slow, somber, melodious, packed with biblical references, the spirituals began to circulate in other churches as well. Where spirituals went, gospel blues soon followed. Jazzier than spirituals, calmer than big-belting gospel, gospel blues presented a compromise for conservative Protestants. "Negro spirituals and gospel blues arrived together," explained Josué, lead singer of Kadoshi. "The churches felt comfortable with this kind of music, because it was slower and more peaceful."

The career of Antônio Bicudo is illustrative. Born poor in 1940 in São Paulo, raised in the strait-laced tradition of the Assembly of God, Bicudo was in his twenties when he began to listen to Aretha Franklin and Mahalia Jackson. Instead of embracing their diaphragm-bending music, however, Bicudo sang gospel blues, speeding them up and making them bluesier. "He always loved to go to the edge of what was acceptable," his widow recalled. The result was wildly popular with Christian audiences: between 1970 and 1990, Bicudo recorded no fewer than twenty-one records and inspired a generation of Brazilian Christian artists, including José Carlos Correa, Luiz e Carvalho, Lorisvado, Washington Alves, and Beltrán.[9]

Yet the magnetism of drum- and electric-guitar music could not be resisted for long. A generation of Christians eager to play faster and harder were chomping at the bit. Among them were two Afro-Brazilian teenage brothers named Josias and Josué, members of a small Assembly of God church in São Paulo's peripheral southern zone. From their father, who played clarinet, the brothers learned classic musicianship; from their mother they learned samba, soul, and funk.[10] (The Beatles and the *Jovem Guarda*[11] they discovered on their own.) Soon they recruited a talented friend; located and borrowed a bass, electric guitar, and drums; and named themselves the Redeemed Ones (Os Redimidos). By the mid-1970s, they were deep into Marvin Gaye, Toni Tornado, and Jorge Ben, and they scoured stores for recordings of Mahalia Jackson, Milton Bronson, and James Moore. "We realized," explained Josias, "that the rhythms of soul were an extension of Negro spirituals, that it was all music of God." They faced strong prejudices. "Many pastors just didn't get it," recalled Josué. "They thought that drums and guitar and loud singing were devil music." Those pastors were serious: in the late 1970s, they excommunicated Os Redimidos.

But the wilderness did not last long. In the early 1980s, pastors anxious to attract young people to their congregations began loosening the rules of

Black gospel singer

acceptable church music.[12] Inspired by Os Redimidos (renamed Atos II in 1980), other young artists began forming heavy-beat-driven gospel groups, such as Os Hebreus, Grupo Semente, A Nova Luz, Mintre, and Embaixadores de Cristo. Soloists began to proliferate: Matos Nascimento became Brazil's Ray Charles; Oséias de Paula, its James Brown; and Alvaro Tito, its Stevie Wonder.[13] In the midst of this new energy, in 1985, a young evangelist named Pedro Liasch organized the soul group Banda Rara and soon opened Pedra Viva (Living Rock), a church which became the Apollo Theater of São Paulo's black gospel scene.[14] "We became the kids who go to Pedra Viva," said Felipe, who in 1991 started attending the church's regular Friday-night shows. "It became something everyone understood—'Hey, are you on for Friday? Pedra Viva?'" The church nurtured a generation of black gospel artists, including the one and only Robson Nascimento. Said Isabêh, the unofficial chroni-cler of the city's black gospel scene, "True vocal virtuosity in black gospel came with Robson. He arrived on the scene in 1993–1994, at Pedra Viva. He took the place by storm. It was never the same after that. He had a sense of the stage. He knew how to make James Brown–type yells and screams. He danced, had a real sense of spectacle. He had a sense of the visceral. He really wanted to shout out. He was so strong, so charismatic. No one, and I mean no one, was singing in Brazil at that time like Robson."

Now it is important to understand that these artists did not have an explicit, self-conscious racial-pride agenda; their goal was to attract souls to Jesus.[15] But in the early 1990s, as blackness in São Paulo became increasingly politicized, it was hard to be politically neutral about race (Nogueira 2004). In 1991, Atos II found themselves in the spotlight due to their use of "Afro" clothing, which they had initially adopted, said Josué, "as a way to stand out, not to make a political statement. Wherever we went, people would ask us to talk about *a raça negra*, to talk about the black movement—so we had to! I had to start learning about these things, so we could answer the questions posed to us." Among other things, the band was invited to perform at the 1992 commemoration of Zumbi's death. "All of a sudden," Josué recalled, "all of that attention—we certainly wanted to have our music heard, and so we did not want to say no—but all of that demanded from us a certain identity. We had to work on the side of identity, for our race, whether or not that had been a priority for us." This meant serving as race-identified role models. "We started to want to show through our conduct that *negros* too can win, that we too are children of God, to help the *negro* valorize himself, help him study, know his rights, to know his value—just by seeing us up there."

Until the early 1990s, it was still possible to count on the fingers of two hands the black gospel acts in São Paulo. But starting in the mid-1990s and continuing until the mid-2000s, the city saw the formation of two or three new black choirs every year and these spun off dozens of other acts. By the mid-2000s, there were in São Paulo over two hundred black gospel choirs, quartets, bands, trios, duets, and soloists, both amateur and professional.[16] Several factors contributed to this growth. First, neo-Pentecostal churches were eager to expand, and to do so, they increasingly adopted a big-tent policy on music, welcoming an unprecedentedly broad range of musical styles.[17] At the same time, the falling cost of VHS players made it possible for a growing number of low-income people to buy and rent videos, including videos of black choirs.[18] It is worth noting that every founder of a black choir I met traced his decision to found such a group to seeing a video of a North American black choir sometime between 1990 and 1997.

Things really took off after 2000. In 2001, the vocalist and music director Sérgio Saas recruited the best singers, rehearsing them for months before

Black gospel singing group

their first concert. His choir, named Raiz Coral (Root Choir) immediately set the standard for the highest vocal quality. The choir's first CD, *Pra Louvar* (2003), became the best-selling black gospel album in the country. In that year, the group opened at Credicard Hall for the world-famous black gospel singer Kirk Franklin, ratifying Raiz Coral's stature as the premier black gospel choir in Brazil. Soon they had sparked dozens of imitators, including Coral Resgate, Coral dos Hebreus, the Mission Choir, and Coral Virtude. Every year now sees the emergence on the scene of at least one new black choir.

Black Gospel in Performance

Let us now turn from history to the contemporary sights and sounds of the best-known black gospel choir in the city. Raiz Coral—thirty-five sublime voices that sing a broad repertoire of US and Brazilian gospel music—will long be remembered as the group whose first CD, released in 2003, sold more copies than any other in the history of Brazilian black gospel recording. They will also be remembered for the fact that the following year a scurrilous rumor circulated that if you played their CD at slow speed, you could hear Satan being praised. The rumor never dented their appeal. Nowadays, a typical week for Raiz Coral includes a day of studio time, two rehearsals, and three shows. When the word goes out that they are going to perform, venues sell out immediately. Some pastors falsely announce that Raiz Coral is coming to their church, just to fill the pews.

It is a muggy Saturday night. I am tapping my fingers impatiently on the subway-car wall as we pull into the Vila Mariana subway stop. Raiz Coral is playing at Pedra Viva tonight. If you are a churchgoing Christian who wants to feel surrounded by historical karma, Pedra Viva is the place to be on a Saturday night. It is a five-block walk to the church, with half an hour to go until the eight o'clock show. We navigate through the crowd on Avenida Domingos de Moraes, deafened by the roars of passing buses, our skin sticky with the diesel-laden air. The sky is darkening. We hurry past middle-class apartment buildings, a car dealership, an art-supply store, a language school, until we arrive at the old converted cinema. The sidewalk is filled with more than four hundred people lined up over two city blocks. Admission on Saturdays is usually free, but demand is so great for Raiz Coral that the church charges ten reais (five dollars) per person. It is a young crowd, mostly in couples, some married, no kids in tow; the men in ironed slacks, neatly pressed shirts, leather jackets, designer caps, fashion glasses, some with ties, some with jackets; the women in pumps and snazzy blouses, tight jeans, and smart jewelry. This is definitely a "*negro*-and-proud" crowd. Hairstyles are a walk through *Raça* magazine: men in stylish dreads and designer buzz clips, women in delicate perms, braids, and carefully shaped naturals.

Some people start dropping little chic phrases in English, like "Hey, brother, what's happening?" and "We are in Harlem, man!" "Yeah, brother!" Someone imitates the broad theatrical gestures of Sérgio Saas and mock-croons a hymn in Sérgio's inimitable style. A young woman starts dancing in place, bobbing her shoulders and thrusting out her chin. Those around her applaud.

At long last, the church doors open, and we move en masse through the old, dimly lit theater lobby, past a table covered with DVDs of Aretha Franklin, Kirk Franklin, Fred Hammond, Isabêh, Sergio Saas, and Robson Nascimento. But no one is buying right now: we are all too eager for the show to begin. Inside the auditorium, we are flanked by dirty white walls under a high-paneled ceiling. Five slow-moving overhead fans struggle to dissipate the humidity. Within minutes, four hundred people are in their seats, and the place is humming. A tall black man in a fine leather jacket appears onstage and raises a hand. "My friends!" he proclaims, "in the name of Jesus!" Eruptions of "Hallelujah, Jesus!" "Amen, Jesus!" "Brothers and sisters," he continues, "we are here tonight for a great show." Roars of approval. The man next to me stands up, shouts, and throws up his arms. "Yes, we are here for a great show," he continues. "But what is the greatest show on earth?" The crowd roars, knowing its lines: "Jesus Christ!" Thunderous "Hallelujahs" erupt all around. The man raises his hand once more, waiting for us to calm down. "My friends," he says, "I ask that before we begin we all give thanks to the Lord for being together tonight." A hush falls on the place, and we all rise. The man shuts his eyes and raises his left hand. "Dear Lord, hear us tonight, oh Lord." "Hear us, hear us," we reply. "We have come here tonight to praise and worship you." The crowd: "Hallelujah, Jesus." The man: "Yes, Lord, thank you for giving us this opportunity tonight. For we know that you wish us to worship you in all ways, that you value all the ways we praise your name, that you love all rhythms, that for you no rhythm is wrong when played with love for you." The crowd: "Praised be the Lord!" "So tonight, Lord, bless this gathering. Bless all these souls who have come together to show their love for you, to sing and dance as they praise you. Thank you, Lord, that you may bless all our hearts and bring us all closer to you. Amen, Lord."

He pauses. "Did I say amen?"

"Amen!" we explode. "Amen! Amen!"

"Well, then, my beloved friends, ladies and gentlemen, brothers and sisters, without further ado, join me in welcoming . . . Raiz Coral!!!!!!!"

The crowd is on its feet, and that is where it will stay for much of the next two hours. The whole place goes dark momentarily; then, suddenly, the stage is flooded by flashing red, green, and blue lights and jets of stage smoke. A drummer appears onstage wearing wraparound sunglasses; he leaps behind his drums and crashes into the bass-line riff for "Louvado," the group's signature song. Emerging from behind the smoke, the bass player appears, followed by guitarist and keyboardist. They launch into the melody, familiar to everyone from the CD, and soon everyone in the auditorium is chanting.

Finally, the choir arrives. Their entrance does not disappoint: twenty men and women in their twenties storm the stage from behind us. Spotlights shine down on the two aisles, and there they are, led by Sérgio, singing in perfect harmony, leaping and twirling and dancing up toward the stage. The men are dressed in shining red and white suits and ties; the women wear glittering sequined red and white dresses; and everywhere there are braids, corn rows, dreadlocks, naturals, and shining bald heads, as far as the eye can see. Onstage, they arrange themselves into groups of four behind five microphones, swinging their arms, bodies bobbing, grinning from ear to ear. The feeling is one of utterly infectious joy. The crowd has not stopped screaming.

Sérgio, dressed in an all-white suit, is totally in control. He plays the audience like an instrument and directs his artists with a raised eyebrow, a flip of the hand, a lift of the knee. He is a dynamo, a blur, constantly on the move, jumping, rocking, flirting, having a fantastic time. He is flanked by Scooby, shorter and smaller, a dense package of energy, weaving in and out of Sérgio's path, leading the audience in clapping, waving, jabbing fingers and fists into the air. Humor flows constantly from the two of them: barbed, funny arrows whose target is always the stiff formality of churches—their own and everybody else's. They take no prisoners. Twenty minutes into the show, we are still on our feet, dancing in place. Suddenly Sérgio calls for silence, knits his brow, purses his lips, and crosses his arms. He raises his hands before him and with an air of annoyance gestures for us to sit. As we start, slightly embarrassed, to do his bidding, he bursts out laughing: "I just wanted to see all you church people follow some rules!" The place explodes into joyous applause, a collective dig at priggish church etiquette. A little later, a woman yells the name of a song she wants to hear. Sérgio shoots her a severe look and turns to Scooby: "Please expel that woman." Roars of laughter. "We cannot have such behavior here!" More roars. And on it goes. The show is all about rejecting pompous decorum, about celebrating a style of music that touches the hearts and vibrates through bodies.

The first half of the show luxuriates in the astonishing talent of the artists onstage. They sing "Caridade" (Charity), all frenetic energy, all Stevie Wonder–like melismas, Aretha Franklinesque belting, Mahalia Jacksonian arias. Both Sérgio and Scooby pause frequently to wipe sweat from their brows with oversized white handkerchiefs. They play a mesmerizing game, in which each pretends to control the other's voice, pantomiming an imaginary dial on which they take turns increasing and decreasing each other's volume. Then comes a series of heart-stopping solos. As each soloist sings, Sérgio flashes a huge grin, spins, walks with faux-hauteur to center stage, eggs on the crowd, raises his hands and calls on everyone to raise theirs, stretches his arms out side to side, crooks his head toward the audience, and places two fingers behind his right ear in an "I can't hear you" gesture.

Then, midway through the evening, the tone suddenly shifts. We move from the raucous, infectious pleasure of music which celebrates the utter happiness of knowing one has been redeemed by Christ to utter somberness. Sérgio turns his back to us and looks at his choir, becoming the truly serious director, and leads them into the indescribably intense hymn "Jesus meu guia é" (Jesus Is My Guide). Seven minutes of music builds slowly, ever so slowly, from an almost inaudible, tentative plea to Jesus, to three choruses, each one more confident and louder than the last, until the choir arrives at two body-wrenching crescendos layered over shouts and wails. I can feel a change in my own body—it feels a weight upon it—and I can see tears flowing down other people's cheeks.

But Sérgio is not done with us. He raises his hands and asks the choir to launch into "Te adoramos" (We Worship Thee/We Love Thee). Gone is the pure joy of the first half of the evening. (Will it ever return? I wonder.) Now, on the strains of this gorgeous hymn, we are face-to-face with death, with the mystery of the universe, with the inscrutability of God's will. The first half of the show was praise; now all that is left is worship. Sérgio and Scooby struggle. They whine and fuss at the hem of the music, hoping to enter it. Then they do. The choir skips a beat, the drums come down like a thunderbolt, and all those voices suddenly combine to plunge all of us into a sonic ocean, deep and clear, as if we could see miles to the bottom. Sérgio's voice enters again, this time without the whine, now pure and hard and sharp, carving out an auditory space like no other, rising voluminously, toweringly, above the rest in a shattering melismatic fugue. You can see Sérgio's vocal cords at work: his neck stretches and shortens, stretches and shortens again. The Voice storms through the auditorium like a hurricane of pure energy, felling all in its path.

The show has been transformed, and so have we. It started as a spectacle of sound, light, color, and play, but now God is manifest, and we realize that we are in the presence of people anointed by him to fulfill a mission. Earlier in the show, the music was all about performance; now it is the purest vehicle for the Holy Spirit. At the start, "churchiness" took a back seat to the music; now the music has become a vehicle for the true church. Four hundred people are now standing with arms outstretched, praying, weeping, our hearts reached, our bodies sliced in two by Sérgio's vocal knife. The power of this style of music, its ability to transform us, has been revealed. Black gospel music has worked its divine power.

The Anointing

Though I have until now directed my attention to the external, visible features of these three scenes, I want to conclude by taking a first step inside these artists' cognitive worlds, by focusing on their deepest commonality: their conviction that they are vessels of anointing (*unção*). *Anointing* as a term of Christian theology refers to the bestowal on a person by the Holy Spirit of a skill, talent, or capacity that provokes deep spiritual experience, reflection, or change in others. Anointing is not just about musical talent: everything from preaching and teaching to evangelizing and writing and all of the arts may be anointed, that is, touched by the Holy Spirit. God anoints a person with the Holy Spirit, and that person is thereby enabled to produce life-changing performances of the skill with which God has endowed him or her.

Let us contemplate the theology of anointing as it relates to the singing voice. A good singer without anointing can move listeners to tears, can fill the audience with intense emotion, can induce feelings of joy, longing, even love. What he or she cannot do is save souls. To grasp this point, we need to understand that evangelical Protestants see the person as composed of body, soul, and spirit. The body—the outer, most superficial layer—is the seat of the senses, physical strength, weakness, hunger, and fleshly appetites. The soul— equated by evangelicals with the "heart"—is the seat of human (not divine) emotions such as love, anger, sadness, loneliness, pride, and arrogance. By themselves, body and soul lack redemptive power, tied as they are irredeemably to humancentric, worldly feelings. Buried deep within the human heart, however, lies the third element of the person: the spirit. While defining this element is difficult, evangelicals agree that it is something like a divine spark that God has placed in all of us so that we might all have a direct channel to him. Only the spirit is capable of feeling divine spiritual love and faith. But alas, most hearts are sinewy and tough, and the divine spark remains locked within, powerless to connect to God.

That is where music and anointing come in. Most music fails to reach the divine spark buried deep within the human heart. After all, much music is composed of rhythms and grooves that stir the physical body, making it move and dance and fill with desire, but little more. Some music goes a little deeper, softening the heart, drawing out its range of emotions, helping people to shed human tears for this-worldly reasons. In the evangelical perspective, the human heart, even when softened, is still filled with original sin. Unanointed singing cannot slice through the tough, sinewy walls of the heart to the sacred spark within; for that, one needs as a scalpel a voice anointed by the Holy Spirit. "You can listen to normal singing," said Silveira, the famous black gospel singer, "and it is beautiful. It can touch your senses and even your soul. But music from someone who is anointed does not just touch; it enters. It penetrates inside the heart. It is like a knife cutting though it, to get within and touch your spirit." The black gospel singer Angélica's account is more graphic still. "There are people who have beautiful voices," she told me, "but they don't have anointing. They can soften the heart, make someone feel very sad or happy. But they cannot grab your heart, rip it in two, and fill it with the Holy Spirit. For that, one needs to be anointed."

The mission of anointed singers and artists, thus, is to be that scalpel. To be anointed is to have been gifted with being a conduit between God and the divine spark within one's listeners, such that the Holy Spirit can penetrate into their souls. Serious gospel musicians today quote from the Second Book of Chronicles (2 Chronicles 5:12) to communicate the essence of their mission:

> The Levites who were the singers, all of them, even Asaph, Heman, Jeduthun, and their sons and their brothers, arrayed in fine linen, with cymbals and stringed instruments and harps, stood at the east end of the altar, and with them one hundred twenty priests sounding with trumpets; it happened, when the trumpeters and singers were as one, to make one sound to be heard in praising and thanking Yahweh; and when they lifted up their voice with the trumpets and cymbals and instruments of music, and praised Yahweh, saying, "For he is good; for his loving kindness endures forever!" that then the house was filled with a cloud, even the house of Yahweh, so that the priests could not stand to minister by reason of the cloud: for the glory of Yahweh filled God's house.

"If we can do that," Sérgio Saas told me, "then we have fulfilled God's mandate. That is our job, to fill the house of the Lord with a cloud. We are the modern Levites."

2

We Are All One in the *Periferia*

Blackness, Place, and Poverty in Gospel Rap

In late June 2003, I met Vilmar Junior, a twenty-two-year-old Pentecostal member of the Brazil for Christ church, dedicated rap MC, accomplished graffiti artist, and proud *negro*. We sat in a McDonald's in downtown São Paulo, near the Praça da República, munching French fries. He sported dreadlocks, wire-framed spectacles, and a T-shirt emblazoned with a map of Africa. Every word he said was suffused with earnestness. I listened for nearly three hours, through the bustling lunch-hour rush into the quiet midafternoon, as he regaled me with denunciations of the sinfulness of racism, stories of how his rapping had changed his life and those of others, and how the Lord had, it was clear, begun to pour his anointing on the hip hop movement in Brazil. I listened to all this with a feeling of great relief. I had been in São Paulo for three months, trying to find evangelical Protestants who articulated the points Vilmar was now making. At long last, much cheered, I turned off the tape, promised Vilmar I would contact him again, and left. Within an hour, I had written the following passage in my fieldnotes:

> June 19, 2003. My conversation this afternoon with Vilmar has forced me to rethink my whole approach to this project. Have I been looking in the wrong places? I have been talking to pastors, people in Bible study, and regular churchgoers. It always feels like I am stretching, like I have not yet found the consciousness I am hoping for. But after talking with Vilmar, I have begun to think maybe black consciousness has been under my nose all along. My thinking is turning to rap. Rappers. Hip hop. Why didn't I see it? Gospel rap. Surely a powerful vehicle for racial consciousness-raising. I think I have been resisting this, perhaps because from an unexamined judgment that music tends not to be a good vehicle for consciousness-raising. But what about rap? Surely there the cognitive can take place. I must turn my attention more to this. . . . Hernani alerted me to this. Maybe he was right.

Guided by the spirit of this passage, and by Hernani's insistence, for the next two years, I searched for racial consciousness among *paulista* rappers. I got to know a dozen amateur gospel rap groups, and as many secular ones, becoming a regular attendee at rehearsals and performances. I probed, prompted, asked, listened, and asked again for commentary—about race, blackness, neighborhood, police, violence, brutality, drugs, gangs, death, sex, God's will, music, and the rappers' art.

I expected that my time with gospel rappers would be rewarded with discoveries of militant black consciousness, synthesizing racial identity, politics, and the Bible. I expected some sort of convergence of religion, identity, and militancy because, like Hernani, that is how I understood rap: as the cultural expression of rebellion, the unification of art and struggle, the quintessential articulation of black pride. But I was wrong. Things were, as they always are, more complicated than I had expected. A month into my inquiry, I attended a meeting of Vilmar's rap group, Território D. Looking forward to a bath of black power rhetoric infused with biblical language, what I encountered instead were four young men, all *negros*, in a house, drinking lemonade, listening to music, and trading neighborhood gossip. I awaited their first rap, hoping for a denunciation of racism. Instead, it was an ode to Pirituba, the neighborhood where all the group's members lived; all that was being denounced was hatred, discord, drugs, and the lack of education, and what was being advocated was the need for salvation through Jesus Christ. The topic of race did not even come up. I scoured the group's rhymes for references to racism or blackness. Nothing. I told Vilmar privately that I was surprised, given our earlier talk, that antiracism was not more present in the group's work. He laughed. "Of course, it's not there. That is not what we rap about. We rap about helping the kids in the *periferia* get away from drugs and gangs and violence. What did you expect?"

That was my first clue that what I would encounter in gospel rap was not the black consciousness to which I was accustomed from my experience in the United States. Over the next two years, I ended up remaining attentive to how blackness among gospel rappers got expressed, articulated, and reshaped in three sites—in the voices with which rappers told their stories, in the ever-present theme of *periferia*, and in the history of the scene itself, recounted in interviews and informal moments between rehearsals. What I found is that among gospel rappers there is a very robust though complex understanding of blackness—but not at all the one I had thought I would find.

A brief methodological note: though I ended up spending equal amounts of time with gospel and secular rappers, the data on which this chapter is based are derived mainly from my time with gospel rappers. I make a point, where needed in the text, of distinguishing between the two groups. That said, one of the key findings of this project is just how similar are the ideas and practices of both secular and gospel rappers. At various points in the text, the reader will find me referencing both groups at the same time with the locution "both secular and gospel rappers." Indeed, in many ways, the two groups are virtually indistinguishable. Both are committed to rap, identify deeply with the *periferia*, seek through their rhymes to paint a realistic portrait of the hard lives young men and women face in the favelas, seek to offer realistic ways out, and invoke God and Jesus. The gospel rappers just do the latter with a good deal more regularity, more biblical accuracy, and, many gospel rappers would say, more integrity. That is, since gospel rappers are baptized members of Protestant churches, seek to walk in the ways of doctrine, and make a point of regular church attendance, they can legitimately claim to be "of the church." Whether this means they are any more spiritual than those who do none of these things I leave for others to decide.

Spatial Practices and Blackness
Hanging Out on Fábio's Roof

There we were, the eight of us, drinking orange soda and sitting on white plastic chairs on the roof of Fábio's house, in the warm evening air, beneath a darkening cobalt-blue sky. A few pieces of pork were cooking over the embers of the little grill assembled that afternoon from a handful of stray bricks. The blood-red horizon seeped through the ragged skyline of roofs and satellite dishes; below, as far as the eye could see, lay thousands of twinkling yellow lights. Those lights were the nighttime face of Tiro ao Pomba (The Shot Dove), an agglomeration of some six hundred houses, one of the innumerable favelas lodged in the hills of São Paulo's vast *periferia*.

The young men looking out on the glittering landscape that evening were all MCs and DJs in local amateur gospel and secular rap groups. All these young men were members of the same *banca*. *Bancas* are a common organizational feature of amateur rap groups in São Paulo. A *banca* is a cluster of groups from the same immediate neighborhood (or, at furthest, adjoining neighborhoods) that support each other by traveling to each other's performances, cheering each other on, offering feedback, and providing supportive audiences to each other's rehearsals. (*Posses*, which have declined in influence in São Paulo over the past decade, are similar to *bancas* in function but are made up of groups from neighborhoods spread across a whole zone, such as the northern zone). The seven young men on Fábio's roof all happened to be members of the Banca Tiro ao Pomba—a *banca* made up of four gospel rap groups and two secular ones.

Next to me was Zero, a tall, lanky seventeen-year-old wearing a T-shirt bearing the face of Tupac Shakur. Not too many years ago, Zero had carried a gun and had been arrested seven times for causes he would not reveal; but that all changed last year when he took a walk on Camaratiba Street, just down the block from here, and heard rap music pouring out of the tiny Deus é Fiel church. Discovering the word of God in rhyme got him to accept Jesus, and soon he was rapping in his own right, in a group he called Caçadores de Almas (Soul Hunters). "I came to know Jesus through rap," he told me. "For me, rap is the voice of Jesus speaking through me." Zero was light-skinned, with a wisp of red beard; he called himself *branco*. He sized up the view slowly, panning from left to right. "God's creation,

Gospel rapper, northern zone of São Paulo

eh? God is good. Look at all that beauty. *Beleza*. Those lights. It's like we're looking at heaven."

"Maybe." The word was laden with skepticism. The speaker was Will. Will, the MC of his own three-person rap group, Profecia Final (Final Prophecy), was a compact sixteen-year-old in baggy shorts, faded T-shirts, and corn rows. He had grown up in a small Assembly of God church and had strayed at the age of thirteen; but in 2003, depressed by the deaths of several buddies, he returned to the bosom of the Lord. He lived one street over. He proudly called himself *negro*.

"Maybe what?" asked Zero.

"Maybe beautiful. But terrible, terrible. Brothers [*irmãos*], what we are looking at is beautiful. But that's the view from up here. Go down from the mountain, go down there, and what do you see? You know what I'm saying? You go into any one of those streets, you know what you see? Not so beautiful."

"Yeah, I know." Elton said. Twenty years old, Elton had lived on this street, two doors down, since the favela arose some fifteen years ago. Dressed in a

Wu-tang warm-up jacket, sporting artfully jagged-shaped sideburns, Elton had founded his own rap trio, Impacto Frontal (Frontal Impact), the year before and was working hard to record the group's first CD. He dabbled in church but was not a convert, and he did not regard his work as gospel. Elton was light-skinned and called himself *branco*, but he also sometimes called himself *moreno*, "because here in Brazil, everyone has some African blood." He continued: "Yes, brothers, it is not so pretty down in the street. There the blood can flow. We have seen that. There the blood can mix with the garbage in the street. Am I right, Elvis?"

Elvis was Elton's cousin, a year younger than he; he rapped alongside him in Impacto Frontal. He was wearing a heavy sweatshirt emblazoned with the insignia of Sexto Sello, "The Sixth Seal," a popular gospel rap group. But Elvis was not a convert, and, he said, he had no interest in joining any church. "I want my freedom," he had said to me. Elvis was much darker than Elton and called himself *negro*.

Elvis nodded. "I know what Zero means—it is beautiful." He pointed down at the blanket of lights. "But they are right—look closer. There, at the corner of Barreto, there, that little square? It looks pretty now, doesn't it? All lit up." Zero pursed his lips, nodded, and finished the sentence: "Yeah, *manos*, that is where that kid was killed last week. No park there, nothing. Next to the wall. The vultures came by to peck at him before the police took him away in the van." Quiet descended for a moment; I was thinking of the appalling image of a vulture pecking away at the body of a dead teenager.

"Brothers," Fábio finally asked, "how many times has the *movimento* [drug traffic] left *defuntos* [murdered people] there?" Fábio was a large, muscled, tattooed nineteen-year-old, his tank top stamped with the face of Jesus. We were on the roof of his parents' home, where he still slept in the room he grew up in, though now he had a computer to help him compose his songs. When he was not composing, rehearsing, performing, or praying, Fábio helped his sister plastic-wrap and sell clothes. He was a pious member of the Deus em Cristo church. He rapped as an MC in a group he had founded called Aliados em Cristo, or the "Allies in Christ." He called himself *negro*.

Everyone seemed to be thinking about Fábio's question. Finally Will ventured, "I can recall at least five times."

"I count seven," said Fábio. "And you know I've been here for a while."

Everyone nodded. Will agreed it must have been seven. A chill wind blew over the rooftops, and I trembled, thinking of the bodies of seven dead people, one after the other, staining the little square below. Fábio went down-stairs to fetch more orange soda and came up with a full bottle and a box of crackers.

I then asked how the favela had gotten its name. "Everyone knows the story," said Choquito. Choquito, twenty-two years old, was a member of Fábio's church and rapped with him in Aliados em Cristo. He was wear-ing a hoodie; big, baggy shorts; and sneakers. He was fairly light-skinned and called himself *branco*. "This favela got its name from one of the origi-nal residents—he used to hunt here for doves." Everyone smiled at the irony. Then Choquito pointed at a high wall down below that encircled a cluster of four high-rise buildings. "Those buildings are the bourgeoisie!" Everyone laughed. "Those were built in, I don't know, 1994 or 1995, for rich people. That was the start of Tiro ao Pomba. The poor people, us, came here think-ing they might work in those buildings. But the people in the high-rises were scared of us. They tried to get the mayor to remove us, but the mayor refused. So the people in the high-rise built that wall."

"The Berlin Wall!" Will exclaimed. The others nodded knowingly. I looked at the wall, which stood strikingly white, about half a kilometer away. It was rimmed with electrified wire.

Now it was Adimilson's turn. Eighteen years old, bedecked in a sharp gray warm-up jacket with "Apocalipse 16" on the back—the name of the most famous gospel rap group in São Paulo—Adimilson rapped with Will in Pro-fecia Final. He lived in a house two blocks away. He was very dark-skinned and called himself *negro*. "People, you know what I'm saying." He opened the box of crackers and began munching. "You know what I'm talking about. The Lord knows what I am talking about. Thank Jesus. Every day we have to look at that wall. And did anyone here—did anyone in Tiro ao Pomba get a job, so much as a maid's job or cleaning the toilets of someone in those buildings? Nothing. That is how the system works. The police work for them. They come in here and beat us. They look the other way while gangs kill each other off. They take their cut, and they look the other way. And the people in those buildings continue rich."

Will stood up, stretched, and began to laugh ironically. "It is like Pregador Luo says. They say, 'You are scum! We don't trust you! We don't want to see you!'"

The box of crackers was making the rounds and going fast. The sun had gone down, and we were facing the twinkling firmaments of sky and favela.

We had just finished talking about the little square below, the deaths there, and the apparent indifference of the police to them. Suddenly, Fábio got up, left, and returned a minute later, a *caderno* (notebook) and pen in hand. Will shot me a knowing look. We both knew Fábio's *caderno*. This, I had learned from my sessions with him, was his portfolio of personal meanings, crammed with his rhymes, poetry, and graffiti sketches. Fábio had pored over the notebook with me a few times, proudly showing his favorite rhymes and sketches. The well-stocked *caderno* was not Fábio's invention; some kind of notebook, whether carried in a backpack or kept close at hand in one's room, was a common accessory for all the MCs I met. Just the day before, Will had shown me his *caderno*, filled with colorful, splashy drawings of hip hop letters, police, crosses, daggers, blood, guns, clowns, skulls, and Jesus.

While Fábio remained engaged with a Bic pen, Zero, Will, Elton, and Choquito began to speak more quietly, though the flow of their conversation continued unabated. Not knowing protocol, I leaned over and asked Fábio what he was writing. He replied with courteous brevity: "I'm writing a rhyme, John. The talk about the square got me going."

Fábio continued hunched over his notebook for a few more minutes, while the rest of us chatted, sipped soda, listened to the breeze, contemplated the view, and absorbed the roar of a passing motorcycle. Finally Fábio came up for air.

"You guys wanna hear?"

Everyone did.

He looked down at the page and began bobbing his head slightly. He paused long enough to synchronize his voice to an inner drumbeat, then began.

> Just one more dead kid in Tiro ao Pomba
> Our *parada*, our *viela*
> Just one more kid from the *periferia*
> One more body fallen on the ground
> Here in the *quebrada*
> Seven times on the ground, seven times fallen

Heads were bobbing gently. Will got the groove, put his left hand to his lips in the form of a cone and used his right to regulate the flow of air, which he expelled forcefully, producing a perfect imitation of a drum.

The police don't arrive, they leave the body on the square
People walk around it, not wanting to see
But it is reality, it is a fatality, it is the final path, life devalued
But God sees all, God doesn't step around it
If only, if only
Seven deaths were seven days of following God
Those boys would be alive and smiling today
Our *periferia* would be a place of life and not death

He stopped and looked up expectantly.

"Well?"

There was a pause. Choquito expressed the general opinion: "Tá bom demais!" (That's super cool!)

One week later, on a Saturday morning, I went back to Fábio's house to witness a rehearsal. The sky was a gorgeous pale blue, very few clouds, unusual for São Paulo. I knew that Fábio and Choquito were planning to spend a couple of hours rehearsing for a performance at a church rap festival that night. When I arrived, Fábio welcomed me in. "John, come in! We're just getting started." He was resplendent in a red baseball cap and loose white jersey graced by the crest of a São Paulo soccer team. Choquito was in the living room with Carlito, Aliados de Cristo's DJ, choosing the CD they planned to use for the rehearsal. Fábio led me into the kitchen, took a pitcher of juice from the refrigerator, poured me a glass, and explained the morning's plans. "We'll be performing tonight in the eastern zone. We need to represent Tiro ao Pomba well. We'll be on stage for just a few minutes, so we're going to prepare two numbers." He motioned me to sit at the small Formica table, then leaned over me, opened his notebook, and pointed out the rhymes for tonight. One of them was "Quebrada Tiro ao Pomba," which I immediately recognized.

"Oh, man," I exclaimed. "That's pretty cool. I was present when you wrote that."

He smiled broadly. "Do you like it?"

"I love it."

This pleased him. "Yeah, I stayed up late that night writing this out, and I have been tinkering with it all week. You know, we need to rap about what happens and how God allows us to overcome these things through his love." He then copied the lyrics onto a scrap of yellow paper—"just in case I forget," he said, with a grin.

As we sat at the table, three boys under the age of ten wandered into the house from the street, friends of one of Fábio's younger brothers. They plunked themselves down on the sofa in the living room to play video games and to listen to whatever they could of the rehearsal. A tall woman in a tank top and shorts, carrying her baby on her hip, also came in from outside, smiling broadly, to chat with one of Fábio's sisters but also to stay and get a better listen of the rehearsal. It struck me that the barrier between the rehearsal space and the neighborhood was almost entirely porous.

Choquito and Carlito had finished setting up the sound. "Oh, brother!" said Choquito. "Are you ready yet?" "Yeah, *mano*," Fábio replied. Carlito popped in a CD and looked at Fábio, who nodded his head with studied gravity. "OK, let's do it." Carlito gingerly removed two long microphones from a snug Styrofoam mold and passed them to Fábio and Choquito. Fábio gave the signal to Carlito to start the CD. The impromptu audience of neighbors sat quiet, respectful, on the sofa. Instantly the house was filled with the pounding of heavy drums, and Fábio became bottled lightning, his left hand over his chest, his right hand holding the microphone lightly, all energy now channeled into his voice. Fábio circled around the room in a large arc, while Choquito crisscrossed his path, accenting every other line by repeating its final words. The audience's heads bobbed appreciatively. A cool breeze swirled into the living room through two windows that opened directly onto the street—still more audience. Fábio pretended that he did not see the teenagers, the three women, and the man who had stopped at one of the windows. The teens' heads bobbed throughout the rehearsal, and when the music came to an end, they burst into applause, as did the four sitting on the sofa. Fábio grinned. "Did you like it?" "We adored it!" said one. The young man at the window, his elbows on the windowsill, was less effusive. He shook his head. "No good?" asked Choquito. "It's OK," the young man said. "I think you need to pick up the pace." Fábio looked to Carlito and gestured with his right hand, making rapid circular motions with his wrist, asking him to give the listener's opinion a try. "Let's take that one from the top, OK?"

* * *

I want now to draw the reader's attention to a series of *spatial practices* embedded in the two scenes I have just described. I will present these practices in detail, then make the case that in combination, they help to generate, develop, and sustain among amateur rappers a specific set of ideas about the racial composition of the *periferia* and, for rappers who identify as *negro*, of what their blackness means.

Hanging Out

On the surface, the social gathering on Fábio's roof seems little more than a simple, accidental occasion of friends getting together to hang out. And this it certainly was. The interesting thing is that every one of the amateur rap groups I got to know devoted a lot of time precisely to being together in this informal, face-to-face way. Whenever I arrived in a neighborhood to meet with an interviewee, I usually had to track him down in one or another of the houses of his groupmates, where I would find them genially sitting, listening to music, watching TV, eating, and talking. Every day I spent with rappers in the *periferia*, at least half the time I found myself in such hanging-out sessions, on stoops, on porches, in backyards, in kitchens, in living rooms, in bedrooms, and, of course, on rooftops. The huddle at Fábio's resembled scores of others in which I participated, during which members of a *grupo*, *banca*, or *comboio* met to eat, kibitz, joke, listen to music, play games, watch TV, talk theology, take notes, read rhymes, criticize, and eat and drink some more. (There usually was some beer drinking, but not a lot, out of respect for the evangelicals present.) An hour or two could pass just watching music videos, raiding the refrigerator, playing cards, commenting on each other's CD or record collections, or, as at Fábio's, philosophizing on the view. At first I thought these parleys were contrived for my benefit; but a month into my fieldwork, I realized they were really part of everyday rap culture. Pastor Ton, an MC of the gospel rap group Rimas Proféticas (Prophetic Rhymes) made this crystal clear when he said, "A lot of what we do is hang out, listen to music, talk, get to know each other better. You can't be a rapper without hanging out. Rap is not one of those professional things. It's a social thing."

Why all this hanging out? Most obviously, the neighborhoods in which it occurred were not exactly bustling with recreational options. A common refrain of urban political discourse is that poor youths have few choices for leisure, and this was a slogan I found by and large to be true. Certainly it was frequently echoed by my informants. "Look around here," said Rodrigo, a secular rapper. "What is there to do for young people? Zero. We don't have a movie theater here. We are poor! Going to the mall? [*Laughs.*] No organized sports. . . . There are *boutequins* [bars], for getting drunk and fighting. There is church, not for everyone. If you want to be a part of something, what do you have?" The hangout sessions thus fulfill a recreational need. That is partly why the neighborhoods are teeming with rap groups: they give young people groups to hang out with that are not narcotraffic. A gospel rapper pointed out, "In this neighborhood, a young person basically has three options: narcotraffic, church, or rap. By rapping gospel, I am doing two out of three!"

At a deeper level, a key reason rap groups meet regularly face-to-face is precisely to nurture and tend the mutuality and trust they need to avoid being confused with or sucked into the world of narcotraffic. Hanging out is precisely the time and place where one of rap's attractions is strongest: namely, in the quality of its relationships. While relations within narcotrafficking gangs are marked by suspicion and fear, relations within rap groups strive to be typified by mutual support and trust. I heard this contrast stated repeatedly by both secular and gospel rappers. Samuel, a seventeen-year-old secular rapper, put it this way: "There [in drug gangs], your brother would kill you when ordered. I was a part of that, and I can tell you, you don't know what someone will do next. You're always afraid." "And in the rap group?" I asked. "Totally different. They say it is like a family in the traffic, but that is a lie. Here [in rap], we are like a family. If you make a mistake, they don't jump on you, because this is about something else entirely." Gospel rappers added spiritual warfare to the mix. "In [narco]traffic, the devil rules," explained Zero. "He came to kill, separate, and destroy, and that is what happens in the traffic. But God has another plan. You can see that plan in rap; here, we love and trust each other." But this love and trust are not automatic; they must be nurtured and tended. "If I am hanging with my friends in rap," said Will, "that means I can't be out there in the street: . . . someone comes up to me, makes a proposition. So it is safe here." Said Zero, "There is a lot of temptation. They come to you and say, 'Wouldn't you love this watch?' or whatever. It is hard to say no to that unless you have others to help you, support you, back you up. And the rap group does that."

Recruiting Group Members

Now look again at who congregated on Fábio's roof that evening, and you will notice another interesting fact: everyone there lived in the immediate vicinity. And I do mean immediate: the longest walk anyone took that day to arrive at Fábio's house was about seven minutes. This state of affairs is entirely typical: in all of the dozen amateur rap groups I came to know, core members (MCs) lived within a five- to seven-minute walk from each other. Israel, Adam, and Anderson, childhood friends, now members of Profetas do Apocalipse, lived within a three-block radius; sixteen-year-old Cristovão formed the duo Guerreiros do Senhor with Nathan, his cousin, who lived on his street; Feisel, Vinícius, and Daniel, members of Família Jesus Cristo, were brothers who lived under the same roof; Mary Ellen and Monica, high school friends, formed the rap duo Gueto em Cristo and lived next door to each other. I could go on. Rappers do, of course, attend fairs and contests and shows and church events, where they meet artists who live farther away, in the next neighborhood over and even across town; yet in spite of this, they usually choose to limit group membership to people close to home.

The pattern emerges from the interplay of preference and constraint. As we have just seen, rappers are sticklers for regular, informal, face-to-face interaction. "To be in a group together, you need to talk, to share ideas," explained Will. "You need to hang out." Quite obviously, it is simply not easy to do this with artists from other neighborhoods. São Paulo is staggeringly far-flung, and travel from *bairro* to *bairro*, whether by bus or subway or car, is draining and time-consuming. Dense traffic and long distances make the average trip from one zone to another easily last up to an hour and a half, even two hours. Interaction on a regular basis requires living close by. "I don't know how I could be in a group with someone who lives across town," said Fábio. "You need to be able to drop by. No question. I was in a group a few years ago with a guy from another zone, and it did not work, because we didn't have enough communication." Choquito added, "When we all live in the same *quebrada*, you know, one of us says, 'Hey, let's go hang out at So-and-So's house'; someone else calls on his cellphone. . . . If you live far away, you don't have that spontaneity." So important is close coresidence that it can trump skill. Ton told me that when his cousin, a talented MC who lived an hour's bus ride away, announced that he wished to join Ton's rap group, Rimas Proféticas, Ton made his disinclination clear. "I told him it just couldn't work. . . . If you don't live nearby, it's hard to hang out." Then there is Samuel, a young man with no prior rapping experience, who was asked by his cousin Duglass to join his rap group. When Samuel reminded Duglass that he had no experience, Duglass smiled and shook his head. "He was like, 'Hey, don't we live on the same street? Man, you just hang out with us. It'll be cool.' . . . They all said, 'No problem. You live right here. You're always around,' you know?"

The exception proves the rule. To be an MC, all one needs is one's voice, a mind, and a pen. DJs, in contrast, are harder to find, because they need equipment, working knowledge of the music, and a respectable collection of CDs and vinyl. Not every neighborhood boasts such a virtuoso; thus, whenever a member of an amateur rap group originated from outside the immediate neighborhood, it happened to be the DJ.

The Writing of Rhymes

I have suggested so far that the amateur rap scene in São Paulo includes intense, regular face-to-face interaction between artists who live near each other in the same neighborhoods. Let us now consider the implications of this type of interaction and recruitment for the process of writing. Gospel rappers, like secular ones, want their rhymes to represent what they call "*o real*" (the real): the sights, sounds, sensations, and characters they observe on a daily basis. This is why MCs like to carry a *caderno* with them through the day: always having the *caderno* at the ready means they can add to it at a moment's notice, as observations of their immediate surroundings occur and as they transmute them into ideas. Part diary, part ethnographic notebook, the *caderno* is living proof of rhymes' claim to being "real." As Will put it, "My *caderno* is the record of my life." Carried about in backpacks, broken out and read from, sometimes written in as others watch, *cadernos* are vehicles of the intimate connection between rappers' direct observation of the world and their ideas about it. This kind of immediate, local knowledge is absolutely central in the creation of the rappers' art. On Fábio's roof, he turned to his *caderno* when he sought to capture the meaning of the square that he and his companions were looking at and discussing. "We have to write about what we know, what we see," he explained later. "What I know is this place, where I live, where I spend my time. I can try to rap about going into the forest only if I go into the forest, or other cities if I go there, but I haven't been to the forest, and Tiro ao Pomba is what I know. This is what ends up in my *caderno*. So my rhymes about this place are real. All I need to do is look around me and see what is happening on the corner right now, and I have the subject for a rhyme."

While rappers often begin the process of creating rhymes in the solitude of their bedroom or kitchen, the process rarely remains a solitary thing.

Rappers do not want their ideas to be expressions unique to themselves; rather, they ardently wish their ideas to *connect* and communicate with audiences, to "represent" them, to "speak for" groups larger than themselves. They thus are always seeking feedback for their writing, eager to read aloud from their *cadernos*, to share drafts of their rhymes, to tinker with them in response, in order to see whether they have captured something meaningful, not just for themselves but for others, too. "If I have an idea," said Will, "I want right away to read it to the other guys, to see what they think. I don't want to write a rhyme just for me." The aesthetic world of amateur rap is thus an intensely collaborative one, in which *trocando idéias* (exchanging ideas)— the process of talking, sharing, listening—is a key ingredient. I frequently witnessed a rapper sitting at a table with one or two others, going over the lyrics to his most recent creations. Usually the goal was not full-scale revision but simply to confirm that the lyric spoke to a concern shared by others. "I always want to be sure that the guys hear what I am doing," said Will, "and I can tell they do when they nod their heads."

The role of the group is not only to affirm what the MC has already written; it is to help him write something new. From this perspective, hanging-out sessions frequently have an important creative function. In many of them, there was usually a moment when an MC would seek input on a new rhyme. As we saw on Fábio's roof, this can be an energetic affair, with rappers responding actively to each other, adding to a common pool of local knowledge by contributing their own take on local events, places, and people. Ton, MC of Rimas Profeticas, described the process this way:

> I would have my *caderno* out, someone would mention something and say, "Did you see that? This happened just down the street. Were you there? Did you see when So-and-So did this or that?" And so we would talk about it, and that lyric would come out of that. 'Cause you're talking about it, and you're hearing these different ideas, and you add your own, and that really improves the lyric. Or someone will start talking about something, you know, anything: a bird that arrives in the room makes you think of freedom, say, or a crack in the wall or the broken sewer pipe makes you think about how the *quebrada* is falling apart and the system is not paying attention. You're looking at it, and you're talking; you go back and forth, and maybe now you see something you didn't see before, right? So you're learning, and so a lyric can come out of that too.

The process of creating Fábio's rhyme on the roof illustrates what Ton is alluding to here, the collective discovery from observation of deeper meanings. We can see this in Fábio's transfiguration into divine parable of his *banca*'s discussion of the murders in the square: in that case, observation (the ironic beauty of the square) and collective discussion (of its terrible local history) became the springboard for a rhyme about evil and redemption. Thus does local knowledge play an essential role in rap's core creative process.

House Rehearsals

Amateur rap groups rehearse at least once a week, sometimes more, usually on weekends, and their preferred place to do so is inside members' houses. Most amateur rap groups have a hard time gaining permission to rehearse in churches, and none has the wherewithal to rent a studio or other restricted-access space. (Amateur rap differs in this respect from black gospel and gospel samba, whose rehearsals almost always take place in church atria, basements, and annexes.) Thus, the choice of Fábio's living room was entirely typical. A key feature of the home in the urban periphery is that it is constantly open to the social world around it. Rappers have little power to exclude from this space household or nonhousehold members who happen to be there. There is no way to cordon off the rehearsal from fleshy bodies jostling in and out, from cooking and bathroom smells, from rambunctious and crying children, from murmuring televisions, from the flow of comment from bystanders. In addition, in the urban periphery, the line between home and street is a porous one (cf. Hansen 2008, 54–55). Keeping doors and windows open to beat the heat means the intrusion into the rehearsal space of people not only inside but outside the house. It is hard, in crowded neighborhoods, on weekends, with windows open, for locals to ignore for long which houses happen to be hosting rap group rehearsals. I often saw girls and boys walking by houses where rehearsals were taking place, and they would suddenly start bobbing and commenting on the virtues of the sounds emanating from within. As we saw with Fábio's group, a rehearsing rap group may be exposed at any moment to an impromptu street audience.

When I first witnessed what I took to be these intrusions, I imagined them to be the negative consequence of rap groups' inability to afford sound-proofed studios. But Fábio had a very different perspective. "No, man," he said, "we *like* this. I don't see anything wrong with it. Our music is for them anyway!" When Fábio says he feels that his group "represents" Tiro ao Pombo, this is no abstraction; it is based at least in part on the interactive flow with listeners in the everyday social exchanges of rehearsal. Physical proximity, lack of soundproofing, porosity between house and street—all contribute to organic connections between rappers and their immediate surroundings, whether household, street, or neighborhood (cf. Turino 2008, 49).

Rapping about Place

Gospel rap is, naturally, about salvation and redemption; but it is also about how these unfold in a geographically specific place: the *periferia*. The *periferia* of São Paulo as a general term refers to the sprawling, chaotic expanse of urban construction that from space might look like a vast cathedral, the nave forty kilometers east to west, the transept sixty kilometers north to south, immense tracts of territory within whose boundaries unfold the everyday dreams, hopes, fears, sufferings, victories, and deaths of nearly ten million people. Gospel rappers, like secular rappers, refer constantly to *periferia* in their rhymes, informal talk, stage patter, and blogs, as well as to the *periferia*'s multiple spatial subdivisions such as *quebradas, getos, vilas, vielas, parques, jardins*, and favelas. Scan the verses of any *paulista* rap group of the past decade, and these spatial terms abound: they are rappers' "reality," their social and physical universe, the setting of all their pain, struggle, solidarity, and overcoming. Rappers, both secular and Christian, rhyme about the *periferia* as a place of danger and deep moral lessons, a place where you must learn to resist the promise of easy money and power, do what is right, know who your true friends are, read, stay away from drugs, and find self-respect through education, family, community, music, and art (Weller and Tella 2011; Pardue 2011). What distinguishes gospel rap is that it frames these lessons as above all spiritual discoveries, as moves from everyday despair to the empowerment that comes from knowing the word of God. (Secular rappers also invoke God but not nearly as often.) For gospel rappers, the *periferia* is thus figured as a grand stage on which the devil tempts youths with the promise of easy money, sex, and power into a world of drugs, violence, and death, from which they can only be saved by accepting Jesus Christ. This image of *periferia* is well illustrated in Epidemia Gospel Rap's "Periferia Amada" (Beloved *Periferia*); one or another version of this narrative structure appears in almost every gospel rap:

> Favela, *periferia*, the brothers *se trelam*, kill each other, crash into each
>   other
> In the constant war for trafficking spots, just see
> The kids, twelve or thirteen years old, already sniffing powder
> Without hesitation, without fear, already shooting without mercy
> In the dark dead-ends of the alleyways, silent, favelas
> Where evil reigns and there are no rules
> Here whoever is bigger is bigger, who is smaller no longer exists . . .
> It is so hard for the man to live here, it is difficult
> He has to move savvily in the middle of the war, gunshots, screams
> The mother despairing over her son
> Here there is so much of this, innocent children who are no longer
>   innocent
> Who want to become bandits

Into this darkness, gospel rappers inject the word of God, as the promise they hold out to despairing youths. Gospel rappers recognize a role for secular institutions to create youth-friendly programs, policies, laws, and job opportunities; but these are for them secondary to engaging the spiritual battle.

> Light will shine in the *periferia*
> Light will shine, bringing love and happiness
> *Periferia*, favela, alleyway, dead brother, brother in a cell
> Rebellion that blinds, wake up and clean off the snot
> Wash that face, Christ is awaiting you
> He is calling, he clamors for you, so get out of the mud
> Forget fame, forget money
> He has something much better for you
> But you are the one who needs to decide
> Don't follow the devil, and don't follow me
> Only to Christ should you say yes[1]

The Identity Outcomes of Spatial Practices

The several spatial practices I have just described have in common the following feature: they all *focus and intensify rappers' attention on their spatially immediate neighborhoods.* Quite logically, calling on rappers to make dense observations about their immediate surroundings increases the likelihood that they will think about those surroundings in densely textured, rather than generic or abstract, ways. Recruiting from the immediate vicinity increases the likelihood that amateur rappers will overlap in their local knowledge. Embedding the creation of rhymes in a collaborative process of intellectual checks and balances makes it likely that rappers will keep each other honest about their shared knowledge and inhibit the temptation to slip into facile, experience-distant claims about their shared reality. Hanging out enriches rappers' attachment to their immediate, neighborhood-based networks. Rehearsing in local homes reinforces rappers' organic connection to their immediate neighborhoods, as do those local trust-building hangout sessions. All of these practices, then, each in its own way as well as in concert, forge between rappers and their immediate neighborhoods strong bonds of realism, dense knowledge, attachment, and identification.

It should come as no surprise that these bonds, in turn, invest the spatial terms that gospel rappers use with densely packed place-based meanings. That is, when Fábio deploys spatial terms such *periferia, quebrada,* and *parada,* he is not describing an abstraction, a generic "any place" in the *periferia*; he is referring, rather, to the specific places that he knows from direct experience, where he grew up, that he has seen from the roof of his own house. It is Fábio's knowledge of his *own* neighborhood that injects gravity into his rhyme. Given the power of rappers' spatial practices to focus their attention on the immediate and concrete, for them spatial terms such as *periferia* and *favela* always remain a small cognitive step away from the reality of *this* intersection, *this* little grassless square, *this* polluted creek, *this* cluster of relatives' houses, *this* stretch of alleyway where they grew up, *this* corridor away from the streetlights where a cousin was gunned down. This is why when rappers travel far and wide to perform in other groups' shows, they invoke their *own* little *quebrada* as their true home. This is why rhymes are so often filled with thank-yous to the *manos* of the named *vila* or *alto* or *morro* or *conjunto* that produced it. Thus, rappers imagine the *periferia* not as an abstract slogan but as infused with their own dense local knowledge, of real named corners of the vast urban expanse, of a textured, personal world with which they are intimately acquainted.

How does this concrete, immediate spatial sense of neighborhood affect ideas about race and racial identity? To address this question, it will help first to recall that for activists in the black movement, spatial terms that refer to poor neighborhoods, such as *periferia* and *favela*, are strongly connected to claims of blackness. Since the late 1970s, the movement has conceptualized such residential spaces as exhibit A in the prosecutorial case against Brazilian racial apartheid. Listen to any black activist, read any black movement publication or blog, and the claim appears: most people who live in poor residential neighborhoods are black. This is why, rhetorically, black activists proclaim the *periferia* or favela to be the modern-day version of the *senzala* (slave quarters). "It is well known and indisputable," said Márcio, a black activist, "that the vast majority of people who live in the *periferia* are *negros*. This is a simple fact. They have been segregated there, just like in the US. It is like the *senzala* of old, but now called *periferia*." Black activist Sergio Vaz refers to "the modern *senzala*, otherwise called *periferia*" (2006); Jessica Balbino asserts that "the *senzala* changed its name and today it is called '*periferia*'" (Balbino 2010), and a recent short film advertises itself as "an audio-visual manifesto on the trajectory of Brazil's *negros*, from the *senzala* to the *periferia*" (Alvez, Souza, and Hilario 2005; Carril 2004). When Netinho de Paula, activist and television producer, created the show *Turma do Gueto*, he insisted on recruiting only black actors because "*a periferia é negra mesmo*" ("the *periferia* is really black"; Veja Online 2001). Or as Tarcia Silva has written, "*A favela é negra!*"—"The favela is black!" (2010). These claims of the *periferia*'s racial homogeneity are based on the view that persons with any African ancestry at all, irrespective of how they identify themselves, should be categorized as *negro*. Whether or not this view corresponds to how people in the *periferia* actually identify themselves, black activists are less interested in this than in claiming numerical dominance.

Now in the United States, of course, when both activists and rappers refer to the "hood," they mean a place that is, in general, ethnoracially homogeneous (Forman 2002; Rose and McClary 1994). In São Paulo, in contrast, poor neighborhoods are in point of fact ethnoracially *heterogeneous*. It is possible for black activists, armed with a strong rule of hypodescent (i.e., that any African ancestry at all makes one *negro*), to argue that poor neighborhoods are inhabited by large numbers, or even (in some cases) majorities, of *negros*. Yet large numbers of people in the *periferia* whom black activists would categorize as *negro* think of themselves as *moreno*; and large numbers of people who live in the poor periphery of São Paulo see themselves and are seen by others as *branco*. The statistics are really quite striking. Every survey conducted in São Paulo's poorest neighborhoods shows that roughly half of the residents regard themselves neither as *negro* nor even as *moreno* but as *branco*—white. The 2000 federal census found, stunningly, that majorities of the population in poor, peripheral neighborhoods identified themselves as *branco*,[2] and this result has been confirmed by other studies. A survey of nearly six hundred youths in poor São Paulo neighborhoods, for example, found that half of the respondents identified themselves as white, a third as "mixed," and only 14.5% as *negros* (Bousquat and Cohn 2003). A 2005 survey found that half of the heads of household in São Paulo's poorest neighborhoods call themselves *branco* (Pasternak 2005). A 2006 survey of eight hundred informants in a poor São Paulo *bairro* found that 18.3% identified themselves as *negros*, 35.4% as *brancos*, and the rest as "mixed" (Lima 2009; Lavalle and Komatso 2008). A recent study of São Paulo's homeless population found that 40% identified themselves as white (Schor and Artes 2005; cf. Telles 1995). The data from Rio de Janeiro echo these patterns: in the favela Cidade de Deus, 36.2% of the population classified themselves as white; while in Rocinha, the largest favela in the world, the percentage of whites was no less than 53.9%. In Madureira, considered one of the symbols of Carioca blackness, more than half of the population (54.5%) declared themselves to be white (Telles 2004, 204). These data suggest that impoverished urban neighborhoods in São Paulo (and Rio) are not exactly racially homogeneous *senzalas*. They are, rather, places where poor nonwhites live elbow to elbow with poor whites. Eduardo Telles, comparing US and Brazilian statistics, found that whites and nonwhites in São Paulo were in fact more than *twice as likely* to live near each other as they were in New York City and *three times more likely* than they were in Chicago. "White exposure to nonwhites," Telles concluded, "is much greater [in Brazil] than in the urban United States" (ibid., 203–204).

Against this backdrop, it is revealing to hear how rappers talk about the racial composition of their neighborhoods. As we have seen, their experience of locality is shaped by practices that focus their attention on the immediate and concrete; and as rappers, they are committed to speak the truth about what they experience. Given this, the activist view that "the *periferia* is black" does not correspond to what the rappers know from concrete, immediate experience, and they feel they must say as much: *that their neighborhoods are ethnoracially mixed.* That is, while all my informants identified themselves as *negro*, they were quite certain that their neighborhoods *were not.* "Look," said Pretto, in rap we must tell the truth, we must tell what we see. . . . And I have to say that when I hear that phrase, "the *periferia* is *negro*," it just isn't true. . . . We are always rapping about the *periferia*, right? So I can tell you, in the periphery, it isn't just *negros*. Look, take my street: there are not just *negros* on my street. There are whites too. Lots of them. Living in the same kind of houses we do. We hang out in each other's houses. We are in the street together. If we drove around my neighborhood right now, in the middle of the afternoon, when people are supposed to be working, what would we see? Young people, both white and *negro*, standing around doing nothing, sitting on benches, sitting on stoops. I leave my house to go to the bus, and I pass ten kids who don't have jobs, both white and *negro*. That's the reality. Anyone who says it is all *negro* in the periphery is saying that for some reason. That is what they want to see. I would tell them to go look: whites and *negros* are there.

Or listen to Fabio:

When you pay attention, get past what some people say, you know, that "the favela is all for *negros*," you see that there are whites and *negros* here, not just *negros*. There are not just *negros* on my street. We rappers have a responsibility to see the truth and say it. And saying that it is all one thing on the street is a falsehood. I know this well, because I spend a lot of time here. I cannot lie, man. That is just the way it is. There are whites as well, who don't have access to a good education, who don't have access to a medical clinic, whose house also suffers from the floods and the sewage and disease and violence. Here, it is the same crap for everyone.

Now, given the importance to rappers of identifying closely with their neighborhoods, seeing and experiencing their neighborhoods as multiracial leads them to a dual identity. On the one hand, they possess, as I discussed earlier, a clear color-based identity of *negro*. Yet, given their scene's spatial practices and commitments, this identity coexists for them with another, place-based identity rooted in the multiracial *periferia*, in which what unites people is their shared experience of a place riddled with poverty and danger. The formula "*preto e pobre*" (black and poor) used so often in rappers' lyrics has been interpreted as implying an identity in which blackness is the cause of the poverty; yet my time in the field suggests a different meaning: while rappers knew the disadvantages of their color, it is their identification with their neighborhoods, and thus with other people who are poor, irrespective of color, that really informs the phrase *"preto e pobre."* For rappers, it means not "I am *negro* and therefore poor" but rather "I am *negro*, and therefore I understand and am in solidarity with those who are oppressed like me." Listen to Pretto: "I am *negro*, yes, of course, and I am proud to be *negro*. But I tell you, what I feel is that I am one with all of these young kids, of all races, my neighbors who live in this shit. We are here together. They can get shot just as easily as I can. As a rapper, that is what I am committed to changing." Or, as Fábio put it, "There are white kids who live the same life I do here. If you look around, that is what I see, that is what I live every day. I cannot talk only to the kids who say, 'Hey, I am *negro*!' Why would I want to limit myself that way? So this is what happens: I think of myself as *negro*, but I also think of myself as a resident, a neighbor, of all these kids. I am what they are: a *periférico*." Most broadly, being black for these rappers functions as a kind of spiritual resource for empathy with the others in the *periferia* who are oppressed by their circumstances. "We blacks," said Will, "have suffered much in the world. We cannot go from that to close ourselves off and say we can only fight for ourselves. Because we look around, and our neighbors, black and white, are suffering too. We must join together. We understand what suffering is, so we must join together."

The Voiced Body and Antiessentialism in Gospel Rap
Telling It Like It Is

It is a hot evening in October, around six thirty, and I am sitting at a little table in a coffee shop in downtown São Paulo with Pretto, a thirty-year-old Afro-Brazilian man. From seven that morning until just a few moments ago, Pretto had been navigating thick downtown traffic on his motorized bicycle, as he does every day, making deliveries of documents to air-conditioned offices—a job for which he earns less than sixty dollars a week. He does not mind the traffic, he says, because it gives him time to speak with God (he is a longtime member of the Assembly of God) and to listen to rap through his headphones. He removes several CDs from his backpack—by Lito Atalaia, Pregador Luo, and Gênesis, all very hot-selling gospel rappers—and shows me his own new CD. He is proud of the fact that he has just produced this, his first CD, independently. The CD's paper insert is graced with an image of himself, looking sulky and wise. He passes his right hand slowly over his tightly woven corn rows as he talks about the CD. All of a sudden, he launches into a rap:

> I know who is who. Yes I know who is who
> I know who my friends are
> I know that they are few so few that I can count them on my fingers
> In the southern zone, practically, I was born
> I was raised here, built a reputation here
> I have never used drugs
> I have never been involved in crime
> But in my area, many have not had the same destiny
> Alcohol, drugs, fights have always made victims in the periphery
> I remember the time when fights were decided with fists
> That's the way that it was at school
> Now fights are settled with bullets
> It doesn't take much, brother
> If you look at a guy wrong, or you look at the wrong girl
> It's already enough for someone to pick up a gun
> The bullet is crazy on the other side

Pretto's voice is gravelly and low; it is an untrained voice, one that vibrates at unexpected moments, gathering strength for a few seconds, then losing it. There is no denying that it is a hypnotic voice, one that commands attention, makes you want to listen; but it is far from a beautiful voice: it cracks and creaks and squeaks and becomes breathy. He continues:

> Brothers seduced by easy money
> Violence is increasing, and young people are being attacked
> You should be vigilant and remain attentive
> Nothing that I say have I invented
> All of this is happening to young people who don't have knowledge of
>   the word of God
> Little by little, the world is getting corrupted
> People just sit back and say that it is normal
> But we who know the word of God
> We know that that's not the way that things are

Preto Jay, of Sexto Sello

> This is the strategy of the enemy
> While no one is watching, the prophecy is being fulfilled
> They have even had campaigns for peace
> But they don't realize that it's only through Jesus that we will achieve
>   that
> The enemy wants to dominate all populations

I am hypnotized. The spell is surely not due to the purity or decibel capacity of Pretto's voice; it has to do with something harder to define—a certain confidence, an earnestness perhaps, that permeates Pretto's delivery, affirming his right to be heard, to take over the soundscape of our little table—of the whole corner of the shop, if he feels like it. I love the rhyme and the flow, but I am struggling to express why. Finally, Pretto comes to my rescue: "Because it has a sincere message. That's what rap is. Using your voice so that people can understand your ideas. A rapper is someone who, when you hear their voice, you learn their ideas." Yes, I agree, that is a big part of it. Pretto's meaning in his rhyme is transparent and sincere, carried by the luminosity of each word, albeit roughly spoken. In the months to come, I find myself returning repeatedly to Pretto's comment, quoting it to other informants, and every time I do so, it is met with slow, knowing nods.

I begin this section with Pretto's comment because it sums up the core creative act in rap: that of using one's voice to speak aloud, rhythmically, and in public *a mensagem* (the message)—ideas and observations felt by the rapper to be significant and true (Forman 2002; Krims 2000; Dimitriadis 2001). For gospel rappers, "truth" (*a verdade*) is using one's voice to articulate one's sincerest and deepest ideas about the world, God, humanity, salvation, and what to do to make things better. Turning to rap as *vocal art*, I wish to draw attention to three ideas peculiar to the scene: amateur rappers' conviction that their art, at its core, is the truthful communication of *message*, their view that their art has fundamentally more in common with *spoken* than with melodic vocalization, and their belief that sonority of voice is not essential to successful rapping. In considering the implications of these ideas for gospel rap's construction of the relationship between "race" and voice, I conclude that they sustain a racially antiessentialist position, in which divine gifts are bestowed not on racialized groups but on individuals. I then suggest that this antiessentialism is reinforced by rappers' experience of non-*negros*' record of performing rap at the highest level of quality.

If Pretto is correct in asserting that "the truth" is what "voice" means in rap, then the primary goal of the rapper must be to ensure that his voice has integrity, that it accurately conforms to his own experience and belief. There is thus a deep individualism at the heart of rap's project. A rapper should, as we have seen, speak a truth that is similar to one felt by others; but what gives his speech weight is that through it *he communicates his own truth*. As Samuel put it, "I always say, 'My voice is my truth; my truth is my voice.' No one else can speak for me; I must speak for myself. So when I rap, it is true because it is my voice and no one else's. I am the one who knows what I saw, what I feel, what I believe, and I must say it." Every young rapper I met regaled me with stories of how rap had allowed him to "*achar minha voz*," to find his voice, to realize what he wanted to say. "This is what rapping is all about. This is why I got involved," explained Samuel. "Someone like me—we have something to say, we want to say it, but no one hears our voice. It is like we are in a box, in a prison, pent up. My voice was caught in my throat, gagging, no way of speaking. So I started to rap, and it is as if . . . I don't know. It's like I heard my own voice for the first time, really heard it."

Now while voice in rap is about the individual rapper's message, that message must be articulated not just in any way but with skillful rhythm and flow. Gospel rappers, like secular ones, know rapping to be a highly skilled art that requires a great deal of practice. It takes time to develop the capacity to keep the flow synchronized with the beat, to modulate back and forth between fast and slow, to articulate rapid-fire syllables. (I would stand for long periods awestruck by rappers who practiced these skills through beat-boxing and freestyling: in the former, they would use their hands and the microphone to distort their voice in intricate patterns that made themselves sound like replicas of drums and vinyl record scratching; in the latter, they would take verbal flight from an object such as a driver's license and rap witty rhymed couplets about it for minutes on end.) Yet I was surprised to find, again and again, that my informants insisted that rapping, despite such articulatory fireworks, had more in common with everyday speech than with any other vocal art; in particular, they asserted that rap was a version of the everyday spoken, rather than the melodically sung, word. Like everyday speech, rap involves short voiced syllables and no sonic sustain, while melodic singing involves sustained pitches and tones. "In rap," said T.H., a young *negro* gospel rapper from Pirituba, "you don't push your voice, like when you are singing. You relax and do what you normally do with your voice when you talk, just faster, making sure each word comes out clearly. You don't have to put a note out there and hold it." He demonstrated by holding a note for a few seconds.

> See? That's singing. To do that you need good vocal cords, you know. You have to train your voice for that. For rap, you don't need such a good voice. Because rap is spoken; it is not sung. It doesn't make you push your voice like that. It's very different. Rap requires a lot of skill, a lot of skill, to learn how to speak fast and stay on the beat. But it's totally different. I think that it uses different parts of the voice than sung music.

From this point of view, "voice" is not about the voice box's inherent sensory qualities; it is about practicing articulatory skills, such as flow, speed, and enunciation—and, of course, honing the content of the message. Marylede, a *negra* gospel rap artist from Tiradentes, elaborated: "To rap, you don't really have to refine the instrument of your voice, I mean, the vocal cords. You practice saying the words—fast, sometimes really fast—but whatever your voice is gonna do, it's gonna do. Some rappers sound pretty, some don't. We really don't worry about that. There are a lot of rappers who just start rapping. They don't have anything special in their voice."

This view certainly influences everyday practice: when commenting on another rapper's performance, amateur rap artists would regularly focus on the content of the message and the style of delivery but almost never on the sound of the voice. I found that when they wanted to show admiration, rappers would remark on how smart and truthful the rhymes were and on the speed, rhythm, technique, flow, and enunciatory clarity of verbal delivery. What they would *not* do is comment on the sonority, timbre, depth, color, richness, gravel, acerbity, or any other sensory quality of the rapper's voice. *It was as if vocal cords were off-limits.* Indeed, I made a point of asking all of the rappers I got to know which aspect of the voice was more important: message, flow, or sound. They made it clear that what was most important were the message and flow. "The sound of the voice is important," said Adimilson, "but it all starts when you sit down and express yourself through words. You want someone to hear and understand those words, and the sound is really just a way to do that." Cassio, lead MC of the Pregadores do Gueto, put it this way:

> I think that lyrics and the flow are more important than the sound of the voice. There are a lot of lousy singers who are great rappers. Let's say you have a really beautiful voice, beautiful. But you don't have anything to say. And you don't have flow. Then it doesn't matter how beautiful it is. And let's say you have a really hoarse voice, or you can't carry a tune, but you have something really important to say, that is great. Then you have to say it, and you can do that in rap.

In practice, too, amateur rappers' treatment of their vocal equipment suggested they did not think of themselves as possessing singing voices but rather highly skilled articulatory apparatuses. They did not take singing lessons. They did not do laryngeal warm-ups before shows. They did not consult with phonoaudiologists. They did not practice scales. They rarely did anything to protect or comfort their voices, such as drinking hot tea or lemon or honey. "You do those things if you see yourself as a singer," said Gilberto, of Discipulos do Rei. "But I am not a singer. I'm a rapper."

So different were singing and rapping in this view that some rappers felt the creeping inclusion into their art of melodic singing to be something like a betrayal. Hard staccato voice was for getting across true messages, even if they were tough and unwelcome; melody was for sugarcoating and romance. Early in my fieldwork, I attended a rap contest at a large, dusty indoor club. It was too hot to wait inside, so I hung out in the yard with a small clutch of amateur contestants. The conversation ended up being about rappers who were not there. Zero was ragging on a group that had been experimenting with *melodia*—sung melodies and harmonies in some stanzas, alternating with stanzas of straight rap. To general hilarity, he stood up and struck the pose of an Elvis wannabe, imaginary mike in hand, eyes meaningfully squinted, free hand caressing his abdomen. "That's how he looks, *manos* [brothers]!" "Now it's all about romance and love and *melodia*. No way! Enough! Rap has to get back to its roots, *manos*: hard, straight message rap; simple, hard, pulsing bass; voice snapping loudly. None of this *melodia*." Zero's position was no doubt extreme. In a later conversation, Pretto remarked,

> There can be some melody, some backup singing, whatever. That's all fine. But if this grows too large, rap will lose its soul [*perderia a sua alma*]. All that melody would become what it is about. Melody is pleasing, but rap can't ever be just about pleasing the ears. It has to be ready to sear them. . . . If they want to sing, let them sing. But rap is not about singing. It is about telling it like it is.

"One Cannot Hear Race in Brazil"

Now I want to suggest that the features of rap's vocal art that I have just described—its connection to the spoken word, its lack of reliance on vocal sonority—diminish the ability of the idea of "race" to inform rappers' understanding of their own voices. Rappers had, quite clearly, no difficulty agreeing that one could "hear" race in the singing of melodic music. "In *negro* gospel and R&B," said Marylede, a *negro* gospel rapper in her twenties, "you can tell the difference. . . . I can't explain, but there is a difference, yes [*three-second pause*]. I don't know how to explain it, but when I am listening to music, I can tell that it is the voice of a *negro* person. I know there is a difference. I don't know if there is some technique or something, I don't know." In contrast, *one cannot hear "race" in the spoken language of Brazil*.[3] In the United States, the existence of an African American vernacular dialect makes it possible, from a cultural point of view, to "hear" African American speech patterns. A recent series of sociolinguistic experiments have shown that in US linguistic culture, African American vernacular English is sufficiently recognizable that speakers of English correctly identify it on the telephone 70%–90% of the time (Purnell, Idsardi, and Baugh 1999; Wiehl 2002). No comparable study has been conducted in Brazil, because there the assumption is that no such study is necessary. Whenever I asked in Brazil whether one could "hear" *negritude* in everyday speech, I was given an unequivocal no. As Marylede put it, "Here in Brazil, you cannot hear whether someone is *negro* or not. We just don't have any accent like that. If you are on the phone, it is simply impossible to know whether the person on the line is *negro* or not." Marylede's views are quite common, even dominant, in Brazil. "There is no such thing in Brazil as a '*negro* accent,'" writes a Brazilian commentator on the Internet. "There are regional accents but no racial ones."[4] Another writer commented that there exists no "spoken dialect or language, peculiar to Afro- Brazilians, common across Brazil,"[5] and still another said, "I have not heard of a linguistic dialect peculiar to Brazilians of African descent."[6]

Given these prevailing cultural views, and given the cultural understanding of rap as speech and not singing, it should come as no surprise that my informants said that *they could not infer the racial identity of a rapper by simply listening to him or her*. When I asked Marylede whether race made a difference in the rapping voice, she replied, "With rap, you can't really identify the race of the person. It's just like on the telephone—if you listen to a new song by a rapper you don't know, it's like being on the phone with someone: no way of knowing whether they are white or *negro*." Vilmar, too, insisted, "You cannot tell the difference between a *negro* and a *branco* voice when you hear them speaking—not here in Brazil. I defy you to do it. Turn away, and you can't tell. Maybe you can in the US but not here. Singing, maybe, but not speaking. So I'll tell you this: there's no way you can distinguish a *negro* voice from a white voice that is rapping. Listen to any CD, and I defy you to try and determine the race of the person who is rapping, if you don't look at their photo."

The conviction that there are no detectable sound differences between the *negro* and white rapping voice supported skepticism toward claims that *negros* have a special vocal essence that permits them to excel in rap. Pastor Ton was eloquent on this point. "John, there is no way we can say that!" he declared. "No way we can say that *negros* are better rappers than whites. How can we say that? If you look the other way, you cannot tell if the person who is rapping is white or *negro*. So how could I think the *negro* rapper is better? They have no special vocal qualities that they bring to this. I defy you to try to find that."

If rappers' definition of their art as an extension of everyday speech leads them to a certain racial antiessentialism, the scene's strongly inter-racial character reinforces it. We have already had a glimmer of this: in São Paulo, *brancos* are a real presence on the scene. Everyone knows and has seen one or more white rappers who have demonstrated their ability to excel in messaging, flow, and rhythm. DJ Alpiste, who is *branco*, is one of the best-known gospel rappers in Brazil, widely cited as one of the found-ers of the scene. Other well-respected white gospel rappers include XDR, Choquito, Dom, Gabriel, Ermec (of Sexto Sello), Anderson (of Alerta Ver-melha), the white sisters of Gueto em Cristo, and Dina D. In addition, there are numerous gospel rappers, like secular rappers, who are light-skinned *mestiços*, such as E-Beille, DJ Joilson, Israel, and EVS, all of whose presence on the scene gives one a sense of the range of racial identities. Thus, Lean-dro, the dark *negro* DJ for Gueto em Cristo, could tell me, "I know lots of excellent rappers who are white or very light. They are great. It has nothing to do with color."

The strong presence on the scene of high-quality white rappers does not obviate the fact that most gospel rappers are *negro*; it just makes it harder for rappers to interpret this preponderance as due to inborn skills rather than learned, trained, or enculturated ones. As Pretto put it, "If a *negro* raps better than a white guy, it is not because he was born with that. It is because he ded-icated himself. Anyone who raps well, that is because of practice, not because of blood." The other side of this coin is that being *negro* in no way ensures competence in rap. Leandro drove home the point about himself:

> Look at me. I'm *negro*, but I don't have a gift of rhyming. My gift is more of creativity. I know how to frame things in the right way in the right chan-nel. . . . And meanwhile, Monica and Mary Ellen [white women] have the gift of rapping. . . . If it were a matter of blood [*laughs*], I would be much more the singer than I am! . . . This is person by person, this is individual. Each person has their own gift. Everyone has come here to do some mis-sion. Each person does the thing that God has given them to do on Earth.

Or, as Pretto, also *negro*, put it,

I know many *negros* who are descendants really from the *senzala*, you know, descendants who are really truly Afro. . . . But in spite of that, they have no way—they are not able—like this, while the beat is going like this [*he does a basic rap beat*], they are going like this [*he imitates a totally disconnected singing sequence*]. So I don't believe that this gift was poured out especially upon *negros* or that this comes from the blood. No. I don't believe that, John. I believe that it is individual! I think that it depends on the capacity of each one, because the most important thing there is to sing exactly what you are thinking and what your reality is. Whether you're *branco* or whether you're *negro*, they are equal: as soon as they are rapping their own truth, they are perfect.

I have argued here that *paulista* amateur rappers' understanding of voice inclines them to be skeptical toward racial essentialism. Rappers speak of skills as individual gifts from God, not gifts bestowed on a whole racial group; and they emphasize that these gifts must be nurtured and developed through learning, hard work, and practice. All the rappers I got to know, both secular and gospel, insisted that the kind of vocal skill called on in rap was not subject to the influence of *uma diferença de cor* or *de raça*, whether conceived of in "natural" or "cultural" terms. Dr. Billy and DJ Joilson have rapped together for many years. Billy is a man in his forties who strongly identifies himself as *negro*; Joilson is younger, in his twenties, and identifies himself as *mestiço*. I asked the two of them whether either had ever come across the idea that "in order to sing a good rap, you have to have *negro* blood." Eyes widening, they both shook their heads. Joilson laughed. "No!" came their cry, in unison. "No, no!" added Joilson:

A person is simply born with the gift. I do not think that anybody who starts singing in this style and raps well somehow feels more *negro*. You don't feel that blood running more in your veins, no. I think this is just something that you acquire when you're little, like I did growing up listening to it. It is just something that I always liked. But it's not because I got to know rap that I'm going to have more *sangue negro* run more in my veins, no; I think that all blood runs the same way.

And Pastor Ton put it this way:

God gives a gift to both whites and *negros*, and then it's up to them to develop their gift. I think the gifts from God are to individuals, not to races. When I am rapping, I am not expressing my race. I am expressing my ideas. I am not expressing my *negro* soul. I'm expressing my own soul. I think each person expresses their own soul. Each person has their own way of rapping. I don't rap the way I do because I'm *negro*.

Historical Narrative in Gospel Rap

In contrast to the experience-near contemporary world of voice and neighborhood, we now enter the realm of experience-distant imagination, connecting ideas of what people have done in faraway times and places to the unfolding will of God.

To begin with, in contrast to black gospel, which, we will see, encourages a chronologically deep historical consciousness, gospel rappers have comparatively little knowledge of musical traditions earlier than the 1970s. When I asked them to tell me the story of their scene, they hardly spoke of precursors, roots, or ancestors, starting instead by naming the first rappers in the United States in the late 1970s and early '80s. The weakness of rappers' knowledge about pre-1980s musical history may also have contributed to their generally low level of awareness of the connections between music and black collective struggle. Few rappers had thought much, for example, about the connections between slave songs and slave rebellion, between spirituals and black spirituality, between blues and psychic survival, between gospel and the civil rights movement. Gospel rappers had heard of these things but only vaguely; for them, black music meant mainly the recreational, "cheerful" music of samba or the idolatrous drumming of candomblé, neither of which they valued very positively. Their lack of knowledge of music history thus reinforced a conception of blackness tethered to an image of play, irresponsibility, eroticism, and superstition and removed from collective struggle for survival and racial justice.

That being said, there can be no doubt that gospel rappers do possess a specific form of historical consciousness. Through listening to their everyday talk, attending their events and teach-ins, scouring rap lyrics, perusing their websites (such as Rap Gospel Brasil and Missão Urbana: Hip Hop Gospel Organizado), following their digital traffic on social networking sites, and questioning them directly, I identified key elements of gospel rappers' historical understanding of their music.

A first pattern that emerges is that all rappers, both secular and gospel, who tell the story of the origin of their scene begin by referring, in some way or another, to *the Bronx*. They have heard older rappers mention this mysterious location as the birthplace of their art and are eager to emphasize it. "Our art began in a poor, very poor neighborhood called the Bronx," said Gabriel, "on the street, man. Ask any *mano*, and he will tell you: it all started in the Bronx. That is a *bairro* in New York City, USA." The point I want to underline is that these narrators do not speak about the *blackness* of "the Bronx"; what the name symbolizes to them is harshness and similarity to poor neighborhoods in São Paulo. "The older guys," said Pretto, "say the Bronx was really a tough neighborhood. I mean, think of some of the places you've seen in São Paulo, in the *periferia*—maybe harder than that." Listen to Pregador Luo: "I saw all the movies that are set in the Bronx. The Bronx is way, way up there, miles and miles away from Times Square. The burnt-out buildings are like our *periferia*—the ripped-up streets, the debris in the streets, the smashed windows. Actually it looks even worse there than here. The violence, the crime, death, drugs, guns—it is all the same." DJ Alpiste compared the Bronx with Capão Redondo, the most peripheral of neighborhoods. "It all started in the Bronx," he said, "the hardest part of the city, the real *periferia*—like our Capão Redondo—really far out. It takes forever to take the subway there, like it's the end of the line." Again, speakers did not refer to the racial composition of the Bronx; they talked instead about the oppressiveness of its living conditions. Indeed, while understanding that early rap was a vehicle for prophetic critique of injustice, none of my informants, whether gospel or secular, recognized racism as having occupied a special place among these objects of denunciation. Thus, what they seem to be focused on is not so much a hemispheric identity residing in being of African descent but rather one of poverty and marginalization.

A second pattern in these narratives is the theme of the moral decline of US rap and the implications of that decline for transhemispheric identity. All Brazilian rappers, both secular and gospel, tell the story of this moral decline, in which the founding generation of rappers, motivated by the high ideals of nonviolence, community, justice, and peace, were replaced by MCs more interested in bling and champagne. This narrative was important to all of my informants. They referred to the visual images they had seen in TV

Gospel rappers praying before the show

specials, movies, music videos, and the *Cribs* series, all of which display the decadent splendor in which famous US rappers live. It is hard to miss US rap videos—they play in music stores, in the homes of friends, and on television—and rappers do not like what they see. "The Americans are destroying rap," said DJ Alpiste. "It used to be about important things, things that mattered; now it is all about materialism and prostitution and drinking and drugs and champagne and cars." Pretto openly sneered when I asked about American rap. "How can we respect that?" he asked. "It's basically pornography! That is what is produced in America."

The take of gospel rappers on this familiar narrative is that the decline is a spiritual one. "God was pleased with what he saw in US rap back then," explained DJ Alpiste. "There was much spirituality in that. This was the word of God in action. The rappers of that period were all about brotherly love, about doing good in the world." But then US rap was led astray by its own material success. The success of rap in the 1990s bred the sins of pride, covetousness, envy, lust, and, ultimately, violence. From its pure beginnings, said Adam of Profetas do Apocalipse, "rap in your country fell into the clutches of the evil one. Once it was all about brotherhood, man! That is how it started. But then it deteriorated when money and wealth came into the scene. That bred anger and violence, and there was all that anger between New York and California, and Tupac was murdered." By the 2000s, as Ton, lead MC of Rimas Proféticas, put it, "Rap from the US is just big cars and bathtubs and champagne and bling. I do not think that any of this is pleasing to God. They went down the wrong path, and now they have distanced themselves from the Lord." Or as Anderson, of Profetas do Apocalipse explained, "Look— rap in the US was once fearful of the Lord. They stood up for values of the Bible—for justice and brotherhood and the good you can do for your neighbor. And God rewarded this with guidance—the Lord's hand was in it."

A corollary of this narrative, told by several of my gospel rapper informants, is that North American rappers are losing divine favor, while Brazilian rappers are gaining it. "God is withdrawing from the US or is being pushed away," explained Pretto. "And these guys are getting worse. But here, we aren't rich. I don't want to say that we'll be immune at some point (though I hope we will walk in the way of the Lord! [*laughs*]). But for now, almost every new group that appears is singing the praises of the Lord. It is like a fire has been lit here in Brazil." Will also observed,

> I don't know anywhere else in the world that has as many Christian rappers as we do here. I have not heard of any gospel rap from the US. But here I believe that this is the fire of the Holy Spirit. Your rappers have not been really fearful of the Lord. They have not sought him out. They do not live a life that is obedient to him. You can see that on TV! So God cannot pour out his anointing upon your rappers. . . . But here, we have not been led astray by materialism—what do we have? Nothing! None of our youth can afford bling! So here our youth want to serve the Lord. We have people who wish to do nothing better than to serve the Lord, so God responds to that and is pouring out his anointing. And now, we are harvesting the fruits.

Now this narrative, that North American rap has lost its way spiritually, weakens the idea that what black Brazilian gospel rappers have most in common with North American rappers is their African ancestry. Listening to the quality of the discourse in rap in the Northern Hemisphere, black gospel rappers feel mainly alienated from it, and the fact of North American rappers'

blackness offers little remedy for this alienation. I asked Will whether the fact
that he shared a common racial identity with North American rappers such
as Fifty Cent in any way mitigated his spiritual frustration with him. Just the
opposite, was his reply:

> Why should I identify with him? He has let rap slide into a mish-mash
> [*uma salada*] of whatever. It has no idealism left. No, no, I would say that
> these rappers are reminding me what my true calling is, and it is not with
> them. Maybe Fifty Cent wants to talk to his friends and get out and do
> their thing and get rich. But how about all the people who are still suffer-
> ing, who don't have bling? Those are my people—my people here, maybe
> there too, I don't know, certainly here.

I asked him to clarify.

> When I hear these guys in the US, sure they are the ones who started rap,
> and I respect them for that. But they aren't my leaders spiritually. Rap has
> to be bigger than a black thing. It is not just about blacks. It is about some-
> thing bigger, which is fighting for what is right, in the sight of God. The
> poor in the *periferia* here, there, anywhere, those are the people I want to
> fight for, no matter what their color.

I encountered this position among other gospel rappers as well: North
American rappers, having abdicated their historical role as spiritual leaders, can no longer credibly make a claim for the inherent moral advantage of
blackness. Gospel rappers in Brazil have found their spiritual path, are being
blessed for it by having their anointing doubled by the Lord; yet in Brazil, as
they point out, rappers come in all colors. Thus, the contrastive experience
of the two hemispheres suggests that for gospel rappers a strong hemispheric
identity is defined not so much by blackness as it is by residence in marginalized, poor, harsh urban environments. Material adversity, not blackness,
is what creates a transnational hemispheric identity. Fábio articulated this
point:

> John, I am black, I am proud to be black. But being a rapper is not for
> me just about being black. I respect my heritage, and I respect the rap-
> pers who founded this all. But I cannot limit myself. Look at rappers in the

US—they are black, but what are they doing? Are they an example to me? I am more inspired by DJ Alpiste [a white gospel rapper in Brazil], who has a vision for the people in the *periferia*. So that is what inspires me: vision, not skin color. If there are rappers in the US who are trying to give voice to the oppressed, then I am with them. I identify with that. If they live in a favela, so do I. And favelas have something in common all over the world.

A final feature of gospel rappers' historical consciousness that decenters blackness is undoubtedly the evangelical suspicion of strong enthusiasms that threaten forgetfulness of God. They call such enthusiasm "idolatry." One thing that threatens idolatry, for gospel rappers, is excessive interest in heroes, including black ones. As the lead MC of Pregadores do Gueto put it,

I think that it's very interesting to learn about heroes from the past, about Malcolm X, about Martin Luther King, about Zumbi. So I do not disrespect anybody who is seeking to learn more about them. But as we become more involved in our church and deepen our knowledge of the Bible, we have learned that the greatest revolutionary of all was Jesus Christ. He was the greatest revolutionary because he didn't need to spill anybody's blood to make a revolution. He had to spill his own blood, and that was all. We respect that each person, each group needs to defend their own vision of revolution. But it is not the vision of the Pregadores do Gueto; it is not our vision to pursue those kinds of worldly revolutions, the ones that black heroes fought for. I think it's fine for others to learn the history of these people. It would be hypocritical, though, for us to be talking a lot about and preaching about the lives of people that we don't really think about much.

On a different occasion, I asked Feijão, an MC for the gospel rap group Ao Cubo, whether Zumbi was important. "He was a great leader," he replied.

But all the stuff about Zumbi still being alive, we see that as a kind of idolatry. Today all this talk about Zumbi is turning him into a kind of idol. . . . I know that in secular rap, they are always running after the heroes of black history. And that's important to know about, but we don't really put that great of a priority on that because we have to be sure that in first place always is Jesus Christ. The greatest man was not Malcolm X. He was not

Pregadores do Gueto

Zumbi of Palmares. He was Jesus Christ. So we involve ourselves more in reading the Bible and learning that history than we do in learning the history of black people.

At the start of this section, I observed that the ideology of gospel rappers, like that of secular rappers, is strongly present oriented, leading them to have little interest in delving into their scene's history further back than the 1970s. Lots of historical knowledge and its accompanying discourse about "roots," Africa, diasporic slave experience, blues, spirituals, and so on are simply off their radar. Consequently, gospel rappers do not have a rich vocabulary that connects musical history to ethnoracial identity. Pretto said, "Rap doesn't really concern itself with things about blues. We hear about that more in the church, from musicians. People in the church comment on this, you know, the blues and gospel musicians. On the side of rap, we kind of forget the origins of our own music." Chris, of Guerreiros do Senhor, stated that his slight musical historical knowledge came not from rap but from R&B singers and magazines. He knew the basic musical genealogy—work songs begat spirituals, which begat blues and gospel—but had *not* learned the genealogy from hip hop culture. "Listening to rappers," he explained, "I didn't hear much about history. They talk a lot more about police and violence and the problems we face now. If I had just listened to them, I wouldn't have been so interested in reading books about black people." Preto Jay, lead MC for gospel rap group Sexto Sello, was brought into contact with music history via his interest in blues. "It wasn't rap that taught me that," he explained. "It was when I started to listen to blues. . . . The idea of harmony, the idea of melody . . . So I was reading magazines about that music, and I picked one that had a whole article about the history of blues and its connection to slavery and its connection to melancholy. I never got that from rap."

Yet in a fascinating way, things are beginning to change among some rappers—precisely those who have begun actively to incorporate *melody* and *harmony* into their repertoire. I found that the more seriously a rapper was pursuing these things, the more that rapper began to regard North American black musical history as something with which he or she needed to be familiar. Rappers dedicated to a basic aggressive beat, samplers, and voice-overs had little interest in becoming conversant with this history; but rappers intrigued by the expressive potentialities of melody and harmony wanted to make more informed aesthetic judgments when working with tonal progressions, backup singers, longer samples, and live instrumental musicians. Consider Preto Jay, a rapper in his late twenties who has developed aspirations to blend a variety of melodic and harmonic forms into his work, such as blues and Brazilian samba. When I asked him whether he had sought to learn more about musical precursors to rap, he replied,

> Yeah, but access to books on these materials is very difficult. But, you see, in my case, I would like to learn how to play the piano. And so I know that to do that I really need to learn a lot more about the whole basis and about the history of music. Because I want to put musicality into my work. My work is musical. But I want to make it even more musical. My next record, I want to have a band.

Indeed, like many other rappers, Preto Jay has been moving toward fusing more R&B sounds as well as samba into his music. Like others, he characterized this trend in his own work as "evolution": "I want to be evolutionary in my music," he said, and this evolution goes hand in hand with greater attention to everything to do with melodic music, including the precursors to rap.

"Now that I am interested in this," he said, "I realize I have a lot of education to do. I need to learn about it all—soul and jazz and spirituals. As soon as I open that up, I need to learn it all!"

Similarly, Samuel has become interested in incorporating more melody and harmony into his music, and as he does so, he has grown more knowledgeable of the deeper roots of rap in blues, funk, and soul. When I asked about the history of music, he expounded tenderly and at length. He had read, he said, several articles about the topic, and his retention of what he had read was impressively detailed. "It said," he explained, with evident satisfaction,

> that a long time ago the black was always in a state of suffering. So that the blues are very melancholic, and the blues were made by blacks. Jazz as well is a very rhythmic music, but if you look closely, it too has this kind of melancholic feel to it. And blues began to be done as a way to externalize what they were feeling as oppression, the oppression by the whites. To think this whole question of the musicality of the *negro*—that the black is more musical than the white or sings better than the white or that the black's voice is more potent than that of the white—I think it all comes from a long time ago. Because I think also of the history of the Africans, of the slaves, how they came singing into the church, when they were chained. They were pulled out of their country, but they came singing. I believe the fact that blacks have soul comes from suffering. Not that I want to carry some kind of trophy or claim any kind of honor for the black; but if they say that the black can sing better than the white, I think that it is because of suffering.

A key point here is that it was the blues, and not rap itself, that led Samuel to learn this history. The key to his historical interest was his "interest in making harmonies":

> It was a time when I had started to listen a lot to blues. . . . And I didn't even know why I was listening to blues. But I was listening to blues and blues and more blues, until finally I realized there was a reason in there, a reason for me to listen to all those blues: for me to absorb a little bit more that rhythm, for me to absorb a little bit more that music that I could then bring into my own style—the idea of harmony, the idea of melody, the idea of bringing in more melancholy, because we have one of our songs which

is very melancholic. So I was very interested to pick up a magazine that had a whole article about the history of blues and its sound and its connection to slavery and its connection to melancholy.

Cristovão, nineteen-year-old rapper in Guerreiros do Senhor, also had an interest in musical history; but like Preto Jay and Samuel, his interest came not from rap itself but from an effort to go beyond the scene as conventionally performed and to integrate more melodic and harmonic elements. He knew about the roots in Africa, about the transformation into work songs, blues, jazz, and soul. He also was clear that it was not his involvement in the rap scene that had taught him this history; it was the practitioners of soul. "Because," he explained,

> when I listened to our national rappers, they talk a lot about police and those things, things that are happening today. Listening to that, I wasn't that interested in learning about a lot of history. In rap, you don't talk much about the history of music. . . . When you talk about the musical history, it's more students of it, those who study it, and the magazines. It's not really the rap groups. But when I started to listen to Kadoshi, they recounted stories of African tribes, how they began to sing all that. The African style comes along with the musical repertoire, there at the root, the foundation, making a choir, the history of black music. I started to see the link with Africa but also to see that Brazil has a culture that is different from Africa and different from the United States. . . . About the voice—I read that in a book that talks about black music and gospel here in Brazil. I'll show it to you later. It's a book or it's a magazine article with Ferrisbeck and the Blackness Boys. Because he is from Angola, and he talks about this.

Rappers who knew that blues referred to a black art form and that "blues was the music of the slaves" stated that they had not learned these details from rapper friends. "Rap doesn't comment on this," said Pretto.

> About this, we hear about it more in the church—about blues. Some people in the church have more knowledge about this, and they comment on it—the musicians—not really the pastors themselves but the musicians. On the side of blues and jazz and singers like BB King, the musicians that

play that kind of music, they seem to know more about the origin of it, and they talk more about that. They know more about it. But on the side of rap, they forget the origins of their own music.

"What Did You Expect?"

Having journeyed through some of the everyday practices and discourses of black gospel rap, let us now return to the rapper whose voice it was that pushed me into this journey to begin with. Back in 2003, Vilmar Junior asked me what I expected. To tell the truth, I had expected (or hoped) gospel rap in São Paulo to be a bastion of surging black consciousness. Before embarking on the journey, I thought I knew what "black consciousness" meant. But my journey revealed a form of black consciousness that I had not expected to find. For black gospel rappers, blackness is important; it is a key part of their identities. It is just not *the* central part of their identities. I learned that what is central to them is their experience of marginalization, forged through adversity and residence in an impoverished, marginalized place, shared with similarly placed people throughout the hemisphere. The black rapper, in focusing on a place in which people of all races suffer similar hardships, is pushed to a heightened identity forged in poverty and hardship, irrespective of race. As Dr. Billy said,

God has concern with the poor, the miserable, the broken, the kid out there who is on drugs or is suicidal. All over the world, this is happening. That knows no race, has nothing to do with it. We rappers are instruments of the Lord's will, to tell this story, irrespective of race, about all races, to all races. You look over the kids who we bring into the church: they are of all colors. And we are of all colors. God is choosing us at this time as his instruments, to carry out his mission and preach the word to every living creature. In rap, we know no race. In rap, we are all one in the *periferia*. We are all one in the Lord.

Still, the fact that "rap knows no race" does not mean that one forgets one is black; it just alters the valence of that knowledge. Black gospel rappers include their blackness as a contributing force in their identity. Listen again to Dr. Billy: "I am black, and I am proud to be black. Being black, I have had certain experiences—let us say, unpleasant things have happened—and

I learn from that, certain lessons: not to be exclusive but to embrace others. Because what I have gone through for being black, maybe someone else in the *periferia* has gone through for being in the *periferia*." To be black from this point of view thus implies an inclusionary impulse, a capacity to empathy, an ability and willingness to feel the pain of others. This is not just evangelical Christianity speaking: it is a consciousness born of a common fate—thus Pretto's lyric:

> It doesn't matter what your color is, nor your race
> White and *negro*, young or old
> Where all people without exception are destroying themselves
> Those who should do something don't, they just watch

3

The Flags of Jesus and Brazil

Body, History, and Nation in Samba Gospel

A Visit to Marco Davi's Office

Marco Davi de Oliveira had recently published a book entitled *The Blackest Religion in Brazil*. He was a bearded young Baptist minister, and I was sipping hot coffee from a tiny plastic cup in his church office in São Paulo while he spoke animatedly about the struggle against racism. I had read his book, which argued that evangelical churches were a key strategic front in the struggle. "If the church recognizes that blacks and whites receive different treatment in this country," his book had concluded, "and that this wounds the conscience of God, Lord of all, other institutions will be able to follow its example and seek a social transformation of the nation" (2004, 112–113). He was gravely serious about this conclusion. "Listen, John," he said, jabbing his cup in the air, "what are the churches that are growing fastest in this country? Evangelical ones. Where are most Afro-Brazilians going for an encounter with God? Our churches. So it follows: we have a huge responsibility. Our churches must face the question of racism. If we don't, this problem will never be solved in this country." I told him I agreed entirely and in fact had been busy studying music precisely in order to understand whether a certain form of black pride might already be taking root in the Protestant arena in Brazil. His eyebrows lifted; he set his cup down, placed his hands behind his head, and leaned back.

"Aaah. Yes." He said, "Now we are getting somewhere. That is good. That is where you should be looking, yes, at music." He paused for a moment to think the idea over. "So what kind of music have you been looking at?"

Until then, I had been spending my time mainly with artists whose music derived from North America, and I said as much. Marco Davi looked disappointed. He leaned forward and wagged a finger at me.

"An error, an error! You are trying to see black pride as it exists already, but you are looking in the wrong places, the wrong places."

"Where should I be looking?"

He raised his hands toward the ceiling.

"John! It should be obvious! You need to look at gospel samba!"

He got up, started walking around the room, and began speaking more rapidly.

"Gospel samba," he repeated, "that is where you'll find what is authentic. That is the future; that is Brazil! These other things are fine, but they are too North American. They are rooted in your country, not ours. If you want to find Brazilian black pride, look at samba. That is where the future of gospel music lies, John, for us who are trying to bring the issue of race into the church. Samba is the true Brazilian music. And it is black music! There is a rich tradition there. That is where you should look if you want to see the next front of black pride in our churches."

He went on: "Just a few weeks ago, I heard this for the first time—I had never heard gospel samba before. It's definitely important. The group is called Deus Crioulos." (This is a pun: *Deus Crioulos* means at the surface level "Black God" or "God of the Blacks." At a second level, it can be interpreted as *Deus Criou-l-os*, meaning "God created them.") "They didn't have conscious lyrics, but look at the name of their group—Deus Crioulos! If I were you, I'd look them up."

I left the office confused and a little concerned. Had I been missing an important piece of the puzzle? Of course, I needed to get to know gospel samba. What was the name of that group? I looked at the note I had taken, and I resolved to track them down on the Internet. Sitting on the bus back to the center of town, I thought things over. I had from the start of the project intended to look at gospel samba, but had gotten sidetracked. I was so swept up in the expressions of black pride I was discovering in gospel rap and black gospel that I had neglected the most Brazilian of the Protestant black musics. Here now was a Brazilian Protestant minister who was also a sociological researcher (who had just published a book), urging me to get moving on gospel samba. As I looked out the window at the buildings rushing by on the Avenida Brasil, I knew Marco Davi was right. I needed to spend more time in the months I had left in Brazil looking at a genre rooted in Brazilian rather than North American music. I needed to focus on investigating whether and how gospel samba served as a vehicle for black identity. And so, starting that very week, I began to attend more performances of gospel sambistas.

In what follows, I navigate among a series of meanings—some obvious, some less so—of samba as imagined and performed by evangelical artists. This is a deep ocean I am wading into here, and I do not claim to have gone deep enough for us to understand what the music means in all ways to its practitioners. In order to get at least knee-deep, I follow the theoretical orientation outlined in the introduction and developed in chapter 1, to pose questions about how evangelicals imagine and practice this music in terms of bodies, place, and history. I move from ideas about samba and the body to ideas about samba and the physical landscape of Brazil, to ideas about samba and Brazilian history. There is inevitably overlap here, but such is social life— that seamless, sutureless thing, in which moments of thought and language are recruited into many different clusters of belief and practice. As I look at the beliefs and practices associated with gospel samba, I pay attention to how they do or do not embrace particular notions of blackness.

Gospel Samba and Ideas about the Body

First, let us turn to gospel sambistas' ideas and practices having to do with samba's relationship to the body. To what extent do gospel sambistas entertain ideas that black bodies have an affinity to samba? To address this question, let us begin by focusing on that quintessential aspect of the relationship between music and the body, namely, the voice. To understand gospel samba's attitude toward the voice, we need to look at the scene more broadly for a moment. For all sambistas, whether secular or gospel, the rule is quite

simple: one does not need a powerful, beautiful, strong, mellifluous, or pol-
ished voice to be considered a good samba singer. Both secular and gospel
sambistas often have quite small, unimpressive voices, and many have voices
that are decidedly rough, ragged, even raspy. All one need do is listen to sambistas regarded as the greats of the scene, such as Nelson Cavaquinho,[1] Dori
Caymmi,[2] or Cartola,[3] and there will remain little doubt that in samba prestige is not awarded to a sambista based on his or her voice's decibel-level
capacity or exquisiteness. The key quality one listens for in a sambista is the
fit between melody and lyric and the minimal ability of the singer's voice to
deliver the latter. This allows us to understand why, for example, Paulo César
Pinheiro is considered a great sambista, though he does not even sing—he
speaks his compositions.[4] At the end of the day, what is most important in
samba are, first, the skill in playing the instrument; second, the interesting,
arresting quality of one's lyrics; and, third, the marriage between them. If the
sambista happens to have a particularly memorable voice, that is fine, but
this is in no way an essential feature of the art. That may be why, for example,
a recent examination of samba singing focused on rhythmic structure and
percussive vocalization rather than on the production of clear, strong, powerful, loud, or smooth tones (Naveda and Leman 2009). "To sing well [in
samba]," writes Juliano Coelho, "is not absolutely necessary—in some cases,
it is not even welcome."[5] David Ramos, a specialist in the history of Brazilian
singing, in a lecture I heard him deliver several years ago, waxed eloquent on
this point. "In Brazil," he explained,

> there was for a long time little interest in really developing a strong sing-
> ing tradition or culture. People sang samba, but samba really isn't about
> singing as much as it is about the playing of the instrumental music, the
> *cavaquinho* and the *surdo*. It wasn't really about singing; it never really
> has been about that. And so there was little development of the Brazilian
> singing voice. It was really only with the influence of American soul and
> gospel music in the 1970s and afterward that Brazilians started to get inter-
> ested in developing their voices, to really exploit the full potential of their
> voice boxes. Samba in no way exploits the full capacity of the human vocal
> instrument. It just doesn't.

The low priority samba places on the inherent technical qualities or decibel power of the voice very likely has to do with the fact that samba arose

mainly as an instrumental scene, focused on beat and rhythm, and that the first places it was played were intimate settings—in people's homes, in small bars, and in backyards—rather than in the wide-open spaces of large clubs or concert halls (Shaw 1999). As the style developed, samba became a way to tell stories and to communicate emotional content. This may be what sambista Candéia means when he insists in his song "Pintura Sem Arte" that "não basta fazer uma linda canção" (it is not enough to make a beautiful song) and what Murilo Mendes meant when he wrote,

> To sing samba it is not necessary to have a beautiful voice. . . . For the song to be well sung, one must . . . sing it with the voice coming from the heart; maybe that is why samba is one of the few rhythms in which the best interpreters are not always the best singers. . . . Samba is the music of the people—it can be sung equally well by the sober and the drunk, by beggars and the elite, by men and women—all that is needed is that whoever is doing it seek to allow emotion to win out over reason.[6]

This sense that the beautiful, powerful voice is not essential to samba was very clearly present among the practitioners of gospel samba whom I interviewed. In practice, what mattered to them was melody and instrumentation, not the singing voice. Alexandre, who played *cavaquinho* for Deus Crioulos, pointed out, "In samba, the quality of the voice is not what is most important. That is the tradition. Those who really know the music don't think this is necessary." Robson, another *cavaquinho* player, explained, "In the house—no, no, no—you don't need to sing well. You need to sing in a way that shows your heart. But what is really more important than singing well is playing the instruments technically well. That is essential. The instruments are more important than the voice." He explicitly distinguished samba from black gospel in this sense. "Choirs at church," he said, "singing like that, that needs a really good voice, a strong one. But for samba, you don't need that." Jairo, the founder of Deus Crioulos, went so far as to say that beautiful singing would sound out of place in samba. He argued that this was because samba is a democratic scene, in which the style of singing needs to be available to all. "When I hear someone singing samba," he said,

> I need to feel, 'Hey, I could do that!' You do not need to have a trained voice—you know, trained in the academy, how to breathe, and doing

scales and all—to sing samba. I think of singing samba as like singing in
the shower. Anyone can do it. There are some very good samba singers—
they are the ones you really feel; they sing the words with great feeling. But
sometimes they are singing them just as if they were in your living room,
talking to you, crying, sad, or melancholy. It isn't that feeling like they are
on the big stage singing operatic arias. That is not how samba singers create feelings.

That samba's vocal tradition is constructed as democratic, nonexpert, and
open to "all Brazilians" is further suggested by the fact that almost none of
the samba artists I got to know had sought formal voice training. In only
one case, a sambista who had decided to expand his musical horizons to soul
and jazz had begun to take lessons, "because for those kinds of music, you
need a better trained voice; you need more control." Of the voice instructors
I met while in the field, I came across none who taught samba singing. "It
just wouldn't occur to me," explained one. I scoured the singing instruction
and tutoring world in vain for specific samba singing lessons. Voice lessons
in jazz, soul, rock, and black music abounded—but no samba. "Anyone who
really is involved in samba can develop the skill he needs to sing samba," said
Isabêh, a voice instructor. "In general, they don't need special instruction."

What is the impact of this aesthetic relation to the singing voice on ideas
about blackness? To begin with, none of my informants articulated a physical, genetic, biological, or essentialist connection between singing samba and
being either black or Brazilian. I pushed the envelope several times on this
matter, asking my informants whether having African ancestry endowed
singers of samba with any special capabilities to generate the music. When
I did so, I was met with laughter, frowns, knitted brows, indifference, even
hostility. It was not so much that gospel sambistas refused to think about
the possibility of an inborn connection between music and blackness—they
admitted they thought black gospel singers might have racially privileged
voice boxes—it was simply that in the creation of the vocal sounds of their
own genre, no exceptional physical endowment or apparatus was required.
It seems that because there is little role for spectacular singing in samba,
there is no corresponding need to think about what might *explain* spectacular singing. As David Ramos put it in an interview, "In samba, people
don't think about such things. How could we? Listen to the singing in samba.
There is not much to think about!"

But what about people of African descent having a special aptitude for vocal *swingue* or *ritmo*—the ability to synchronize vocally with the polyrhythms and microsyncopation that are at the heart of the genre? My informants here were a little more interested in ideas of Africanity; yet even in this connection, Africanity was sharply constrained by a sense of the common endowments of all Brazilians. Gospel sambistas acknowledged that there might be something to the theories of an "African vocal rhythm," passed along either by blood or culture; but they were skeptical toward the notion that more or less African blood implied greater or lesser capacity to produce samba polyrhythms. It was as if a logic of quantity offended a deeper ideological commitment to the national *comunitas* of Brazilian identity. Listen to gospel sambista Rogério, whose comments capture this feeling, as well as the ideological synthesis of "blood" and "culture": "Maybe some people have better rhythm," he said.

> Maybe that has to do with having black blood. I don't know. But you know, we live in such a miscegenated country that we all have some black blood, so I think all Brazilians are able to sing samba, if they want. So I don't really think it matters about some people having more than others. If you are Brazilian, you have some African blood—and Portuguese blood. Samba is a mixture. It isn't just African blood. It is about the Europeans too! It is all this mixed together. Any Brazilian, if he wants to really apply himself, can play samba. It is our music.

In a moment, I will return to this notion of racial mixture and samba; for now, I just want to underline that it here supports a rejection of a "quantum" idea of blood that might reinforce a racially essentialist understanding of voice.

But what about that quintessential site of racialogical thinking, the dance? To understand the peculiar relationship of gospel samba to dance, we need to visit a church on an evening when the sounds of samba fill its spaces. Although it is midweek, the Brazil for Christ Church in Freguesia do Ó, a working-class neighborhood on the north side of the city, is packed. Two hundred people crowd into the oversized ex-garage. It is an evening of celebration, as the congregation congratulates a rap band (which includes a member of the church) on the release of its debut CD. It is a warm, muggy night, and many young people who have nothing to do with the church are milling about in front of it. Some of these find themselves pulled through the church's wide-open blue steel doors by the magnetic sounds issuing from within.

As four young men set up their instruments, the church is filled by the buzz of excited voices—"Here they are!" "What do you think of that?" I ask the young man next to me who this group is. He breaks into a huge smile: "That? Those guys are the church's samba group!" It turns out the group is fairly new to the church, having come into existence only a few months ago. All around us, there is a sudden whoosh of bodily vitality, as if someone has just plugged everyone around us—or, at least, the younger people—into an electrical outlet. But it is a highly controlled electricity. A shimmer of prepa-ratory shaking is happening in front of us: five young women stretch their arms up to the ceiling and gyrate their shoulders, but, as far as we can see, they carefully avoid gyrating their hips. From behind us, three female teen-agers make their way laughing toward the front of the church, entering the space between the front pew and the pulpit. They too perform little shoulder shimmies and tight three-steps—again, studiously avoiding any sway of the hips.

All this sudden bodily motion is not out of the ordinary here. This lib-eral church is accustomed to gospel rap and rock groups provoking move-ment, from simple bopping and bobbing to swirling and breaking in the center of rings of appreciative, clapping young people. So again now, as the little church fills with the sounds of *cavaquinho* and *surdo*, young people in the front row stand up and join the girls near the stage, happily swaying, singly, in place. Behind them, some of the old-timers cross their arms and purse their lips, but what can they do? Dancing in place is, as the pastor said, "showing how happy we are to be standing in God's grace"; it is a sign of "pleasure to be a part of God's creation," a "joyful celebration of the Lord."

The real trouble begins about halfway through the first number, when over in the corner, near a huge potted fern, a teenage boy and girl start to dance with each other. That is a line no one is supposed to cross. Bodily motion in church can occur singly, not with a partner and certainly not with someone of the opposite sex. Sometimes girls dance playfully with each other (though boys never do), and that is tolerated though not encouraged. So how can these two young people not know that they are violating a taboo?

It turns out that this pair have frequented the church for a couple of months but have not yet been baptized and so are not yet fully versed in church decorum. The girl, whose name is Fernanda, begins to swivel her hips, and the young man, whose name is Samuel, dares to place his hand on the small of her back, at a dangerously low altitude. This breach of etiquette goes on for almost a full minute. Then something startling occurs: rather than triggering general disapproval, the couple's daring catches on. Within the second minute, four other young couples, including baptized members of the church, find themselves testing the limits of their church's tolerance. The *surdos'* drumming now mixes with exclamations of surprise, pleasure, and censure from the congregation.

All this is more than Pastor Sérgio can take. Marching to the podium, his annoyance visible on his face, he signals to the drummer and guitarist to fall silent. The dancers freeze, and the muggy air fills with tension. The couples who have been dancing fidget nervously, and one of the girls plants her eyes on the floor.

"It is time," Sérgio shouts, "for me to say a word of discipline!" Hallelujahs erupt from deep within the crowd. He launches into a ten-minute sermon about how we must keep our eyes focused on the Lord, not allow ungodly thoughts to enter our heads, that here we must glorify and praise only his name, not each other, that protocols of modesty and moderation were being violated, and so on.

His voice grows plaintive.

"I have permitted all kinds of music into this house of worship," he says, pacing the pulpit, sweeping his arms in a wide arc. "And you know—those of you who know me, who know my work—you know my love for the Lord. You know I have allowed this music because I am convinced that the devil can have no victory, that all glory and victory belong to the Lord."

"Hallelujah!"

"And I know," he continues, "some brothers and sisters have criticized me, saying this was going down the wrong path. And I have prayed and sought the guidance of the Lord and turned to the Bible again and again and read the passages about the Levites. Glory. Hallelujah. So you know I have always responded that God called upon us to glorify him with tambourine and drum and with our voices, in all ways, and that there is no music that does not belong to the Lord. And I have said I have trust in the discipline and faith of my congregants."

"Glory!" "Thank you, Lord!" "Hallelujah!"

"But some of you have disappointed me today."

The place falls almost frighteningly silent.

"Let us not give our critics a reason to keep this music out of the church. I will ask that you reflect on this, that you pray on it, that you seek guidance from the Lord. Friends, I refuse to let the devil win this battle. I will not allow the devil to steal back samba in this house. We will take it from his clutches. But not today. Today the music is over."

There are gasps all around. The tension is almost unbearable.

"Yes, I know, many of us came here today to listen to music. But there is a music that is higher than any of this. It is the music of heaven. It is the music of the Lord. So we will invite our friends back another day, after our young people have had time to pray and think about these words."

The physically painful silence continues for a few seconds more; then, finally, a "Hallelujah." The samba group packs its instruments dejectedly, sheepishly, while the young offenders slink back into the crowd, ready for a long hour of testimony and preaching and no more samba.

The samba troupe does indeed return several weeks later to play, this time with everyone carefully abiding by the single dancing rule.

Now, while this episode shows a pastor successfully disciplining his church, it also illustrates why many pastors are nervous about inviting samba groups to come in. Evangelicals fear samba because they worry it will unleash ungodly thoughts and draw young people, whose religious convictions are just starting to firm up, into an inner place of sin, to be followed by who knows what. What worries the pastors is not so much the music itself—the instruments and singing can be tolerated as long as the lyrics are godly—but the intersex dancing in church, which the music has the power to incite. "In church" is the key phrase. Pious believers are not thrilled by the idea of people dancing in couples to gospel samba outside the church, but they acknowledge it is not necessarily a sin. I saw gospel samba performed in various nonchurch contexts—an outdoor Christian music festival, an interfaith meeting in a hotel, a hall rented for a university-based Bible association—at which some men and women danced samba together and were the target of no (obvious) negative commentary. It is dancing samba in pairs *in church* that is the real problem, the Maginot line. Pastors and the pious expect people who dance in church to do so in place, singly or in circles, but never, never in pairs. "Outside the church, if people want to dance, that is OK," said Angela, an older member of the Universal Church. "But inside the church, this is sacred. It sends the wrong message to our young ones. God is offended that his house is used like a dance hall." It is thus not surprising that when samba gets played in churches, it tends to be limited to opening services, commemorative celebrations, or special events organized by youth groups. It is rare for gospel sambistas to play during solemn occasions, such as Eucharistic celebrations or prayer vigils. "This is one thing that has not yet happened," Jairo remarked when I asked whether his gospel samba group had yet played during a church service. "I have tried," he continued, "to talk about this with some pastors, but our culture is still very against this. There's a fear of what the rhythm is capable of doing. In a general meeting of the church, we can't simply say, 'Let's play a samba.' This has not yet happened."

Antisamba sentiment may be read in the fact that while hip hop and black gospel are sweeping through evangelical churches, gospel samba remains relatively rare. Search *samba gospel* on the Internet, and you will get ten times fewer hits than with either *rap gospel* or *black gospel*. Gospel sambistas complain much more than do gospel rappers or black gospel artists about not getting gigs. The latter routinely play multiple concerts each week, in their own churches or as guests in other churches, in festivals, in clubs, in squares, and on the street. In contrast, I found it took much effort to find a gospel samba show. One of the most successful gospel samba groups in São Paulo could go for months without performing.

Now the fact that dancing samba in church is cause for severe disapproval deprives congregants of the opportunity to develop, refine, or exhibit dancing skill. Anyone who dares indulge in very skillful samba moves quickly falls under suspicion of lacking piety, or worse. "Church is not the place to be an exhibitionist," said Angela. "It is OK to move around some, when they play samba, but all in order, all with decorum."

Now, how does the taboo against letting go and dancing samba in church influence sambista ideas about blackness? Because there is no room in evangelical churches for the development or exhibition of samba-dance virtuosity, it appears that there is little opportunity for evangelicals to witness particularly impressive dancing and thus to be stimulated to ponder the sources of such prowess. The taboo on samba pair dancing thus seems to ensure that congregants are deprived of regular exposure to the extraordinary skillful samba maneuvers that develop over time and practice; consequently, the whole project of trying to explain such extraordinariness is simply not present.

In this context, ethno-essentialist ideas about the body—such as the idea that people with more African ancestry have more *ginga* or *swingue*—appear to have little room to grow tendrils among gospel sambistas. Every sambista I asked about this acknowledged that "being black" might contribute something to dance skill, but these statements were peculiarly anemic, as if the sambista had heard them somewhere but had little to attach them to. Listen, for example, to gospel samba guitarist Edy: "I know they say that *negros* dance better than whites do. Maybe that's so. I don't know." Since people with any kind of ancestry within the church clearly had not developed much *swingue*, there was little room to develop strong ethno-essentialist kinds of thinking about dance. Rather, what I heard from samba musicians was a certain vague social determinism about dance skill, which acknowledged the inside-outside church contrast created by practice. Thus Rogério: "Out in the world, yes, in the fallen world, that is true. There, because that is where black people hang out in the world—in samba, in bars, drinking, and dancing. So they become very good at this. That is something you can see at Carnaval. But in here, we don't accept that. No one can dance like that in church." I asked, "But what are you saying, Rogério? Does African blood endow people or not with a natural ability to dance?"

He laughed at this and shook his head. "I don't know. I think that may be a stereotype, you know, John? Look, in here, no one with black blood is dying to dance samba. Young people like to dance, sure. But once that passes, I think it is all the same. I think that people just learn to relax, to use their bodies in other ways. I don't know. To be honest, John, I haven't thought much about this."

While lack of opportunity to develop dancing skill in church narrows the scope of thinking about associations between blackness and bodily movement, my ethnographic material also suggests that young people are chomping at the bit to dance more, and with each other. It is entirely possible that young nonmusicians may have begun to cultivate, among other things, a certain essentialism about dance and youth—that their young bodies are "in need" of more vibrant, even intersexual dancing. The few conversations I had with young people who were at gospel samba performances suggest to me that they bought into this kind of youth essentialism. It is also possible that as they begin to naturalize and essentialize dancing in this way, they may begin to embrace the idea that dancing skill is somehow linked with blackness. Unfortunately, I did not gather systematic evidence from nonmusicians that might address this question. The sambistas I interviewed were no longer teenagers; they were in their twenties and thirties. All I can say with confidence is that none of the samba musicians I interviewed had thought much about the blackness-dancing association; for them, it existed as a vague abstraction, not as lived experience. It was simply not part of their existential world.

Gospel Samba and Narratives of Musical History

A growing number of gospel sambistas regard it as part of their mission to speak in public about the history of their scene, motivated by the desire to convince church leaders to open up church doors to allow their music in and to de-demonize the instruments of samba. The effort by gospel sambistas to correct this state of affairs may be found at numerous gospel music websites; it can also be heard during Q&A sessions after performances, in conversations with church leaders, and in informal talk. Jairo explained in an interview published on a gospel music website, "Church leaders simply do not know about the origin of the instruments, of our music. It is part of our ministry to confront the culture that was imposed on the evangelical churches. The Brazilian church does not have a musical identity, and whoever has no identity has no history."[7]

A first pattern is that the stories told by gospel sambistas about their scene's development lack depth of knowledge about the music's African origins. While they acknowledge that samba is "uma música com raizes africanas" (a music with African roots), this is a formal statement disconnected from detailed knowledge. In general, gospel sambistas' invocations of "Africa" mean simply that drums are involved, based on the rough equation of "drums = Africa." After an informant said, "Yes, samba has African roots," I would ask to hear more about these; but I was usually disappointed. "I must confess," explained Rogério, "I do not have a very clear concept of this background. . . . I know that the drums came from Africa, but I never really interested myself in origins, you know, like which groups in Africa, of the drums, or how it all began." I asked why he had not worked harder to learn about his scene's African roots. "I am not sure," he replied,

> but I can tell you this: I'm not sure I want to spend time learning about something that is just going to remind people about Africa. Africa—that

we have African roots, that's fine. I am happy about that. I am proud of it. But if I go into a church and start preaching to them about all the African roots of this music, a lot of people are going to feel I am bringing the devil's music into the church.

A second, related pattern in gospel sambistas' stories was ambivalence toward their scene's connection to Afro-Brazilian religiosity. Among secular sambistas, one often hears the story that the music began as a way of dancing in candomblé. This idea has entered into a kind of popular common sense. The comment of Carlito, a secular sambista, is entirely typical: "This music of ours is really a religious music, or should I say, *it used to be*. It began in the *senzalas* [slave quarters] when the slaves were worshiping their gods, as a way to dance, and in candomblé. This is well known!" Well known or no, this putative genealogy created two contradictory responses among gospel sambistas. Some actively denied any such association, feeling uncomfortable with being too closely connected with a religion of the devil. Other informants, however, acknowledged the association, while being careful to frame it as an opportunity for an evangelical takeover of a space occupied by demonic forces. Listen to gospel sambista Hernani:

> Yes, yes, they say it started that way, and the devil uses this music in his own way, too. They dance samba in their religions, where they worship the devil. Like the devil uses rock music or anything else. But he doesn't own this music. He cannot control it. He is terrified of us, that's for sure, because we have the Lord with us, and there is nothing that the devil can do if you have the Lord by your side. Say the name of Jesus, and he falls down.

I asked him to explain how gospel samba could move beyond its historical association with candomblé.

> Just by playing those same rhythms, but putting words that speak of the Lord, that praise Jesus. Before Jesus, the devil always falls down, always shrinks. He cannot take it. Look, if you go to these places, these temples they call candomblé, what do you find? Samba. And you will find it in the places where the devil uses people. He possesses people and gets them to say all sorts of lies. Macumba—they dance samba there, yes. I have seen it.

They say that samba started there, that it is there now. That is what we are doing—showing the devil that he owns nothing, he is a pauper, he is bankrupt, he cannot keep the Lord from taking back what he has tried to steal and put his own stamp on it. We are retrieving it from him, and he knows we will triumph.

Now consider a third pattern. Artists, editorial writers, and politicians have claimed ever since the 1930s that what "makes Brazil Brazil" is the nation's history of miscegenation. Racial mixture, so the claim goes, nurtures tolerance and harmoniousness, virtues manifested perfectly in samba. Secular sambistas never tire of saying that their music unites African rhythm and European melody, African drums and European strings, and that samba is the home of the *mulata*, the quintessentially Brazilian mixed-race woman (McGowan and Pessanha 1998; Chasteen 1996, 30; Shaw 1999, 36; Sheriff 1999; Parker 1992; Bastos 1999; Pravaz 2003; Vianna 1999; McCann 2004, 77–78, 93–94). Thus, just as samba is Brazil's cultural synthesis of European and African musical elements, so too the *mulata*'s body is its biological synthesis. The ideology of the *mulata* insists that African descent endows her with rhythm and irresistibility; European descent confers on her self-discipline and high-status beauty. To take one of the innumerable such tributes at random, consider Netinho's samba "Garotas do Brasil" (Brazilian Girls):

> So much mixture
> So much beauty
> From the purest of which I am certain
> *Ginga* [swing] of the *mulata*, hair of a *gata* [hot chick]
> kisses of hazelnut, body of a mermaid
> parading on the sand, desires of the apple
> So much mixture
> So much beauty
> The girls of Brazil
> Do not fit on the planet

Natasha Pravaz observes that "Gilberto Freyre's conceptualization of Brazil as an inherently hybrid society went hand-in-hand with a eulogy of *mulatagem* (mulattoness), particularly in its female or feminized form. If *mestiçagem*

had been the process par excellence of formation of national identity, mula-
tos stood as the most Brazilian" (2008, 96; see also Goldstein 2003; Caldwell
2007).

Not surprisingly, for gospel sambistas, this account, given its emphasis
on sex, needs a good deal of refining. The *mulata*, reputed to like sex of a
decidedly disreputable kind, disappears from evangelicals' narrative of Brazilian history, leaving only talk about miscegenation. The notion that samba
is the result of a mixture, characterized not by exploitation but by recipro-
cal exchanges, came frequently to my gospel sambista informants' lips. Their
talk flowed smoothly from samba to culture mixture to race mixture. "The
cavaco [a samba instrument]," asked Robson rhetorically,

> where does that come from? It is a Portuguese instrument! From Portugal!
> Now the dance part of samba, that comes from a dance that has its origins
> in Africa. . . . Today samba can't be considered Portuguese, can't be con-
> sidered African; it is Brazilian. This mixing of cultures is the same thing as
> the mixing of peoples. It was through miscegenation, because our culture
> is a totally miscegenated culture—totally. Just for example, we have a black
> neighbor woman here who married a Japanese, and they have a child who
> is a black Japanese. Beautiful, beautiful, beautiful! No other place in the
> world are you able to see that!

Here, what is highlighted is samba's hybridity, its synthesis of multiple
influences, its evolution into a distinctively Brazilian art form. We are in
the presence of the nationalist story of mixture, a story not of conflict but
of exchange, cooperation, and creativity, a story not of suffering and adversity but of reciprocity. There is also in this account an easy slippage from the
meeting of cultural artifacts to the physical melding of whole peoples. This is
clear with Jairo:

> I can tell you everything you want to know about the way the *cavaquinho*
> united with the *surdo*—these are the instruments—this happened because
> people got together and played music! But I wouldn't be telling the whole
> story, because beneath this or—I'm not sure how to say it—alongside or
> above it, you also have people coming together to make families and chil-
> dren and neighborhoods, right? So the Brazilian people are coming into
> being. It is about the music but also about this whole people!

Overall, the picture of the past that emerges from these patterns of story-telling is one in which the embarrassments of Africa and enslavement have receded into a misty background, while the proud accomplishments of cultural synthesis, the mixture of peoples, and the aesthetic achievements of modern composers take pride of place. This is not a historical consciousness that places pride in blackness or black identity.

Gospel Samba and the Place of the Nation

Gospel sambistas have, of course, many ideas about different places; yet one place recurs repeatedly in their lyrics and iconography: that enormous imaginary place called "Brazil." Through their paraphernalia, images, and lyrics, gospel sambistas articulate the territory, landscape, and idea of Brazil as the ultimate center of their collective identity, subsuming and decentering any other subnational or transnational identity, such as blackness.

One of the first things I noticed when I started to hang out with gospel samba groups was the ubiquity of icons of the Brazilian nation. At every turn (and in marked contrast to gospel rappers and black gospel artists), gospel sambistas use the word "Brazil" in their band names and mottoes. Right away, I was hearing about groups such as Samba Gospel Brasil and Borel Brasil and learning that Grupo Ide's motto was "Brasil é o Território de Jesus" (Brazil Is the Territory of Jesus). There is something tangibly territorial, geographic, even cartographic about gospel samba's relation to this place called "Brazil." The group Divina Unção, for instance, uses as its emblem a map of Brazil with the dove of the Holy Spirit hovering immediately above it, and Deus Crioulos emblazons its T-shirts with a map of the country, in the vibrant yellow and green of the nation's flag. In the concerts of gospel sambistas that I attended, there was a self-conscious deployment of Brazil's national banner. By going on YouTube, one can see how Divina Unção always positions a big Brazilian flag behind it at concerts.[8] The lead singer of Samba Gospel Brasil regularly performs while draped in the flag.[9] I saw Valentes de Davi perform flanked by flagpoles, and the group's CD inserts feature the word "Brasil" in iridescent yellow and green. Some samba groups stamp their tambourines and T-shirts with the flag, the word "Brasil," or, in the case of the group Samba Gospel Brasil, an image of the national pastime, a big soccer ball. Onstage, members of Borel Brasil sport snazzy green and yellow T-shirts (the color of the flag). Members of Deus Crioulos point to

their T-shirts' map, colors, and the motto "Christ, Samba, Brazil" as expressing their national pride. I asked the director of Deus Crioulos to talk to me
about the T-shirts. "This is to show our pride in being Brazilian," he said.
"We love our country. We want people to know that."

This feeling for Brazil as nation is also conveyed in gospel samba lyrics.
The majority of those lyrics are about salvation and redemption, like any
other gospel scene. Yet amid all the calls to be saved, what I found striking
was the frequency of lyrics that evoke Brazil, but not just Brazil as abstract
political idea—say, the "progress" and "order" proclaimed in the nation's
motto—but as a real, physical territory with real dimensions of height,
breadth, and topography, a place favored and chosen by God to be an example to the world. Listen to one of what could be dozens of examples, Grupo
Perseverança's "Gospel Brazil," by Carlos Moyses:

> Brazil, my Brazilian plays the tambourine from north to south
> Brazil, my Brazilian shows the foreigner who Jesus is
> Green, yellow, white, blue
> These are the colors of the Brazilian flag
> In it, one hopes for true wealth, the sky of peace
> For Jesus rules this country of land and sea
> Brazil, my Brazilian plays the tambourine from north to south
> Brazil, my Brazilian shows the foreigner who Jesus is
> Cuíca, berimbau, chocalho, give it your all
> Cavaco, pandeiro, surdo, I am Brazilian
> Samba without borders and Jesus Christ in our flag
> Country that is a giant and that awoke to the whole world
> It can feed many nations with its harvest
> In it there is a living bread that sustains and satisfies
> Whoever eats of it will never feel hunger again
> Jesus champion and King of salvation
> In the game of life the only way
> Only he returned to life and this samba is for my Lord[10]

I encountered nothing approaching this love affair with Brazil among either
gospel rappers or black gospel artists. While the latter kinds of artists speak of
their love of country and declare themselves to be patriots, that love does not
translate into the dense imagery and lyrical content present in gospel samba.

Gospel samba's fondness for national imagery needs to be understood, first, in the context of samba as a whole. The enduring association between samba as art form and the Brazilian nation as collective imaginary goes back at least to the early 1930s, when a growing intelligentsia in search of cultural authenticity, along with a state policy dedicated to cultural nationalism, and the rise of radio stations with nationwide reach combined to turn samba into the de facto music of the nation (McCann 2004, 74ff.; Shaw 2002; Vianna 1999; Chasteen 1996; Paranhos 2005). By the end of the 1930s, the sense of Brazil as a rising nation was famously given form in samba after samba, lovingly painting word pictures of the nation, connecting its natural landscape to a set of ideas about the nation's racial composition, history, and favor in the sight of God. Of these, Ary Barroso's "Aquarela do Brasil" (Watercolor of Brazil; 1939) became the country's unofficial anthem (McCann 2004, 70).

> Brazil, my Brazilian Brazil,
> My good-looking mulatto.
> I'm going to sing you in my verses.
> O Brazil, samba that gives
> A swing that makes you sway.
> O Brazil that I love,
> Land of Our Lord,
> Brazil, Brazil, for me, for me!
> O, open the curtain of the past.
> Bring the black mother out of the pastures.
> Find the Congo king dancing the Congo.
> Brazil, Brazil!
> Let the troubadour sing again
> To the melancholy light of the moon
> Every song of my love.
> I want to see the Holy Lady walking
> Through the halls, wearing
> Her garments of lace.
> Brazil, Brazil, for me, for me!
> Brazil, good and pleasant land
> Of the beautiful brown girl
> With the indifferent gaze.
> O Brazil, greenness that gives

The world cause to wonder.
O Brazil that I love,
Land of Our Lord,
Brazil, Brazil, for me, for me!
O, this palm tree that yields coconuts,
Where I tie my fishing net
On clear moonlit nights.
Brazil, Brazil!
O, these murmuring fountains
Where I quench my thirst
And where the moon comes to play.
O, this Brazil, beautiful and wheaten,
Is my Brazilian Brazil,
Land of the samba and the tambourine.
Brazil, Brazil, for me, for me![11]

In the decades that followed, the bond between samba and the idea of Brazil as a physical landscape that infused and shaped the national character grew ever stronger. The 1940s saw samba nationalism reach new heights in the form of *samba exaltação* (exaltation samba), a genre built around the motif of enumerating the tangible qualities that made Brazil a great nation. A samba in this tradition was Herivelton Martins's 1943 "Lourindo," which described the nation's wartime mobilization, its place on the world stage, and its ultramodern thoroughfare Avenida Presidente Vargas (McCann 2004, 67ff.). By the 1950s, as the Brazilian tourist industry grew and images of Brazil began circulating in international cinema, samba became, for both Brazilians and non-Brazilians, an icon and index of the country (Vianna 1999, 95; Stam 1997). The 1960s and '70s brought an explosion of international interest in Carnaval and the spectacularization of the *mulata* as national icon, phenomena that solidified samba's role as a central feature of Brazilian identity (Pravaz 2008, 96). It was in the 1970s that samba earned the distinction of being the only Brazilian music to have its own nationally recognized day of commemoration, observed ever since by the federal minister of culture in an annual ceremony.[12] In the 1980s, as the Brazilian market for North American rock music grew exponentially, sambistas took on the role of cultural conservatives, fighting a rearguard defense of Brazilian culture against the "imperialists" (Vianna 1999, 99).

Over the past two decades, samba has continued to be woven into Brazil's national cultural fabric, from Brazilian cinema to soap operas to TV commercials to pop art to sport—always with the presumption that it somehow holds the key to "what makes Brazil Brazil" (Shaw and Dennison 2007, 220–225). Many sambas are composed as a kind of travelogue, with the composer taking the listener on a grand tour of his or her beloved country. Fernanda Abreu's 1996 samba "Brazil Is the Land of Swing" intones,

> The Brazilian is swing
> The Brazilian is dance
> The Brazilian is partying
> The Brazilian has Carnaval in his blood
> . . . Brazil, Brazil
> Brazil is the country of swing
> Come with me and dance
> In Belém of Pará
> In the festival Tupí
> Come with me, come dance
> The reggae of Maranhão

The song continues its peripatetic, place-bound advance, commemorating the dances of Ceará, Santa Catarina, São Paulo, Bahia, Pernambuco, Rio Grande do Sul, Rio de Janeiro, and most other states of the nation, until Fernanda concludes, "Brazil is the country of swing!"

Wherever samba appears or with whatever it is compared, it is thus assumed to be a window onto the Brazilian soul. Writers and critics never tire of pointing out the commonalities between samba as dance and Brazil's undisputed national pastime, soccer. The artfulness, savvy, and emotion of Brazil's "beautiful game"—soccer played as footwork, body feints, and sheer grace—are, in this view, a mirror image of samba. Pelé's moves on the field are regularly compared with samba steps, and it is often said that the best training for the soccer player is to dance samba—and vice versa. Sambas have been connected to World Cups multiple times: in 1994, the group Gera Samba composed the samba "Copa 94," and for the 1998 World

Cup, Gilberto Gil composed "Copa 98" (Behague 2006, 84). Thus, music and sport become two windows onto the Brazilian essence, presumed to be a unique blend of shrewdness, agility, and passion. Or consider that most Brazilian of public performances, the annual ritual of Carnaval. If Carnaval is what makes Brazil Brazil, it should come as no surprise that Carnaval and samba schools are sites of intense nationalist sentiment and symbolism. A favorite Carnaval costume is to paint one's body with the colors of Brazil, and the official colors of many samba schools, such as Unidos do Peruche or the Grêmio Recreativo Escola de Samba Independentes de Mandacarú, are those of the Brazilian flag. In 2007, three samba schools parading in São Paulo draped their floats in the Brazilian flag (*Folha de São Paulo*, February 20, 2007), and in 2009, a samba school set up a float that represented the different regions of the country, all in the national colors. Today it is common to hear sambas built around the classic motif of singing the praises of Brazil's natural resources, gorgeous landscapes, irrepressible cheer, natural rhythm, impish playfulness, and irrepressible cordiality—hence the samba of Escola Santa Cruz in 2009:

> I am a son of this land so green, the mountains
> Give hope
> That the water send waves of consciousness . . .
> I am Brazilian and this is my place

Overall, then, secular sambistas are happy to be regarded as the carriers of "a música nacional." Composer and musician Delcio Luiz conveyed the sense of being the guardian of national patrimony when asked to name the capital of samba. "There is no way you can pick one place over another when it comes to samba!" he replied, laughing. "I am not going to say Curitiba, or São Paulo, or Brasilia, because samba is Brazil, there are just no two ways about it. Samba is Brazil, like soccer and happiness."[13]

Now, many gospel sambistas were secular sambistas first. Of the twenty gospel sambistas I got to know, all but four had played samba as amateurs or professionals before their conversion. "I already was used to the world of samba," said Jairo. "That was my world. All that I added was Jesus." Thus, the iconicity of secular samba with the imagined place that is "Brazil" is at work in gospel samba as well. It should not surprise us that practitioners of gospel samba, like their secular counterparts, identified themselves as carriers and stewards of a great national tradition, their love for their musical scene a direct expression of their feeling for country. "I for one," said the gospel sambista Nelson, "am extremely patriotic. If you play the national anthem, I become very emotional. Because I love my country. . . . This is our national treasure. This is our national music." I heard real national pride in gospel sambista Rogério's observation, "Anywhere in the world where people talk about Brazil, you will hear people speak about samba. Anywhere, whether you're in Japan, I don't know where, you say 'Brazil' and they say 'samba'!" I never heard such talk from either black gospel singers or gospel rappers.

But if gospel samba's patriotism is a reflection of secular samba's nationalist zeal, it is not only that. Evangelical Christians live in their own complicated spiritual and institutional world. Once converted to an evangelical church, sambistas will no longer attend Carnaval or secular musical performances and will avoid witnessing either on television. They will listen to secular samba but will spend most of their music-making time composing, practicing, rehearsing, and performing not secular samba but its gospel version. And while they may be influenced by secular samba, their most fervent desire is to resonate with the people inside their own church. Gospel sambistas' motives for emphasizing Brazilian nationhood must therefore be sought within the evangelical milieu itself.

For starters, national symbols are very important to gospel sambistas, not only because, as good Christians, they respect the state (as called for biblically by the Apostle Paul in his letter to the Romans)[14] but also because these symbols help these assuage their coreligionists' prejudices and fears. To understand this, we must recall samba's deep association with carnality, the erotic, and alcohol. Indeed, because of this association, in spite of the fact that many evangelicals now believe that to save souls one may play rap, reggae, rock, and MPB (música popular brasileira), samba to this day presents major difficulties for them. "I won't allow it," said Geraldo, a deacon in the Assembly of God. "Any other music is OK. They can have Christian lyrics. But I feel that samba is a way for the devil to ingratiate himself into the home. You think you are hearing Christian words, but it is the devil dressed up as a lamb." One pastor explained why he had decided not to allow the playing of samba in his church.

ARTURO: It is just too risky. Our young people are not prepared. I went to a performance of this in another church, and I was shocked, because the kids were dancing, dancing like the church was a club.

JOHN: What about outside, in the street? Would you permit it to be used to evangelize people in the street?

ARTURO: No, no. What will people say? How will they know that the church is different from the world? They can go hear those things in a club. The church must be clean.

Arturo grudgingly accepted that samba accompanied by Christian lyrics might be useful to evangelize in the street, but he drew the line at the church door. Bringing *surdos* and *cavaquinhos* into the church, he said, would be "like tracking muddy shoes into the nicest part of your house." How, he wondered, could he tolerate music associated with liquor, bars, drums, idolatry, and liaisons of the most vulgar kind? "I have nothing against any music," he insisted, "but the church is not the place for samba."

It was, as we have seen, precisely such sentiments that led Jairo to found Deus Crioulos. One of Jairo's most consequential moves to allay such sentiments was to impress on his coreligionists how *patriotic* this music was. "I thought, 'Let's put the flag on our T-shirts,'" he said, "to show this is a patriotic movement. This is not about bringing anything bad into the church, to get anyone to drink *cachaça* [sugar-cane liquor]." Samara, a middle-age congregant, showed the strategy was working. "You know," she said, "there is a lot of prejudice against samba, but . . . I think that seeing the flag on their T-shirts helps, because I can see that they had good hearts."

There is yet another layer to evangelical sambistas' use of patriotic symbols: they are reacting against the popular idea that Brazil's Protestant churches are dependent on the United States. There is an anti-imperialist flavor in gospel sambistas' constant affirmations that their music is "very Brazilian." Said gospel sambista Edy, "The problem with North American music is that we either translate or we try to imitate. And we lose our own culture. That is my big fight. We need something of our own culture in our own music. Samba is a very Brazilian rhythm. I want to raise the flag of Brazil!" Rogério's resistance to the United States was even more vigorous. "I have nothing against rhythms from the US," he said, "but I feel myself indignant about the fact that this music has occupied so much space in our nation, in our people. They suffocate our musical culture. Because when you think about what is our national musical culture, it is samba."

Gospel Samba and Antiessentialism

Overall, the kind of consciousness of body, history, and place cultivated among gospel samba artists, as I have discussed in this chapter, leads them to develop skepticism toward racial essentialism and to a blackness that may be partly diluted by an overpowering national identity. The combination of low bodily investment, emphasis on Brazil's history of miscegenation, and deep investment in national rather than subnational identity all work to decenter blackness and render implausible the claim that *negros* have a special affinity with samba. Listen to Edy:

> I would say that samba is not just for people with black blood. It is some-thing that is in the blood of the Brazilian. Brazil is a country where there is a lot of miscegenation. All of us have a little bit of everybody in us. My brother, for example, is a black, and he's married to a white woman, and my nephews are white but with black blood. And there is a lot of that in Brazil. So I would say that because Brazil is a miscegenated nation, samba left off being a music that was just for blacks, and it became a Brazilian music for everybody.

The notion that samba is not ineluctably connected to the "black race" was reinforced by the existence of samba groups that included gifted white artists. Robson, a very dark Afro-Brazilian who identified himself as *negro*, explained:

> Look John, I have traveled all around this city. I have seen samba groups in the northern zone and eastern zone and southern zone and western zone. There is just no way to say that samba groups are made up mainly of black people. In fact, the groups are all very mixed. In those groups, you have whites who play just as well as blacks do—often better! . . . In my samba group, there are ten players, and of these, four are white! And they all play fantastic.

Even those secular and gospel sambistas who believed that blacks have a greater aptitude for music than do whites agreed that the actual distribution of skill on the samba scene shows that "blood" is a useless predictor of talent. Nelson knew too many excellent white samba drummers to place much stock in racial determinism. "Maybe in the old days it was like that," he said, "but now you see whites playing samba perfectly. That's what's happening, here in Brazil. So this thing about 'only blacks can play samba,' it's just not true." Gospel sambistas have not given up the notion that biological inheritance influences musical skill; it is just that *mestiçagem* (race mixture) has made it hard to draw one-to-one correspondences. "Sometimes you hear that blacks are the great percussionists," Armando, a middle-age sambista, explained, "and that the great guitar players in samba are whites. But there are great guitarists who are black and great drummers who are white. It doesn't make any sense to say one race is better at this or that. Race doesn't really matter. Here in Brazil, everything is miscegenated, everything is mixed. Anyone can play as long as you're in the community. It is all mixed."

A few gospel sambistas went further and rejected the idea that musical skill could be carried by the blood at all. "With regard to music," said Rogério, "what exists is not blood but rather the desire to sing and to grow. Blacks play samba not because they have some special ability to do these things. It is not that they have it in their blood. It's not that blacks have better voice. I've heard people say that blacks have a prettier voice. But I don't see it that way. Just look at who plays samba—who sings samba: in equal measure, across the board!" Or listen to Edy, who identifies as *negro*: "I would say that when I play samba, I'm not really expressing my blackness; I am expressing my musicality. I am expressing all of my feelings, all of my knowledge, and channel that all into a music that I enjoy. I am black, but when I play samba, that is not what I am expressing."

We are now prepared, I think, to answer Marco Davi's question. It should be clear that the practices and discourses of gospel samba—its nationalism, the ideology of miscegenation, the peculiar appropriations of Afro-Brazilian history, the deemphasis of the highly skilled voice, and the devaluation of the dance—all contribute to the development of an identity that is light on blackness and heavy on Brazilianness. As one after another of my informants told me, this scene was decidedly not about gravitating toward a black identity; it was not about celebrating blackness; it was not about "raising the banner of the black cause." It was about being Brazilian. Said Jairo, "I helped create this group so as to bring Brazilian culture to the church. It was not created to raise the banner of racism. It was not created to raise the banner of the black, to defend the black." This did not mean that Jairo was not proud to be black; it was just that gospel samba was not what made him proud of the fact. His peacefulness about his blackness was derived from other sources, not from playing samba. As he put it, "Blacks are already doing fine. They do not need an exclamation point in samba to raise their self-esteem. I have self-esteem— I am happy to be who I am. Am I proud to be black? Yes, but samba does not makes me proud to be black. Samba makes me proud to be Brazilian."

4

A Voice So Full of Pain and Power

Black Gospel and Blackness

When black gospel artists in São Paulo engage in routine practices to master their art, forces of racial identity are unleashed. I argue in this chapter that an array of practices that belong to the black gospel scene shape the racial consciousness of artists, strengthening feelings of blackness, developing ideas about black history, and sharpening beliefs about the role of black people in God's plan for humanity. To build my argument, in the first section I examine the practice of seeing videos of US black churches—for black gospel artists, a central *place* of their scene—and argue that this seeing carves out and reinforces a specific, aspirational middle-class blackness. In the second section, I focus on the core aesthetic practice of the black gospel scene, vocal technique, suggesting how the experience of that technique and reflection on that experience have a strong affinity to heavily essentializing discourses about black voice and identity. In the final section, I look at black gospel singers' love of black music history and consider how the versions of that history recounted by singers reveals an enormously complex view of the connections between biblical prophecy, the African diaspora, and Brazil's black population.

The Church as "Um Lugar do Negro"

When young singers become involved in the black gospel scene in São Paulo, they find themselves surrounded by an array of practices that focus their attention on the indebtedness of their art to North American blacks. During choir rehearsals, they overhear allusions and see knowing looks about groups such as the Harlem Gospel Choir, the Brooklyn Gospel Choir, and the Atlanta Gospel Choir. During voice workshops, they listen to stories of pilgrimages to the US South or Chicago or Los Angeles, to visit black churches (*igrejas negras*). In the lobbies of churches before and after performances, they see CDs on sale of US black gospel artists such as Fred Hammond, Yolanda Adams, and Kirk Franklin. In informal conversation before and after rehearsals, they hear that Brazilian black gospel singer Robson Nascimento sounds just like Stevie Wonder, and Isabêh just like James Brown. And on a regular basis—in some cases almost every day—they sit down in front of a TV screen, either by themselves or in the company of other young singers, and watch videos of US black church choirs.

The practice of watching videos of choirs appeared in virtually every interview I conducted with black gospel singers. In long interviews, they referred sooner or later to how videos of US black churches had featured in their decision to become singers: how inspired they felt by those videos, how connected they felt to the people they saw in them. Several of my informants were inspired by the videos to found their own choirs. Michael Santiago, musical director of a Church in Christ in São Paulo, insisted that the sight of a US black gospel choir lay at the root of his own motivation as a teenager to start one in Brazil. "It was like a thunderbolt," he said. "The pastor showed it [the video] to our singing group. I sat there and watched those *negros* in that church, and my heart was racing. I broke into a sweat. I never felt like that before. I knew from that day that that was what I had to do with my life."

Narratives such as this led me to pay special attention to the watching of videos. I soon discovered that this practice was a key routine in Brazilian black gospel artists' training. Isabêh, the much-sought-after voice

Black gospel singer

instructor, made this clear one rainy morning as I was sitting in his studio, sipping strong coffee, my feet perched on cables that crawled over the floor like an octopus. Against the far wall, a row of purple robes was swaying on a thirty-two-inch screen, on either side of which DVDs were piled twenty high. When I asked how he used the DVDs, he grinned. "Teaching! Because you see, John, the first secret to good singing is *seeing* how it's done. The best way to learn how to 'sing black' [*cantar black*] is to see how they do it—not just to listen to CDs but to see. Then you really understand the force of black singing." On first meetings with new pupils, he explained, he always showed a DVD of Beyoncé singing in her church. When he began working with the student on more intensive techniques, he would show him or her a DVD of the Harlem Gospel Choir. One of his favorites was of Kirk Franklin and the Nu Nation burning up the stage in a huge church in Houston. I once saw Isabêh in a workshop illustrating the power of belting by popping in a tape of Aretha Franklin in her church in Detroit. "I really love this one," he told the audience, as his fingers caressed the monitor. "You can see how Aretha is singing in her natural habitat, how that voice sounds in the church. That's where it started. That is an American church."

As I got to know the black gospel scene better, it became clear to me that getting aspiring artists to watch videos of US black churches was widely regarded as essential pedagogy. Ton Carfi, one of the scene's great sopranos, kept dozens of such videos and DVDs in his studio and showed them regularly to his private students. Robson Nascimento did the same. So did Silveira. Showing tapes and DVDs of US black churches was a kind of rite of passage, a way of defining insidership: those who had seen them referred to them by name, and in informal contexts small nods and knowing looks of recognition signaled that one had been initiated into the world of US black church videos.

The videos were an important technique for getting artists' juices flowing before rehearsals and shows. They drew the viewer into physical scenes exploding with color, texture, sound, and drama, placing the viewer into vast caverns filled with gorgeous lights, populated by swaying masses of people. Often as I watched the videos alongside Brazilian singers, we would sit transfixed. One memorable Saturday afternoon, I attended a rehearsal at the home of Sérgio Saas, musical director of Raiz Coral, and found myself seated for over an hour in his cramped living room, watching DVDs of US church choirs. Leg to leg on the old couch, I watched Sérgio's star singers, chins in their palms, soak in the sights and sounds of a black church in Houston, whispering "oohhs" and "aaahs," humming along, standing up from time to time to imitate a particularly expansive gesture. At one point, Scooby, the group's small, angular, high-strung alto, stretched out on his elbows on the cold parquet floor right in front of the TV and sang along in hearty faux-English. When gospel star Donnie McKlurcken appeared on the screen and launched into a furious belt, Scooby jumped to his feet, shot his arms out in a direct mirroring of

McKlurcken, and erupted in a belt of his own, prompting the others in the room to burst into applause and laughter.

Seeing these videos, while important for refining artistic skill, also had the effect of exposing young artists to a new and exciting model of blackness, one that many of them had never seen before and that would, I want to argue, shape their ethnoracial consciousness. While the artists I got to know had been used to calling themselves *negros* before seeing the videos, they admitted that the term had been mainly one of description, not a focus of pride. These videos presented them with a model of blackness about which they could feel proud: for here were blacks who were prosperous, suffused with self-respect, in control of a respectable institution, unified, and—of major importance—*Christian*.

Consider the videos' panning shots, of church interiors and audiences. Every video had at least one such shot, filled with evidence of impressive material *prosperity*: vast, cavernous spaces, gleaming cherrywood stages, plush carpets, endless pews; congregants bedecked with designer dresses, pashmina scarves, broad-brimmed ribbon- and flower-encircled hats, and pressed double-breasted suits. Here were black people blessed with material bounty—importantly, visibly *respectable* bounty—thus confronting and challenging Brazilian assumptions about black people. "From day one," said Michael Santiago, "all we hear is that black people are addicts and gangsters and *sambistas*. If the black rises at all, it is because he is a *malandro*"—that is, a trickster or double-dealer. Yet in these videos blacks are none of these things; they are well-off, God-fearing Christians. "I thought, 'Look at those churches,'" said Michael. "'They are rich, they are surrounded by abundance, but they are serious, they are Christian.'" Valter, a saxophonist in the Azusa church, put it this way: "It is amazing to see blacks who are doing well, wearing those clothes, and also good Christians. We have a lot to learn from that."

My informants responded in particular to the *self-confidence* they witnessed in the videos. There was something in the posture of these people, in the way they held themselves, that communicated self-respect. "I love looking at those people in the American churches," said Angélica. "It is an example for us. Because the *negro* here [in Brazil] is really different. He is unsure of himself. But your *negros*, it seems they are not afraid of anything." I asked her to be more specific. "Look, the way they stand, hold their chins up. It's hard to explain." Marcelo tried: "When they wave their hands, walk across the stage, it's like they do not care who is looking at them, because they feel confident. They have an attitude that we don't." He added quietly, "I want to have that attitude."

Seeing this kind of blackness in the videos had consequences for what some viewers thought possible for themselves. "When I saw that tape," said Michael,

> it seemed to me incredible that there existed on the face of the earth *negros* like that, that had no inhibition about expressing themselves to the Lord. Because we in Brazil are still timid! From that moment on, I was not the same. From that tape, I could feel God saying to me something serious was going to happen. . . . When I saw those *negros* acting that way, I was not able to sleep. It was a tremendous moment in my life. Because I was poor, I was *negro*. And when I saw that tape, I said to myself, "My Lord, what is this?" I'd never seen *negros* who were so happy, with their heads raised up. . . . That made me feel I could be different, I could be that way too.

Important, too, was the fact that my informants registered *surprise* at the sight of large churches made up entirely of "*gente negra.*" In Brazil, churches reflect the phenotypical makeup of their surrounding neighborhoods: in both working- and middle-class neighborhoods, this means people of a wide range of colors, from light to dark. Although proportions vary, there are in São Paulo no homogeneously "white" or "black" churches. Many of the artists I interviewed were intrigued by the sight of entirely homogeneous black churches. Felipe's reaction was typical: "I'd never seen anything like it. . . . It was a church. I could see it was a church. But what amazed me was there were only *negros* sitting there. I had never seen a church like that before. Never. And I thought, 'What in Lord's name is this? A church just of *negros*?' Here in Brazil, you don't see that."

Readers may be familiar with reports from elsewhere about the rush that a member of a social minority may experience when suddenly confronted with the sight of being in a majority. When, for example, Samuel Delany saw for the first time the "massed bodies" of gay men in the St. Mark's bathhouse in the early 1960s, he suddenly could think of himself in collective terms. "What this experience said," he wrote, "was that there was a population—not of individual homosexuals, . . . not of hundreds, not of thousands, but rather of millions of gay men" (qtd. in Scott 1991, 773). If such feelings are good, seeing oneself in a majority doing things one feels proud of can change one's self-perception. This at least was the view of the Christians I got to know. They were all too familiar, for example, with the black religion of candomblé, but that was, in their view, nothing to be proud of. Similarly, they knew about black music groups such as samba bands, but those were, for them, dens of dissolution. In contrast, the church videos displayed large gatherings of black people in church. Here were people about whom they could proudly say "black like me." For Marcos, the sight was life changing, because it showed him a whole new model for being black, allowed him to reject the negative models, and enabled him to embrace as his own a Christian black identity. "Look," he explained, "here in Brazil, whenever *negros* are in the majority, it is for some kind of trouble. Here, if you see a majority of *negros*, it must be for Carnaval, it must be for samba, it must be for *macumbaria*. But a church, a place for believers? No one believes we can be doing something good, something pleasing to God, celebrating his name. Those videos show we have more possibilities." Or, as Michael put it, "You can't imagine the impact that had for us. To see people like us, all in one place, just *negros*. We don't see that in Brazil. Not in a respectable place! You can't imagine, to see that for the first time, it is indescribable. For the first time, we could really be proud—proud to be *negros*."

The Black Gospel Voice and Racial Essentialism

If serious singing in general cultivates in singers a consciousness of the human voice as physical instrument, as a complicated structure of organs and cavities and resonators and teeth (Dunsby 2009), black gospel singing in particular, by requiring among the most physically strenuous vocal techniques in the world, cultivates *hyperconsciousness* of the voice's physicality.[1] That is, I suggest that singers of black gospel music in Brazil engage in practices that get them to focus on the thickness of their pharyngeal membranes, the sensation of their larynx withstanding explosive passages of air, and the dense vibrations of cartilage in the deepest recesses of their nasal cavities. As they focus on these things, they come to think about their vocal apparatus as tough and robust, physical qualities that owe little to training or skill. Most pertinently, they frame these qualities as due to inheritance from their African ancestors. The experience of singing black gospel is thus interwoven with the cognitive understanding of voice (Mohanty 2000).

Black gospel music is built from a bundle of vocal practices (Williams-Jones 1975), of which I will consider three: the belt, the growl, and rich timbre. A true belt is an astonishing thing. Belting, we are told by voice science, is achieved by closing the vocal folds tightly, building up pressure against them with air pushed up from the diaphragm, then blasting them open (Miller 2004, 152). To get a sense of belting's remarkable power, consider Angélica, a black woman in her thirties, who recently stood in front of a hundred congregants in her church to sing (in Portuguese) the classic Christian hymn "There Will Be Peace in the Valley." She began tentatively, her voice hardly audible. After about a minute, a bold guitar riff helped steel her resolve. She closed her eyes, clenched her microphone, and tilted her face down. I could hear her rich soprano begin to rumble. "And the lamp is alight," she sang, "and the night, night is as black as the sea." Her chin traveled slowly upward, her eyes glistening, her breathing heavy. The keyboardist sprayed a gentle rain of notes, prompting her tongue to form the first word of the next line. Then, all of a sudden, with a flick of her wrist, she erupted. With her chin now pointing at the ceiling, her knuckles white, Angélica lengthened her throat, turned it into an echo chamber, and blew out an enormous, explosive gust of sound toward the church's farthest rafters. She was belting.

To produce a vocal belt requires making use of the whole body, with "a high degree of physical 'anchoring' . . . to provide the physical support in the back, neck, spine, and torso to produce high sub-glottal pressure and 'support' loud and full vocal tone projection" (Jungr 2002, 106). This is hard physical labor. "Belt," writes Barbara Jungr, "is very evident when singers seem on the edge of their voice. . . . One can almost hear the physical effort employed to make the sound" (ibid., 107). A full-throttle belt subjects the vocal folds to more physical stress than does any other type of singing. Jo Estill, for example, notes that "belting requires much harder work than opera because it involves not only the vocal folds, but also the *extrinsic vocalis* muscles" (Estill 1988, 40; see also Kayes 2004). Not all voices can endure such exertions over an extended period of time. That is why Julius Cheeks's voice "was lacerated from its twelve years on the road. . . . Some say he just about sang himself to death, impervious to the warnings of doctors, until his voice—never a refined instrument in the best of times—began to sound like gravel in a tin bucket." Cheeks's voice was the "rawest of gospel's baritones—moving and painful in its evocation of the roughest side of the mountain" (Broughton 1996, 85–87). The gospel singers I interviewed likened belting to

Black gospel singer

an overwhelming force traveling through their bodies. Angélica compared it to a wave coiling through her torso. "It feels like a tsunami," she said. "I can feel it climbing up from my lungs, hitting the roof of my mouth." Others compared it to a hurricane. Thus, it is not surprising that my informants insisted that their own voices were made of the right stuff to tolerate the strain. "Not everyone has a voice that can take it," said Angélica. "I am lucky that God blessed me with one that can."

A second vocal practice common in black gospel is the growl. Growling in black gospel began among itinerant jack-leg preachers in the United States in the early twentieth century, as their routine of street-corner singing and exposure to the elements created a rough vocal sound (Oliver 1984). The intense growls of preaching spilled over into singing when preaching-singing became common in black churches (Darden 2006; Floyd 1995, 80–81; Middleton 2006, 46–47). Eventually, growling would become familiar in blues, jazz, and rock as a way of communicating anger, hurt, dismay, or despair (Keil 1966, 124; Berger 1999, 167). Black gospel has its own way of using the growl: singers alternate from husky growls to silky melismas, with the best singers performing vocal pivots in the space of a single note. Growling, like belting, can take a toll. The "growl is not a natural sound," writes one voice specialist. "It's forced. It's the sound of friction and friction causes heat and eventually swelling."[2] Yet despite the rigors of the growl, gospel singers insist that their voices can withstand it; in fact, they feel such endurance is crucial from a religious standpoint, for moving from guttural raspiness to sweet smoothness symbolizes lifting oneself up out of the valley of death. One of the world's greatest black gospel singers—Karen Clark-Sheard—infuses most sung stanzas with an alternation from sparkling aria to "hollow, stylized growl" and back again (Ramsey 2004, 206, 209). "I watched how she had a raspy sound," one woman said, watching a black gospel singer on videotape, "then she went into a real smooth, melodic type thing. Then she went right back into it" (Hinson 2000, 267, 269, 279). The "coarse" voice can sometimes gain status in gospel, as it does in blues and jazz (Courlander 1963, 23; Williams-Jones 1975). The key aesthetic pattern in black gospel, however, is not the continuously coarse voice but the alternation between coarseness and mellifluousness. "You hear what happens, when my voice gets ragged and rough," explained Angélica. "But in a flash, the power of God reassures me, and there it is again: my voice fills with that confidence, and I am soaring."

A third vocal practice of black gospel is its cultivation of *rich timbre*. Unlike phonation, articulation, and respiration, vocal timbre (or *resonation*) is hard to change through intentional action (Mendes et al. 2003). A well-prepared singer can learn to perform an impressive trill, growl, belt, or melisma but purportedly can do little to make his or her voice sound rich (Monks 2003). *Rich timbre* is a way of describing the sound of distinct vibrations, generated by air jostling over the physical landscape of the mouth, getting shaped into simultaneous frequencies and intensities. The crannies, orifices, hillocks, crevices, and cavities of the mouth that confront the moving air generated by the larynx are resonators, the mouth's mountainous topography, which acts on air that moves over and through it by slowing it down here, accelerating it there, pooling it here, eddying it there. The combination of all that slowing, accelerating, eddying, and pooling is what is meant by *timbre*.

Developing rich timbre presents a considerable challenge to the singer, for the topography of one's mouth is fixed—how, then, to cultivate vocal timbre? Black gospel singers do this by working to ensure that their God-given resonators produce the sounds of which they are inherently capable. For my informants, timbre was something they were born with, yet they thought about what they could do to bring it out. Training their voices' tim-bre occurred, first, through systematic listening to other black gospel singers. Most of the singers I got to know listen every day, sometimes for hours, to recordings of their favorites. They frequently sing along, calibrating the tone and pitch of their own voices to match the recording. Singers do not just imitate recordings; they listen to each other, copying the sounds they like. Daniel (nicknamed "The Mouth") frequently demonstrated his timbre to his cosingers, and on numerous occasions I saw them follow up by imitating a coloratura here, a melisma there. As they did, they also imitated Daniel's tim-bre, as they strove to reproduce the sound of crisscrossing vibrations that give his voice its distinctive depth. I would also include under the rubric of developing timbre singers' daily rounds of exercises intended to warm up, loosen up, and increase the voice's agility and flexibility. Before and after rehearsals and before performances, I saw singers regularly give their voices a workout, not just by going through the usual scales but by coughing, clear-ing, spitting, drinking water, massaging jaws and throats and cheeks, rubbing teeth until they squeaked—that is, interacting with their vocal apparatus in an eminently physical, hands-on way, apparently believing that the instru-ment's sound could be improved by such physical manipulations. Sérgio explicitly connected manipulation to timbre: "You have to get your voice ready, so that its timbre can come through. All the exercises, all the loosen-ing, that all helps."

Timbre, then, is an eminently physical experience. When I asked singers to talk to me about whether they could "feel" timbre, they responded in the affirmative. They spoke of feeling "vibrations," of the production of saliva, of sensations of tiny movements of cartilage, muscle, and bone. Angélica was perhaps the most eloquent: "I can feel my timbre, yes, I can. As I sing, I feel a million little vibrations, all at once, filling my mouth. I can feel down to the marrow of my bones, vibrating."

Now I want to suggest that the practices of black gospel singing, by gen-erating hyperattention to the physical organs of the vocal apparatus, may be partly responsible for many black gospel singers coming to adopt racially essentialist ideas about their own voices. Experiencing themselves as doing extraordinary things with their vocal cords, many black singers are per-suaded of the truth of certain racial ideas circulating in Brazilian society. A key carrier of these views to singers are practitioners of voice therapy. Many of the singers I got to know had at one time or another consulted with a voice therapist, or *fonoaudiologista*, who, they reported, had given them a lecture on the physiological differences between *negro* and white vocal apparatuses. Marta, a singer in the Mission choir, told me that once when she had pharyngeal pain, she consulted a therapist who, after prescribing hot tea, lemon, honey, and a morning gargle, taught her about the physical uniqueness of the black voice. "She showed me that picture," she said, referring to a cross-section of the head. "She showed me that *negros* have a different-looking voice box from whites. Ours is a strong box. It is stronger. She showed me that."[3]

While I assumed at first that the offhand comments I heard on this topic were isolated, I soon discovered a pervasive belief among many black singers that their voices' capacity to endure exceptional stress and to produce gorgeous sounds was due to anatomical endowments conferred by their African blood. I encountered such claims in everyday situations such as car rides, after-performance debriefings, rehearsals, workshops, collective viewings of DVDs, CD listening sessions, and meal-table conversation. In these contexts, when talk turned to the sound, strength, or grain of the voice required by black gospel singing, someone would usually comment on the distinctive anatomy of "*a voz do negro*" (the black voice).

I heard this idea for the first time on a rainy evening as I rode in the car with members of a black gospel group to a performance in a church deep in São Paulo's periphery. In the cramped Volkswagen, five members of the group, in their teens and early twenties (three self-identified *negros* and two *negras*) were laughing and joking about their church, music, movies, and love interests. In the car too were two young *brancos* not of the group but in their church. As we lumbered over potholes in stop-and-go traffic, conversation turned to the North American film *The Fighting Temptations*, starring Beyoncé, which was very popular with Brazilian churchgoers. Claudio, a young singer, was talking about Beyoncé. "That huge voice!" he cried. "I loved when she finally decided to go for it. Man, that huge black voice [*aquela vozão de negra*] just had to come out!"

Lucia said, nodding, "Sooner or later she was going to have to sing. It's the blood, the blood."

Nods all around.

I could not resist. "What do you mean, 'It's the blood'?"

A pause, then general merriment. Claudio patted me on the shoulder. "It's the same thing in your country! You haven't noticed?"

"Noticed what?"

"It is hard to avoid, John. If you hear two little girls singing in the street, the *negra* will always be stronger than the *branca*. I'm not saying that *brancos* can't sing. But *negros'* voices are stronger. They have better timbre."

The little car was suddenly filled by crisscrossing opinions. Duglass, the *branco* driving the car, joined in.

"Right, right, back me up, back me up . . . "

"Right, *branquelo* [white guy], tell us what you think."

Duglass adopted a professorial tone. "You see, John, in a really good choir in church, maybe you have a few *brancos*. But they are not the lead singers."

Lucia: "That's true!"

Duglass: "And they are always in a minority. You look around, and who are the artists who really stand out? Silveira, Robson [Nascimento]."

Márcia: "Right. And Sérgio Saas and Daniel and Ton Carfi—all *negros!*"

Duglass again: "Yeah, maybe you'll see one or another *branco*, but rare, rare, rare."

"Nonexistent!" Samuel added. "I'll tell you—ask anybody—you look at all these choirs, they are 100% *negros*."

Lucia, to ensure I understood the point, offered the popular saying "A raça que canta é a raça que encanta" (The race that sings is the race that enchants), and Duglass responded with his own: "O que Deus tirou de lá ele colocou lá" (What God took away from up here he placed down here). The conversation then turned to other matters—to the upcoming show, to the arrival in São Paulo of Kirk Franklin, to last week's birthday party, to the rain.

The taken-for-granted tone of the conversation, its embeddedness in robust preexisting ideas, discourses, and turns of phrase, led me in the months that followed to pay attention to the milieu of comment and presumption in which black gospel singers moved, listening for and asking how and whether they believed that ancestry made any difference in the singing of black gospel. What I heard, across the board, was a resounding yes: that people with African ancestry, *negros*, acquitted themselves better in this scene than did whites. And I discovered a well-developed credo about *negro* vocal anatomy: African ancestry, I heard repeatedly, bestowed a set of anatomical features on the mouth and throat that enabled, if they did not ensure, excellence in the techniques of black gospel singing. Thick vocal cords and a wide vocal tract made possible especially good belting; robust and sinewy membranes in the throat permitted sustained growling; and capacious sinuses and other cranial resonators created a rich, multitrack vocal timbre that infused the voice with a deep, beautiful, unmistakably "black" tone.

Listen, for example, to Marta, Lucinda, and Didinha, members of Raiz Coral, as they expounded on the anatomy of their own voices. The subject of conversation was their need for training. While acknowledging that they needed to "polish" their voices, they insisted that their physical endowment as *negras* gave them a clear advantage. "We have to work," said Lucinda, "but not as hard. They just don't have the equipment we have." Marta explained that "the *negro*'s throat muscles are thicker, stronger, more numerous, more resistant than the white's." Didinha agreed. "In order to sing like a *negro*," she said, "the vocal cords must be thick. Have you noticed that in our type of singing we sometimes have to rise up and bellow? You have to have the cords for that. That is why *negros* are so good at this."

I heard talk from others about the timbre of the *negro* voice being based in air passages larger than those of whites and in a facial structure filled with multiple nooks that create the echoes necessary for rich resonance. I heard this last point articulated on many occasions, but a particularly memorable one was during a workshop for new singers led by Isabêh. Standing in front of an anatomical cross-sectional diagram of the human head, he carefully pointed to the facial cavities. "This is where timbre happens," he said. "In the faces of *negros*, there are more cavities, and they are larger. That means more resonance, a richer tone. It is a question of the nasal cavities. There is more room in ours for the sound, with more waves. This affects the timbre of the voice." He demonstrated. "A European will sing like this." He produced a dry, monotonous phrase of music. "Now listen to the *negro*," he ordered, then sang the same phrase, this time infusing it with the rich, deep tonality of the "black" voice, ending with a growl. The room burst with appreciative laughter.

The Telling of History

It is difficult for outsiders to appreciate how seriously black gospel artists take music history. I will not soon forget my first meeting with Sérgio Saas, music director of Raiz Coral. It was a Sunday afternoon, and the members of the choir were congregating at his house in Capão Redondo. I arrived in Sérgio's backyard just as lunch was being served. In the humid shade of peach and acacia leaves, members of the choir sipped guava juice and savored white bean and sausage stew. Daniel, a member of the choir whom I had contacted earlier in the week, introduced me to Sérgio as an "anthropologist interested in black music." This description had a kind of catalytic effect. For the next hour, Sérgio spoke breathlessly about the origins of black music in Africa; its transmission via slavery to Brazil, the Caribbean, and the United States; the importance of field hollers and work songs; the difference between rural and urban blues; and the rise of jazz, R&B, rock and roll, soul, and funk. "You see what happens when I get started?" he asked finally, laughing. He had not touched his stew.

Sérgio's detailed knowledge of black music history, though perhaps better developed than most, was not unusual among black gospel artists in São Paulo. I found that these artists had a profoundly historical attitude toward their music and seized upon chances to show it. I spoke with numerous black gospel artists whose knowledge of their scene's history was no less detailed than Sérgio's, their enthusiasm for sharing it no less keen. There was Isabêh, the voice coach and music educator, who crisscrossed the city with missionary fervor to run music history workshops. There was Pastor Sérgio, head of the Azusa church, who insisted his singers learn about the roots of blues on plantations of the US South. There was Michael, who distributed multipage fact sheets to his choir members that traced the history of the genre from Africa to slavery to the civil rights movement. There was Marcelo, the choir director of the Mission Choir, who said to me, "You really can't be a black gospel artist unless you know its history."

This enthusiasm is, I want to suggest, rooted in several motives. First, black gospel music artists ardently wish to make their music legitimate in the eyes of church leaders. It may surprise North Americans that the reaction of many Brazilian Protestant ministers to black gospel music is negative. They worry about its beats and rhythms, which they view as at odds with decent church order, and its gestures and clothing, which they believe may unleash pride, lust, and idolatry. I met elders in the Seventh-Day Adventist church who were suspicious of Raiz Coral precisely because of how spectacular they were. "I do not doubt their sincerity," an elder told me. "But how can a young person distinguish between the good and bad? They go to a show, and they get swept away by the sound. They forget God. They just want autographs." In response to these views, black gospel artists are eager to demonstrate their genre's historical association with Christian beliefs and values. The "truth about our music," said Daniel, "is that it began as a spiritual, not secular, music. We need to let everyone know. That is how we can fight these ideas. This music has always been very spiritual. . . . It has been in the church a long time! But people don't know that, so we have to teach this history." Said music promoter and producer Ferrisbeck, "We must show people that our music is rooted in the Christian church." Or, as Marcelo, the choir director, put it, "We need to be able to defend ourselves, to show pastors this is music that belongs in church. We need to know our history to be ready with arguments when they challenge us. We must show them that the soul singers started in the church."

Knowing history also strengthens professional identity. Black gospel artists regard their art as exceptionally difficult to master. Choir director Marcelo is convinced that to become a serious black gospel singer one has to acquire detailed knowledge of the music's traditions and forebears "all the way back." He explained, "We are guardians of a great tradition, with aesthetic standards. We are professionals." That was why he made sure all his choirs studied the music's history. "A lot of young singers," he explained, "hear the music and think, 'I want to do that, to impress people with my melismas.' But black gospel music is not about our individual desires. It is not about individuals showing off." How, I asked, were young musicians learning this lesson? "The way you get that," he said, "is by learning the history." Robson Nascimento, who has spent over a decade running singing workshops, insisted that knowing history improved vocal technique, made one a "better professional." "When you know the history of the essence," he explained, "your manner of execution is going to be much more committed. It will be fuller of the feeling that has been present through the whole history of the music. It will be more professional. Now you sing thinking about all of that. That makes you a better singer. It is reflected in your technique, tone, everything."

In almost every rehearsal I attended, musical directors articulated ideas about black history, ideas that their hearers connected to slaves toiling in the nineteenth-century US South. Sérgio Saas would not permit his choir's rehearsals to end without making at least one such reference. On one occasion, he and his codirector, Scooby, were calling on lead singers to infuse more energy into a difficult musical phrase. When the singers hesitated, the dynamic duo launched into a minute-long verbal jam on how melismas were what slaves used to be percussive in the absence of drums. "See, in Brazil, they let the slaves have drums," Scooby said, "so they didn't need to develop their voices." "Yeah!" Sérgio joined in, cracking his tongue like a whip. "Like this! You see? Like this!" He cracked some more. "The slaves didn't have drums! They were robbed! So you have to compensate, compensate! Your mouths have to become like a drum! Your mouth is a drum!"

At every turn, I encountered such verbal connections between current technique and black history. Felipe, an R&B guitarist, alluded to history during rehearsals. I once witnessed him ask a singer "to make the sound more black." Seeing her quizzical look, he devoted several minutes to recounting how slaves were obliged to call to each other at great distances on cotton plantations. "Think what it would have been like: you can't see who's hearing you," he explained. "So they learned to use every last drop of their voices! That's the sound we're looking for. You really have to project!" Kedma, a singer in the Degraus choir, in the neighborhood of Brasilândia, insisted that her choir director was always talking to them during rehearsal "about the roots of the music." Some choir directors prepare carefully typed handouts that recount the history. Michael makes a habit of distributing such handouts in the first session with each gospel choir he organizes. "I have condensed all the things I have learned," he said, "about the history of blacks and the history of black gospel, about music, about choir, and placed it in that handout. I make copies before rehearsal and give it so that people can have something in their hands when they leave."

Voice lessons, too, are an important occasion for the telling of historical narratives about field hollers, work songs, and spirituals. Robson Nascimento devotes the first session of tutoring to history telling, thereafter integrating historical comments occasionally into his one-on-one work. Isabêh instructs his students to get on the Internet to discover whatever they can about the artists on a list he gives them, including Mahalia Jackson and Thomas Dorsey. "That's the only way," he told me, "they'll really understand the music." Then there are the half- to full-day workshops, in which instructors offer lectures, show videos, write on whiteboards, and engage participants in lively banter. The workshops take place in churches, usually instigated by the congregation's musical director, and come complete with snack, lunch break, photocopies, and free pens. The demand for the workshops is strong and growing: in 2005, I came across seven of them, and I am sure I did not locate them all. The demand proved large enough that a recording of one of Isabêh's workshops became a commercially successful DVD. At workshops, the trainers devote a minimum of one hour to telling the story of North American slavery: the arrival of masses of enslaved Africans on the North American continent, the prohibition of drums, the development of percussive vocal techniques, and the integration of singing into everyday labor.

A few pastors organize events devoted to a public recounting of black music history. Joilson, pastor of the Mintre church in the city's northern zone, sets aside one Saturday night every October as "Black Power night," to celebrate the black music of the 1960s and '70s. In October 2005, I attended one of these, dancing sweatily in a packed church for forty-minute sets while the bands pounded out Christian funk, soul, and gospel. During two fifteen-minute intermissions, pastor Joilson and his resident historian, Sidney, sat on stools at the front of the packed house and talked about history. "This music didn't just appear out of thin air," Joilson declared, wiping the sweat from his brow. "It was part of a movement. It was a way for American blacks to fight for their rights."

History telling has also been vital to special Christian study groups. One of these, formed in the late 1990s, brought together a dozen black music artists, moving from home to home each week. Participants discussed what they knew of history for hours on end. According to one participant, the study group had been a formative experience, convincing him of his need for deeper historical knowledge. I found another study group made up of six members of Raiz Coral, who met regularly in 2004 to study the history of black music. Group members copied pages out of books and encouraged each other to look for materials on the Internet. A heavy concert schedule eventually forced this brave little network to suspend meetings. Still, they had succeeded before they were done in disseminating black music history and in stimulating an innovative musico-racial theology. "It was in that study group," reported Daniel, "that we figured out how this music fits into God's divine plan." I will return to the nature of this theology momentarily.

One other context of this rich tradition of history narration are the performances themselves. Once black gospel artists feel they have mastered some history, they often try to educate their audiences about the subject. Several singers I got to know made it a rule to offer historical commentaries between songs. Sérgio, Silveira, Tina, and Marcelo frequently made historical asides while on stage. I heard Sérgio spend three minutes holding forth on "how we cannot forget that this music was brought over by our ancestors on slave ships" and that music helped North American blacks "to survive the oppression of slavery." Whenever the black gospel group Fat Family's lead singer, Deise, rendered the Negro spiritual "Sorrow" (in English), she would explain how slaves were denied drums and had to rely on their voices, how they had to communicate at a distance with each other, and how they needed spiritual comfort under the whip.

What is the narrative that artists learn and disseminate in all these contexts? While they do not walk around with neatly formed histories in their heads, it is possible to discern the rough outlines of their shared view of black musical history. It goes something like this. In chapter one, enslaved Africans carried to the New World a passion for percussion inherited from African musical styles. In Brazil, masters rendered indifferent by their Catholicism allowed slaves to continue playing drums, while in North America, masters made narrowly pious by their Protestant zeal banned drums as tools of the devil. (None of my informants approved of this ban.) Thus, while Brazilian slaves, free to drum, had no incentive to develop vocal skill, North American slaves, longing for percussion and unable to use drums, developed their voices instead, as instruments that produced a broad percussive range. "That's why," explained David Ramos, "we in Brazil never developed our singing like the blacks did in America. Here we just played drums and never needed to develop our voices." How different from North American slaves, forever honing their singing voices in ring shouts, field hollers, work songs, and brush arbor songs! I once heard Isabêh deliver a fifteen-minute lecture on how gospel singing depended on the lower diaphragm, because it had started in America's large open fields, as a way to "cry out to heaven and have other slaves hear you, in the plantation work songs and spirituals."

The second chapter of this narrative tells how Brazil's slaves, suffering from the neglect of good-for-nothing Catholic masters, satisfied their musical needs at night and on weekends, playing drums in un-Christian gatherings where they worshiped demons; in contrast, North American slaves were exposed by their masters to Protestant ministers. Thus, according to this view, while Brazilian *negros* remained mired in superstition, North American *negros* became good Christians and set about living lives pleasing to the Lord. "The Americans were hundreds of years ahead of us in finding the Lord," explained Ferrisbeck. "Here in Brazil, we were worshiping idols and drumming candomblé. There in the US, they were building churches and praising the Lord. So of course this music became strong there and not here." In this account, the hidden clearings on cotton plantations in North

America became the place where slaves intoned, in secret, their passion for the Lord. "We know," said Michael, "that the slaves in your country were deeply religious. They accepted Jesus and abandoned the superstitions of Africa. So they would gather on days they weren't working in the fields, and they would sing in their own way." Their "own way" was a mix of the guttural percussive style inherited from Africa and the melodic sounds they heard wafting over from their masters' churches. As Michael's handout argued, "These blacks . . . heard on Sundays coming from the white man's church services the traditional songs and hymns from England. . . . So after hearing these hymns they were amazed and went to work just humming these melodies at the start, since they did not yet know English."[4] At the end of the day, however, slaves' singing was, in this view, a way for them to cope with the terrors of the system they lived under. As slaves, according to Michael's handout, they suffered under the system "that brought them a life in subhuman conditions, humiliation, and death." Faced with such horrible conditions, music was a means to survive psychologically. "Singing in the North American cotton fields," the handout declared, "was a way for slaves to survive hard work and beatings."

In the third chapter of this narrative, North American slaves combined their inherited musical prowess with their knowledge of the Lord to create that jewel of world music, the spirituals. In this version, slaves founded their own churches and filled them with the sounds of spirituals. The spirituals expressed longing for liberation from oppression. "The slaves sang spirituals," Michael's handout stated, "that had to do with the liberation of the people of Israel from Egypt, thinking that this would be a song of praise and protest, asking God for their own liberation." Sérgio Saas, during a rehearsal in his home, explained to his choir the liberationist longing in "Go Down Moses": "Black people identified with the Old Testament," he told them, "with the people of Israel who suffered." Isabêh, too, spoke about the messages embedded in the spirituals. In one public lecture, he asserted, "The slaves placed indirect messages about escape in the spirituals, because they were very persecuted. . . . What they usually sang about was racism and sadness. It was often sung by blind people or someone with some kind of physical disability. . . . So these were people who were very sad and just threw up their hands and said, 'Leave me in peace.'" They also developed the blues. "The blues," said Isabêh, "was the voice of the slave crying out when he wasn't crying to God."

What were Brazilian slaves doing in the meantime? Inventing samba, of course. For black gospel musicians, samba is closely associated with the urban world of bars, dancing, Carnaval, the erotic, the lusty *mulata*, secularism, and sin—a world, in short, at odds with the church. Several informants insisted that their critique of samba had nothing to do with a lack of national pride; it had, rather, to do with samba's immorality. "I could never accept samba," said Daniel. "When you look at the history of that, it has always been surrounded by drinking, sex, and drugs."

In the last chapter of this story, in the twentieth century, three things happened: first, North American soul singers got started in church. This is a crucial piece of the narrative, which helps black gospel artists justify their art. For, in their telling of it, it was the church that gave Ray Charles his inspiration, and Sam Cooke was a preacher's son. "All the great soul singers started in church," said Isabêh. Second, blacks continued singing the blues. As Isabêh explained, "Black people in the United States, they were still suffering, even though they weren't slaves any longer. And so they kept on singing the blues." Combining the blues with gospel, he explained, a whole generation of black singers in the United States bridged the gap between the church and the world. "They would sing in the church or in the street; they brought that emotion into the church to praise God, and they brought that love of God into the street to sing the blues." And finally, black gospel music played a key role in the civil rights struggle. "For those of you who don't know," Isabêh lectured, "Martin Luther King was a pastor. That's right! A pastor who fought so that there could be equality in the United States. They could not have done this without their music." In this narrative, Mahalia Jackson's voice was recruited by Martin Luther King Jr. to sing at demonstrations. Michael Santiago once spoke for ten minutes to his choir about the civil rights struggle and the role in it of freedom songs. "The blacks suffered horrible oppression," he explained, "but they suffered it until they finally won that struggle. The civil rights movement won so that the blacks finally could have the right to vote. . . . It was the hymns they sang in church that kept them going when they were fighting for their rights."

The narrative elements I have just described invest blackness with chronological and political depth. Chronologically, the narrative goes back centuries, drawing listeners into scenes that unfolded in Africa and on the colonial plantations of North America over three hundred years ago. Politically, the narrative claims that while black music may have expressed black people's love of rhythm and percussion, it was very much about coping with oppression and suffering. The idea of black music as fighting social injustice is perhaps taken for granted in North American Protestant culture, but in the Brazilian evangelical context it is a revelation.

Over the course of numerous interviews and life histories, I detected identity effects of knowing this history. Kedma grew up in a working-class family in Brasilândia, a poor neighborhood in the northern zone of the city. Her father was a janitor, her mother a seamstress, and both insisted their children stay in school. After seeing her older brother graduate from high school and pass the college entrance exams, Kedma wanted to become a fashion designer and break into advertising. "I know I have talent," she said, "and I work hard. I really love to sew, which I learned from my mother." Kedma began singing when she was in her early teens, but the first choir she was a part of "didn't have any interest in black music. It was just a regular choir, in another church, in Renascer [Renascer em Cristo]." It wasn't until she switched to Brasil Para Cristo in 2002 that she discovered black gospel music. "It was there that I found myself," she said. "There I found freedom, freedom to sing how I wanted, in a way I never had before. As soon as I heard those voices, I knew—I knew I had to become a part of this."

Becoming "a part of this" meant, for Kedma, among a variety of things, years of *learning* about black music history. "No one had ever told me anything about Africa or spirituals," she said, "or blues, or anything. I knew nothing about any of that. But Joilson said that if we were going to be singers, we had to know this. Before that, no one had ever spoken to me about blues. I had heard some blues, but no one commented to me about this history. I didn't know about the difference between blues and jazz. For me, that was all the same thing. I didn't know the blues had anything to do with the slaves. I just thought of 'black music' in general. I just thought it was a kind of a mixture of different things." Kedma's innocence of black music history was typical. In my other interviews with black gospel artists, I learned that they regarded themselves as blank slates with regard to this history before getting involved in the scene. Felipe told me, "No one had ever taken the time to teach me anything about this history. Really, it was the first time I learned about this. They don't teach this stuff in school."

I asked Kedma to tell me what difference knowing this history had made to her. The first effect, she said, was that it had led her to see that she belonged to a people that had suffered. Before learning this history, she had heard about slavery in Brazil, had seen it all in movies and on TV. But she had not understood it: "It was like it happened to strangers." What helped her understand the history finally was that she learned that in North America they had used their voices, that they had sung. "I think," she said, "it is hard to identify with the slaves on TV. But when I heard that they sang, that captured me."

"But Brazilian slaves made music too, Kedma. What do you feel about that?"

"Yes, that is true. But their music didn't speak directly to me. Maybe because it is about drumming and samba? I don't know. The thing that I feel is singing. I saw that in those North Americans."

Learning how song expressed suffering stimulated Kedma, she said, to think more deeply. "You know," she said, "you hear about 'suffering slaves,' and you feel like, 'that's too bad: suffering slaves.' But the slaves were out in the fields singing. They got together and sang. That is something else. If I had lived at that time, I would have been a slave too." Knowing this history, and identifying with it via song, stimulated Kedma to infuse into her singing a melancholic timbre, suffused by the awareness of collective black suffering. "I would say it has deepened my singing," she said. "Now when I sing, I think about where these songs came from. . . . I can picture the slaves who were suffering. When they were singing the songs, that is where the music comes from. . . . I think I sing more seriously, that is, a different feel to what I'm singing."

Exposure to history also set in motion for Kedma the desire to study the lives of famous black gospel artists—and of the civil rights struggle. Kedma remembers what Joilson said to the choir: "that we should read about these musicians, that we would learn a lot. And I thought, 'These guys are all from the church, so I should look into their lives.' And I did. I went to the Internet, went to the library. . . . I learned a lot more about how these people were singing, not just for singing but to change people, to change the law."

Kedma was not alone in this trajectory. Rafael, a twenty-year-old singer in the southern zone of the city, was moved by what he learned in his choir to do his own research: "So I learned everything I could about North American blacks, the ones who invented this style of singing. I needed to know more, how this had happened. So I learned they had stood up and fought back. They stood up and fought. Martin Luther King and marches and Black Panthers. I love this. I learned all about it." Stefania, a singer in the poor northern-zone neighborhood of Guarulhos, recalled what she did when she first learned of the connection between music and the civil rights struggle: "read, read anything I could, on Martin Luther King. I began to see how this whole movement of theirs was in the church, that the church really made a difference." And when Angélica started to sing black gospel, she said,

> My mind opened up. I started to want to know everything I could about the origin of this music, where it all started. I longed for that. I felt there must be a secret here, a secret to this music, and I had to find it out. And heaven be praised, I find myself in a church that encourages that—really encourages it. My mind wants to know more knowledge! I need to know these things. I need the support, because now my mind is opened up to new things, and I want to drink it all in! So my voice teacher suggested I read this book, about the life of a slave in the US South. He brought this book about the life of a slave to our lesson one day, and he said, "Angélica, you are going to really like this. This is going to be a very interesting book for you." And he was right, because this book really stirs up my roots, because it's a very important book. It talks all about the blacks in the southern part of the United States and about how God was so present in their singing and how the slaves would get together in the arbors and sing praises to the Lord and that this helped them in the midst of their worst suffering. I tell you, this book completely changed my life. Because now when I sing, I realize that this comes from that time of slavery. I feel them singing with me.

Up to this point, I have been considering the largely secular dimension of this history. But it should surprise no one that the artists I got to know were interested in interpreting in spiritual terms what they understood to be the distinctive physical vocal endowment of black people. Why had God given them apparatuses capable of producing such extraordinary sounds? What was his purpose in doing so? "You can see and hear the gift that God has given specially to *negro* people," said Claudio. "That timbre of voices is unmatched. But why is it that God gave these vocal cords to the *negro*?" I heard this question several times from the lips of singers, posed in a kind of rhetorical flourish, almost always right after having praised the black voice as an instrument. "The black voice is so pretty," said Monica. "Why has God given us such pretty voices?"

Some singers had pondered this question. Claudio, for instance, said he thought about the question every morning, in the hours before sunrise, before the hurly-burly when his family would distract him. Looking into the early morning darkness, Claudio would, he said, "think a lot about this question, all by myself. I remain alone with God, in my room. I seek out why God has done this, why God permits it, why God has given this incredible voice to *negros*." Daniel, too, feels the importance of the question and raised it regularly in his biblical study group. "I ask us to think about this," he said. "I think we need to analyze this by the light of the Bible. What is God's will? Why has he given us this huge voice? For it is God who has done this, not us. We are born with this voice. If God wishes us to have a voice so full of pain and power, there must be a reason."

I found that singers of black gospel in São Paulo believe their voices fit into a divine plan in three main ways: the first has to do with prophecies in the Old Testament, the second with the slave trade, and the third with the rise of Brazil. For the reader to grasp these beliefs, it is important to recall that anointing, in Christian thought, is the capacity bestowed on a person by the Holy Spirit to provoke in other people deep spiritual experience, reflection, or change. Skills such as preaching, teaching, evangelizing, and writing are all subject to anointing, as are such arts as singing, dancing, and painting. As I suggested in chapter 1, many gospel singers see themselves as descendants of the Levites, the people anointed by God in the Second Book of Chronicles with the gift of music, with which they moved the people of the Temple to praise God. According to this view, God deposits a measure of the Holy Spirit in the person, not the performance—hence the claim of my informants that black people's voices have been anointed by God. As evidence, they refer to black gospel singing's unique evangelizing power, its ability to melt listeners' mental armor and open up their souls for an inflow of Holy Spirit. "When I sing with all that force," said Angélica, "that sound rips open the heart and lets in the pure spirit. It tears the body in two." The black voice, in this view, brings listeners to God—hence the proposition of black gospel singers: God chose black people to be his special instruments, through their voices to evangelize the world.

Several of my informants claimed that this proposition was supported by references to Ethiopia in the Old Testament. I heard this version for the first time from Sérgio Saas onstage at the Pedra Viva church, in front of a crowd of several hundred. At the end of one song, Sérgio brandished a large, cloth-bound Bible and opened it to a dog-eared page. "My friends," he said, "the eighteenth chapter of Isaiah speaks of a people from a land beyond the rivers of Ethiopia. Here is the seventh verse of the eighteenth chapter: 'In that time shall a gift be brought unto the Lord by a people tall and of glossy skin, and from a fearsome nation; a nation that is sturdy and whose land the rivers divide.'" Sergio raised the Bible animatedly above his head. "Do you see?" he cried. "It is a prophecy! We are fulfilling the prophecy! God is talking about us, *a raça negra* [the black race]. The prophecy there says that there will come a time when we *negros* will offer a gift to the world." He paused meaningfully. "And do you know what that gift is?" He paused again. The church went still. Then he exploded. "Music!!" Shouts and hallelujahs. "Do you see?" he continued, pacing the stage. "God had given *a raça negra* a great mission, a great task. He has chosen us to go forth, to bring our song, our voices! Because he knows that with our voices and with our suffering, we can move mountains, we can move the world toward him. And now we are fulfilling the prophecy!"

I heard this divine musical story in other contexts as well. When black gospel artists spoke in study groups and workshops about the origins of their music, I sometimes heard them say that God bestowed on the people of Kush the mission to bring the unsaved to Jesus. "Don't you see?" Ferrisbeck asked me. "It is a gift that *o povo negro* have that they offer to the Lord. That is the prophecy, in Isaiah. People of glossy skin from the place where the two rivers divide—that is us, *o povo negro*, from Ethiopia. . . . God endowed *os negros* with ability: when we let ourselves sing, we give God back that gift, as it is stated in Isaiah—that we would bring gifts unto the Lord." Later, Daniel explained that "God was pleased that American *negros* turned to him. So he anointed them with the Holy Spirit. In the United States, *negros* gathered in their churches, and they started influencing all the music of the world. So the prophecy of Isaiah is being fulfilled."

A second cluster of ideas went a step further than the prophecy itself, by claiming that the history of slavery played a key role in this divine plan. If God endowed black people with a physical apparatus capable of creating powerful sounds, their history of suffering ensured that blacks' voices would have the necessary pathos to soften the hardest of hearts. The coherence of this view became clear to me one cool afternoon in Angélica's living room, when she explained to me, in a matter-of-fact tone, the connections between black singing, black oppression, and God's will. In her view, God had visited on the descendants of the people of Kush, she said, much suffering, so that their voices could move listeners to their very core. "God wanted it to be that people can always hear a tear in our voices," she explained. "*Negros* have the sound of weeping in their voices. God needs our voices to be full of pain. . . . I believe that God needs this kind of brokenness, because this feeling of brokenness touches the hearts of listeners. *O povo negro* are part of the dream of God for humankind because our voices reach other people. It is through our voices that God will save the world." Later she added, "I think that even slavery happened for a reason—not that God planned that we would be enslaved. That is the evil of man, that is sin. But God sees and uses everything for the good. And God needed the tears we shed. He needed the pain, the emotion, the sadness in our voices. It is through us that God will save the world."

A third cluster of ideas explains why black gospel is finally catching on in Brazil, after its birth and growth in the United States. According to this view, North American blacks have long been more serious about their Christianity than have Brazilians, but this is finally starting to change, with the result that the Holy Spirit has begun to shower down on Brazil. "The cloud of God's anointing," said Sérgio, "is passing from the United States to Brazil. We are starting to fill the churches. We are fulfilling the prophecy. We are offering the present to the Lord of all of these souls converted by the power of our music." Indeed, in this view, God is actively searching for a nation to make up for the growing deficit in North American blacks. "*Negros* in the US no longer lead the world in their spiritual force," said Ferrisbeck. "You look up north, and what do you see? Spiritual cooling. Your *negros* have become materialistic. They are bowing before idols of gold. . . . As the spirit cools there, it heats up here. That is why it is now us, here in Brazil, we are now singing like *negros* from your country." The language suggests an anti-imperialist critique. "We are still a poor nation," said Sérgio. "We do not have as much material wealth as you do. But we know that material wealth sometimes means people forget God. And we Brazilians have not forgotten God. So God is pleased with what he sees on our continent, and we are being rewarded richly with anointing."

What I want to underscore about these three clusters of ideas is their transnationalism: the idea that God has a plan for the descendants of Kush in general, wherever they may be. North American black musical dominance was extensive but fundamentally temporary; what endures is God's selection of the people of Kush, wherever they are, as carriers through song of his evangelizing mission. It is this transnational vision that allows the same artists who celebrate North American black musical vocal mastery to claim that, as Brazilian blacks convert to the Lord, remain immune from the temptations of idolatry, and cultivate their God-given vocal skills, their destiny is to become the world's musical leaders. "North American *negros* filled their churches with praise before we did," explained Sérgio. "But now he is lifting us up, raining down the Holy Spirit upon us, and we are fulfilling the prophecy of Isaiah. Now is our moment; now it is our turn."

This chapter has sought to show how musical practices unleash certain kinds of emotions, attitudes, ideas, and subjectivities among their practitioners. Here, among Brazilian evangelical Protestants, a fortress of ideological universalism, in which every Christian is radically the same as every other, in which all worldly identities are supposed to melt away—here, involvement in black gospel unleashes powerful, deep, enduring ethnoracial feelings. These feelings have generated complex theological ideas about black people's place in the cosmic design. These are astonishingly novel, strong ideas, and, as we shall see, they have political consequences.

5

The Bible Is Full of Prophecies

Black Evangelical Musicians and Black Politics

I have up to this point examined how the routine practices of different styles of black gospel music shape practitioners' ideas about blackness. In so doing, I have limited myself to ideas about identity, history, and theology, steering clear, for the time being, of how such ideas translate into plans for the public sphere. The time has come to consider such plans, what one might call politics. What political views are embedded in the musical styles I have examined? To what extent and in what ways do these styles foment ideas for public action about black rights, grievances, needs, and justice? To address these questions, I asked my informants to comment on whether they believed they as Christians or their churches had any responsibility to address matters of concern to black people, and if so, what might such responsibilities entail? While I followed whatever path my informants opened in response to these questions, I frequently primed the pump by describing issues important to the *movimento negro evangélico* (MNE). These discussions tended to gravitate toward the following topics: the seeking out and public valorization of Africans in the Bible; the seeking of guidance from the Bible about what to do about blacks' this-worldly concerns; the articulation of such concerns from the pulpit and in other church venues; the involvement of churches in educational programs for *negro* youth; the cultivation of *negro* church leadership; the idea of forming a church led primarily by *negros*; the encouragement of churches to act in solidarity with secular black movements; and public support by churches for specific policy initiatives such as affirmative action. I also examined a range of documents, including newspapers and on-line news, that suggested connections between gospel musicians and any of these topics. Based on this research, I argue here that each of the three main styles analyzed in this book is associated with a distinct cluster of political views and that these distinctions have everything to do with the styles' differing attitudes toward blackness, as detailed in the preceding chapters.

Black Politics and Gospel Rap

In chapter 2, I argued that the practices of gospel rap cultivate and sustain a distinctive form of consciousness, in which blackness exists in articulation with a powerful attachment to the class- and place-bound identity of the *periferia*. On the one hand, I suggested, gospel rappers recognize that the dangers of the periphery affect poor people of all colors; on the other hand, they also recognize themselves as black subjects who have suffered discrimination for being black. At the end of the day, in this consciousness, place/poverty seems to have taken precedence over blackness as a political project. Rappers take pride in their blackness as individuals, but they do not thematize it as insistently in their lyrics as they do the *periferia*. What they thematize is their identity as people coping with, and struggling against, the everyday violence, fear, misery, and falsehood they face as low-income denizens of the urban periphery. This is an identity that cuts across colors. I argued that this identity highlights transnational identification with poor people living in peripheries around the world, and it carries a particular ambivalence toward the United States: positively, as rap's origin and ongoing artistic inspiration; negatively, as a major site of the materialism, licentiousness, and cultural imperialism that rap lives to denounce.

What, then, are some practical implications of this consciousness? Certainly it has led some gospel rappers to become involved in secular projects of nongovernmental organizations, intended to help the youth of the periphery avoid gangs, gain marketable skills, and develop self-esteem. As Derek Pardue found in his studies of secular rappers in São Paulo (2004a, 2004b, 2005, 2008), gospel rappers see their mission as including what they call the "fifth element" of hip hop: *o social* (the social). I discovered that numerous gospel rappers were involved in popular educational programs supported by the municipal government. What is notable in this action is its dedication to *poor youth*, of all colors, in a place—the periphery—inhabited by people of all colors. The projects included little explicitly black-oriented collective action. Gospel rappers' motives for getting involved were nicely summarized by Elizeu, lead MC for the gospel rap group Profetas do Apocalipse:

> We who take this step, who can write and be the voice for others, we who read a bit more and study, we have a responsibility. A responsibility: we need to help show our brothers and sisters in the *periferia* that there are many ways out of this hell. Of course, the most important one is Christ. But not everyone is converted, and even the brother in Christ needs opportunities! So that is why Profetas do Apocalipse participates in these programs. When the city comes here and says they need volunteers, we volunteer! We sometimes get paid, too.

But when it came to bringing collective black projects into church, gospel rappers were more circumspect. Consider the idea of a black church. On the positive side, several gospel rappers said they sympathized with such a project's ability to help an oppressed minority develop self-esteem in a racist society. I heard this view, for example, from Lito Atalaia, a gospel rapper who belonged to the Mintre church. "You know," he said, "I am sympathetic. I am. I am a hip hopper, and hip hop is all about standing up against injustice, right? I think that if we formed a black church, this is a kind of self-defense. . . . Whites don't need this kind of defense; blacks do." Yet in the end, he could not quite swallow the idea, out of concern that such a church could slip into racial exclusivity. Listen to Lito's subsequent reflection: "Well, I'm not so sure how I feel about this, as I think about it. Because you know, if the church gets together just for the color thing, then

I have concerns. I think that if it slips into being exclusive, that is no good. If it's just—you know, you have a black church, because we want to have a bunch of black people together, then I think there is a danger there." I heard this ambivalence expressed repeatedly by other gospel rappers. Several expressed misgivings that the model might be coming from the United States, that hotbed of materialism and imperial arrogance. Naldo, a rapper in a church in Brasilândia, said, "I don't object in principle to the idea of a black church, but if it was just a photo of the American model, that would bother me, because why should we just copy what they have done in the US?" Others feared that an overzealous commitment to blackness in church would contradict not just Christian universalism but hip hop universalism as well. Listen to Dr. Billy:

> Hip hop encompasses all races, all classes. Hip hop is universal, just like God. Isn't God universal? God has no color! Music is universal. And God created music. If you immerse yourself in study, you find that music is universal; it does not have any color. It has no color. So that is why I am not sure I could go with a black church. . . . The idea of hip hop is to bring together all the different peoples of the world, all the different tribes. So I have reservations about this idea of a black church.

Other gospel rappers, meanwhile, felt there were so many other more urgent issues—violence, poverty, drugs, hunger—that an emphasis on blackness seemed misguided to them. As Eduardo, of Pregadores do Gueto, put it, "You know, when the agenda of the church starts going toward this whole idea of supervalorization of *negros*, that worries me. I am black, and I value myself. But I am also poor. I am also a resident of the periphery. There are so many different things to fight for—why fight just for being black?"

At the same time, gospel rappers were receptive to the idea of talking about racism in the church. The idea resonated with their commitment to debate, challenging authority, speaking out, having your voice heard. If people were feeling aggrieved in church, they reasoned, should they not have a right to say so? But again, this view was not without ambivalence. For while public discussion of racism could be a good thing, gospel rappers did not want to discuss "just" racism; they wanted to bring into the church even more urgent issues. "I perfectly understand and like that idea," said Lito. "The church is a place that needs to take this up, to be responsible to society. So I think that the church would be a good place to sponsor debates about racism, what is happening like that. But we shouldn't limit these discussions. We can't just talk about racism—we need to get the church to deal with all the challenges that we face in the periphery."

Gospel rappers were even more ambivalent about the search for blacks in the Bible. Such a project struck some of them as potentially worthwhile: after all, the goal of achieving more learning resonated with their ethos of "study," and the idea of discovering blacks in the Bible resonated with their desire to help nurture young people's self-esteem. Yet they could not see themselves taking a leadership role in any such project. "I guess that I just don't think we should be working a lot in that direction," said Samuel. "We have so many problems facing us in the periphery, so many. We need to all come together. Why should I worry that Jesus was black or whatever? He came to save all of us. And hip hop is here to try to save all of the young people in the periphery, not just the blacks. We have suffered, but so has everyone in the periphery. I think the idea is interesting. I just couldn't see myself as leading that."

The question of leadership is central here. Gospel rappers are *sympathetic* toward collective black projects but also ambivalent toward them, with an ambivalence generated by their abiding identification with the interracial periphery, their sense of the urgency of class- and place-based issues, and their commitment to "hip hop universalism." Put differently, if invited or welcomed, gospel rappers will attend the meetings and volunteer their opinions, but they will not call the meetings themselves. "All this stuff about race, I find interesting, but I'm not sure it speaks to what I want to spend my time doing," said Lito. "I am happy to support and go to the events, but I am not sure I want to organize those events myself." The same pattern applies to gospel rappers' stance toward events of the secular black movement. "I will go if invited," said Samuel. "I think that these things about blacks are right. I am glad people are fighting for them. It is just not something that I would plan on doing myself." And what would he plan on doing? "I like these projects that the city is putting into place, courses in dance and cooking and computers and language—German and English and French. This all seems more practical to me. I think we need to deal with giving young people options—[young people] of all races."

Black Politics and Gospel Samba

As I argued in chapter 3, three main sets of practices influence gospel samba practitioners' stances toward blackness. First, the history they are taught decenters African roots and enslavement and privileges ideas of national racial harmony. Second, gospel samba valorizes an idealized Brazil that celebrates race mixture. And third, the low barrier of entry into samba singing and the widespread knowledge that many nonblacks excel as sambistas weaken the idea that samba skill derives from African ancestry. Taken together, these practices reinforce among gospel sambistas the view that blackness, while important, is less important than Brazilianness in particular and Christian universalism in general. How, then, are gospel samba artists situated in relation to the *movimento negro evangélico*'s agenda of valorizing blackness and working toward authentic racial democracy?

Let me begin by considering the MNE's call to evangelicals to learn about, valorize, and celebrate *negros na Bíblia*. In interview after interview, gospel sambistas evinced little enthusiasm for this call. "To tell you the truth, I've never even thought about that," said Robson, in a typical refrain. A few sambistas said they had heard, yes, that some people believed Jesus was *negro*, but they found the belief irrelevant to Christ's mission. "I know that some people say that Jesus Christ was a *negro*," said Alexandre.

> And I suppose he walked a lot and was exposed to the sun, so he must've gotten brown. But I think that people who work on this point are really wasting their time. Because that's not the principal objective of Christ. He came to save people and to do his miracles. I think that when we start asking, "Was he white? Was he black?" we lose the principal objective, which is salvation of all souls, and souls have no color.

Rogério went further, arguing that those who focused on Jesus's color might be running afoul of biblical precepts. He said,

> I know that there are people who say it would've been impossible for Jesus to have those features [in paintings]. But it doesn't matter what he looked like, whether he was Japanese or white or black, whether he was Russian

or North American. I don't see this as having any importance. Jesus speaks about our similarity to him, whether you're white or black or you have blue eyes or brown. It doesn't matter if you resemble him! Jesus Christ never separated out anybody. Biblically, those who talk about Jesus's color so much are trying to separate people.

Like Rogério, other gospel sambistas invoked Christian universalism and their own moral color-blindness to suggest the pointlessness of searching for *negros* in the Bible. Consider Edy:

The important thing is to understand the word of God. Whether that word was spoken by a white or black doesn't add anything to it. I'm not interested in finding out who was black and white. Personally I've never thought about this. The idea that the wife of Moses was *negra*, as you say— that's something I've never thought about. I myself don't separate peoples out like that: white, black, Japanese. God says to all creatures, "Come to me, all those who have thirst for justice and eternal life." He doesn't direct himself to one group or another.

Gospel sambistas were similarly skeptical about the idea that black church leaders should receive any special support or the notion that some churches should be led by black leaders. In their view, any such privileging of leaders according to color would be dangerous, for it would foment divisiveness. "I don't believe," said Rogério, "that there should be a change like that. If anyone tried to set up a black church here in Brazil, that would exclude others. I know that today they're saying that there have to be more black mayors, more black leaders. . . . But I think that what we really need are honest leaders, independent of color." Aurélio agreed: supporting "black leadership" invited division in God's community. "Look," he said,

you have that in your country. OK. But brother, here in Brazil, that is a very profound subject. This is very complex. Because even if they don't intend it, even if it's not the goal, you start talking about a church of blacks, there is going to be a division. If a white person arrives there, they are going to look at him differently. There's just no way that can work! . . . If a black is a leader, the white should be a leader too. Because after all, God is interracial. So I don't agree with this idea of a black church.

In contrast to people who wanted to set up a church led by blacks, he spoke of what gospel sambistas like him wanted above all:

> To place Brazilianness [*brasileiridade*] into the church, through samba, not to place the *negro* into the church! What we're trying to do is to tear down barriers, not raise the banner of *o negro*. Because it isn't the *negro* who is doing this; it is Jesus Christ who called us to do this. Jesus had no favorite children, no favorite sons! We in samba have no desire to evangelize any particular color of people; all we want to do is to evangelize people.

Robson, meanwhile, rejected the idea of a church led by blacks by invoking the values of Brazilian exceptionalism. "I don't agree at all with the idea of a black church here in Brazil," he explained.

> I think we really need to understand that we are a Brazilian people, and who can tell what color our parents are? Who can say who is white and who is black? I don't want to become like you in the United States, segregated, with every group having their own neighborhood, with the blacks in their neighborhood and the whites in their neighborhood. Of course, we don't live in a perfect society. But that's not a reason for us to start forming our own little separate groups.

Alexandre combined these points with an affirmation of both samba's and Christianity's value of universality. "I see no reason for this [forming a church led by blacks]," he declared. "That sounds un-Brazilian to me. We play samba not just for blacks but for everyone. A church of blacks—I just don't accept the idea. Because God does not separate people and prefers no man. Christ died for everybody. And so if I'm a white, and I enter a church that has this kind of direction, I'm not going to feel welcome. That is not right in a Christian church."

While gospel sambistas were skeptical of the value of valorizing black church leadership or blackening the church, they were more receptive to the idea that the church might serve as a venue to discuss racism in Brazilian society. They were, however, less interested in the topic of racism itself than in the more general idea that the church might be a venue for discussing matters of public concern. "Yes, I think that the church has a role," said Rogério, "a responsibility even. Yeah, I can see that. For all the challenges

of society—we should talk about racism like all the others problems: violence and drugs, the family—to educate people in the church." Racism on
its own never arose in my discussions with Rogério, or with the other gospel
sambistas, to the level of a "problem." "Look," said Jairo, the lyricist of Deus
Crioulos,

> the church has a responsibility to raise the flag of truth, of sincerity, of
> honesty, the flag of the gospel. Maybe it can take some time to talk about
> racism, fine—but it has to take care not to get distracted from its mission,
> which is to bring everyone, regardless of color, to Jesus. So maybe they
> can talk about this a little, but not to lose the most important focus of the
> church, which is the word of God.

For the majority of my gospel sambista informants, then, the ideology
of mixed-race nationalism cultivated by their musical scene seems to have
suffused their consciousness, such that they remain unimpressed by calls to
organize around the rights and grievances of black people. Of all the gospel
sambistas I interviewed, none reported that he or she had participated in the
last year in any activities oriented toward blacks' collective rights.

Black Politics and Black Gospel Singers

While I found gospel sambistas to be less than sympathetic toward blackness politics, black gospel singers were, in contrast, consistently enthusiastic defenders of church-based collective black projects. Indeed, there exists
a significant reservoir of support for the MNE's agenda among the choirs,
quartets, and soloists of the black gospel music movement.

Consider the question of *a igreja negra*—a phrase which, in my conversations with black gospel artists, could mean either a church with mainly black
members or one led by blacks (they liked both). In contrast to gospel sambistas, many black gospel artists had actually thought about this matter and had
developed fairly detailed images of what a Brazilian *igreja negra* might look
like. Among the most elaborate came from Daniel, the powerhouse tenor. He
said,

> The stimulus came from the music. Because I saw this in your country, and
> I liked what I saw in the videos. Because there I see there are churches only

of blacks and only of whites. Brazil doesn't work that way. But I think it would be good if it did. Because today in the church in Brazil, the majority of churches are very racist. They have a hidden racism, that like when you pick up dirt and throw it underneath the rug, people come to your house and say, "Ah, it's so pretty!" but the dirt is right underneath the rug! The church has a lot of this—hidden racism. I would like to debate with people in church, because this kind of thing happens, even though the Bible says that we are all equal, that he is the father of all. That he does not separate people. So if Christians are following a God who does not separate people, why do Christians do so?

Daniel's views were stronger, and perhaps more extreme, than those of most of his musical companions. He argued for a church "only of blacks." He explained,

You cannot stay someplace where people don't treat you with equality. They all have their own places of worship, their own places where they can worship God. But we don't. Everyone who goes to the US wants to go visit a black church. . . . We see this. I watch those videos. I have seen them. I spoke about this to Sergio. We talk a lot about this. If we could create a church of blacks—which is a plan that we have, and I believe we are going to do this. No, we have to be careful—because if we arrive with this idea, there are people who are going to think that we are acting with racism against the church. But our goal is to end this kind of thing and to have our own identification. Because the European, when he arrives here [in Brazil], he knows where his family is. He knows where his ancestors are. The people of Asia know who their ancestors are. They know who their grandparents are, their great-grandparents, their great-great-grandparents. But the black doesn't. The black doesn't have this. You know, we study this. We singers study this. We know this story. We know what happened, that the slaves were brought here and their families broken up so that the masters could make their money. So our families were destroyed. We singers know this. You see, the European can brag about his family all day.

Daniel was speaking more slowly, his tone lowering. I adjusted myself in my chair.

But the black can't do that. Where can he start? Where can he end? All I know is that my great-grandparents must have been from Africa; that my grandfather was taken as a slave, was brought to Brazil, and the other who was taken and thrown to Europe, who was separated from my grand-father—how can I brag about that? The European can. The black has no identity. His identity had been lost. So the thing we are finding is that we must give blacks a new home, within the church. That is why we need a black church.

Other singers hoped not for an all-black church but for one led by blacks. "I would like *negros* to be in a church," explained Sergio Saas, "that encour-aged them to be united, to pursue their rights. I think I would like to see a church led by blacks, though it would be open to everyone—led by them, without a doubt." He continued: "Look I think there really ought to be some-thing like that. We talk a lot about this. I have thought about this. Maybe I'll do this when I have the resources. If there is the Luso-Brazilian church, the Germanic, the American church, the Japanese church, then there ought to be an Afro-Brazilian church. I would love to found one myself."

Sergio had a plan to create just such a church. It would be based in Adven-tist ideas, since that is what he grew up with, but it would be an "Adventist church of blacks" (*uma igreja Adventista dos negros*). In several long conver-sations, he confided his plan to me. He spoke about the persecution he had suffered in the Adventist church because of his commitment to black gospel music. "You know, John," he said, "this whole thing about starting an Afro-Brazilian church here—that is very important." He and several of his choir-mates had allowed this idea to advance beyond a daydream. Pen had gone to paper, and exploratory car rides had been taken. "We have even looked at some plots of land," said Scooby, Sergio's choir codirector. The bottleneck for Sergio and Scooby was their lack of theological training. "For me to do this, to start a church inspired by these ideals," Sergio lamented, "I would have to be educated in theology. Several times we have put together study groups to talk about this idea, but it is hard to keep it up without resources. But I promise you, John, this will happen!" He then waxed eloquent about the social projects such a church would have, including an "introductory class to *música negra*" and a class on "*música negra* for kids." For him, *uma igreja afro-brasileira* would welcome people of all colors. The uphill battle he faced to turn this idea into reality he explained as due to "resistance."

Our churches have a lot of resistance to black singing—about how loud it is, its clapping, about percussion. In my view, this is a lack of good sense. But you know what? Amen. Fine. This will all occur naturally in due course. Because whether or not we want it, it is going to occur. It is there in the prophecies. It is not apartheid. It is something that is going to emerge naturally. Nobody can worship God with music that is forced upon them. . . . It's going to happen naturally, because the fact is that people want to have an alternative, to be able to meet together with people who see things the same as they do. Today there is the church of Germans, there is a church of British people, there is a church of Spaniards, there's a church of Japanese, and so there will come to exist also a church of *afrodescenden-tes*. . . . The people in our churches today are prejudiced and fearful: they see someone with loose pants and braids in their hair, and they do not want to support that. So they're suppressing the culture of the *negro* in the church. I think that this is going to have terrible consequences. It is chasing away *negros*, who now just wander from one thing to the next. That is why we need our own church. The only thing that we lack is money. We need to have space. No nation is a nation without having territory. And we don't have anything. But we must reach and attain that which is ours, in the same way that they have already attained what is theirs.

Then there is Debra, evangelist and soloist for the Wings of the Eagle Pentecostal church. She told me how she felt after viewing videos of US black churches: "I began to really want to visit the United States, so I can go to some of those black churches. That's my dream. Because it's like it would be going to visit some distant relatives and cousins, because whenever I've seen those singers on video, I feel like I'm looking at a cousin or relative that I really need to connect with." Debra has concluded that creating a similar institution in Brazil, "especially with *afrodescendentes* in mind," would be highly desirable, as "a way to express [Afro-Brazilian] culture." "Listen," she said,

other people have their own churches, so it should happen with us. It would be a church that is very encompassing [*muito abrangente*] in the area of musical praise; it would work a lot with four or five voices; because churches that like to work with black music like to work with the bass, tenor, and soprano. It would include the choir a lot more than churches do now, in all of the work of the church. A church based in *afrodescendentes* would have music in every moment of the life of the church, and the main music would come from the choir. And that choir would be very participatory! The preacher would be preaching, and the choir would be participating in the message. Because the Levites of the church should participate in all the ministries of the church. The style would be to have the choir remain at the back and onstage throughout the entire service to give backup to the preacher.

Debra is pushing here, in her imagination, beyond anything currently in existence in Brazil, let alone in São Paulo. The church of Brazil for Christ in Brasilândia, strongly influenced by black gospel music, has a choir that opens the service for about twenty minutes, then leaves the stage. In Debra's conception, the choir needs to stay visible, onstage, for the whole service, as she imagines occurs in the United States. The key idea for Debra, and for others who spoke to me as she did, is the model of the call-and-response between preacher and choir. "I think of an *igreja negra*," she said, "as one in which you go back and forth, when the preacher reaches a very emotional passage, so that the singers would be able to join in and participate in that. That is my dream, that whoever is in front would be able to really lead the church in musicality and touch all of that beauty." Further, with all that energy circulating between preacher and choir, the audience would be in motion as well. "In such a church," Debra continued,

> both the singer and the congregants would feel the freedom to dance—not just the singer making those gestures up front, but everybody in the church would feel that they could stand up and move their bodies. People worship the Lord with great freedom. They're able to really dance and move their bodies in spite of all the suffering of bad things they've gone through. And that's valid! Let's see it happen here in Brazil.

If founding a black church in Brazil was the long-term dream of some black gospel singers, many of them had more immediate aspirations. In contrast to the gospel sambistas, most of the black gospel singers I got to know welcomed the idea of "looking for blacks in the Bible," and some had actually thought through what was needed to do so. Samuel, Daniel, Sérgio, and Isabêh were certain that Jesus was a *negro*, and Sérgio and Isabêh had consulted books that proved it. They all agreed that their churches should bring the study of the role of Africa and Africans into classes about the Bible. "It is only logical," said Daniel. "We must tell the truth, and the truth is that Africans are in the Bible." The head minister of the Mintre church, Joilson, himself a musician who worked energetically to support and expand his church's black gospel bands, directed his Sunday-school teachers to cover the question of *negros* in the Bible. Several young gospel artists I met had gone further: between 2002 and 2005, they participated in evening study groups to discuss the interconnections between the Bible, music, social history, and slavery. Isabêh described one of these groups:

> I made copies of things—articles, chapters in books—and we would bring our Bibles. We read books together, about the *história do negro*. And we discussed them. We couldn't keep this up all the time, but here is what we are trying to do: to understand the Bible's message for *o povo negro*. That's where we discovered that the Bible is full of prophecies which show us that *negros* have a special role, that our voices were anointed by God. So naturally we are interested in *o povo negro* in the Bible.

Given the presence of such ideological tendencies, it is not surprising that black gospel singers have become increasingly visible participants in activities having to do with the collective pro-*negro* movement. The Pão da Vida church, home of several black gospel singing groups, regularly organizes educational forums on blacks in the church and buying from black-owned businesses. Black gospel groups have been directly involved in planning these events and take the stage during such discussions to set the tone. Black gospel singer Sérgio Melo's church, COGIC-Azusa, is at the forefront of the *movimento negro evangélico*, through the organization of interchurch meetings of pastors to talk about racism and the need for more proactive, pro-black polices within churches. After performances, Sérgio Melo never misses an opportunity to speak about racism and the special responsibility churches have to eliminate feelings of racial inferiority among the saved. He regularly uses his pulpit to proclaim the virtues of affirmative action, the valorization of black beauty, support for black entrepreneurs, and nurturance of black leadership. In Azusa's Bible-study classes, Melo has insisted that teachers help students recognize the presence of *africanos* in the Holy Scriptures. He has led trips to Nigeria and Angola, to raise awareness among his followers of the deep connections between Christianity and the African people.[1] Melo is increasingly visible, giving interviews in on-line media to talk about racism in evangelical churches.[2]

Furthermore, in the few churches that have developed reputations for being "black" and that have organized events to talk in public about issues facing black people, head pastors have called on their congregations to establish black choirs. One such church, Igreja Apostólica Renovação, has become the home of a major black gospel choir—the Coral Renovation Mass Choir— which regularly performs at "Blackness and Faith" events. Coral Kadmiel, one the country's great black gospel choirs, recently partnered with Afrobrás to sing at events to promote the agenda of affirmative action and social inclusion,[3] and in 2010, it established a special chapter as the choir of the University of Citizenship Zumbi dos Palmares.[4] There is now a growing presence of black choirs, such as Coral Resgate, singing at events organized by the *movimento negro evangélico* to discuss racism and the need for a new Protestant black theology. Over the past few years, high-profile black gospel singers have helped organize and publicize the annual march for black consciousness in São Paulo.[5] Jamile Zeidan, a black gospel singer on the *paulista* circuit, has been notable for her leadership in these mobilizations.[6] Her sister, Daniela Zeidan, minister of music of the Pão de Vida church in São Paulo, has increasingly appeared in interorganizational forums to speak about the need for evangelical Christians to take a stand against racism.[7] Black gospel singers are increasingly creating webpages devoted to "Blacks in the Bible," "Black heroes," and black history (with the history of Zumbi, James Brown, Martin Luther King Jr., Nelson Mandela, Matilde Ribeiro, Milton Santos, and others).[8] It is thus no surprise that when Hernani da Silva, a leader of the MNE, wrote an on-line article (2004) arguing for the increased dialogue between black gospel musicians and the black evangelical movement, it quickly went viral, with hundreds of approving reposts. Clearly, black gospel singers are not just thinking about the need to struggle against racism; they are increasingly directly involved in the struggle.

The differences in blackness politics that I have analyzed in this chapter were on dramatic display during the process leading up to a workshop on the history of the black power music movement organized by the Mintre church in the fall of 2005. The pastor, a black gospel artist, took the lead, trying to ignite in others the same passion he felt about the idea of the workshop. The reception to his imprecations was a mixed bag, with the degree of interest

mappable strikingly onto musical scenes. In the end, most of the heavy lifting to prepare the workshop was accomplished by the church's main black
gospel band. The gospel rappers attended the workshop as listeners but participated very little in organizing it and made no presentations at the conference. The small gospel samba group did not participate at all.

Conclusion

Evangelicalism, Blackness, and Music in Brazil

My aim in this study has been to tease out from the bundle of forces that form racial identity the specific strand of music-making. How, I asked, do the practices of music shape the racial identities of their practitioners? To investigate this question, I compared musicians from three different São Paulo music scenes, holding constant their color (all called themselves *negro*) and religion (all were evangelicals). Here is what I found. First, being a gospel rapper means learning to identify with the *periferia*, absorbing chronologically recent musical history, and deploying vocal skills that rappers claim to be available to everyone, irrespective of race. These experiences, in turn, nurture a black identity that downplays essentialism and is filled with ideas of non-racially-based community with poor people everywhere. Second, being a gospel sambista means identifying with the Brazilian nation, internalizing the narrative of national hybridity, and becoming trained in a vocal style that purports to be available to all races. This, in turn, develops among its musicians a black identity skeptical of racial essentialism and insistent on Brazilianness. Third, being a black gospel singer means learning to identify with the North American black church, absorbing chronologically deep history about the connections between music and suffering, and mastering profoundly tough vocal skills. This experience, knowledge, and skill, in turn, unleash and sustain a proud, essentialist black identity, an identity so strong that it spills over into support for problack struggle. Finally, while gospel sambistas and gospel rappers sometimes speak of the struggle for racial justice, they are less interested in that struggle than are black gospel artists.

In this conclusion, I wish to discuss several implications of these findings: that scholars need to produce more research about evangelical blackness in Brazil, that they need to think not just about "blackness" but about "blacknesses," that the analytical approach adopted here has wider applicability, and that my empirical findings have strategic implications for Brazil's black evangelical movement.

The Need for More Research on Blackness and Evangelicalism

Over the next decade, the debates about race-related affirmative action in Brazil are likely to remain intense, the number of Brazilians identifying themselves as Protestant is likely to continue to grow, and the percentage of evangelicals calling themselves *negro* is likely to increase.[1] Given these trends, it will continue to be important to improve our understanding of the relations between evangelicalism and black identity in Brazil. This book contributes to that understanding, by showing that Brazilian Protestantism is fuller of ideas about blackness than has hitherto been appreciated. Yet studies of this theme are still rare, due to the presumption that looking at the intersection of religion and race in Brazil means studying the Afro-Brazilian religions candomblé and umbanda (e.g., Sansi 2009; Capone 2010; Lucena and Santos Lima 2009; Willeman and Lima 2010). Given that evangelicals outnumber *candomblecistas* in Brazil by thirty to one, surely it is time for more scholars to embrace the study of racial identity and Brazilian Christianity.[2]

Such research is especially timely now because, in contrast to the assumption that Brazil's evangelicals avoid racial struggles (Kelly 2010, 97; Oro 1997; Gonçalves da Silva 2007a, 2007b; Birman 1997; Giumbelli 2007; Selka 2010,

296; Contins 2008; Dawson 2008, 269; Motta 2009, 178), there is evidence that their participation in such struggles is growing. The number of projects and organizations of Brazilian evangelicals articulating an agenda of black identity now number at least sixty-five (cf. Burdick 2005). Consider the following examples. The Pastoral da Negritude, founded in 2005 in Macéio, Alagoas, currently involves about two dozen evangelicals in an effort it describes this way: "to awaken the evangelical community to a greater black consciousness, to rediscover among ourselves the African presence and culture in biblical history, to work toward the social inclusion of Afro-descendants, and to struggle against racial discrimination."[3] In 2010, the group partnered with other, nonevangelical black movement groups to educate *negros* about the census, sent a delegation to the census bureau to petition for more outreach to the black population, and assisted UNICEF at the local level to raise awareness about the impact of racism on children. Consider too the Fórum Permanente de Mulheres Cristãs Negras of Rio de Janeiro, which brings together two dozen women from a variety of Christian churches to organize seminars and workshops on black women's health. The group collaborated with other black movement groups in mid-2010 to defend the federal Ministry of Education when it instituted a new policy of editing children's literature by adding footnotes to provide historical context to racist language,[4] and it works regularly to place pressure on the public media to cover black issues. At the national level, meanwhile, the Aliança de Negras e Negros Evangélicos do Brasil is dedicated to promoting and strengthening the black evangelical movement. To realize this goal, it coordinates regional and national conferences such as the "Third Afro-Christian Meeting," held at the Methodist University in São Paulo in May 2011. At that conference, the theme was to develop strategies for combating racism within evangelical churches, including promoting courses on *negros* in the Bible, organizing public forums in churches about racism in Brazilian society, and supporting educational events that teach congregations about affirmative action. Clearly all such projects cry out for close examination: to what extent and how do these initiatives reflect and effect ideological shifts inside Brazil's evangelical churches?

More generally, there is some evidence that even evangelicals not involved in such groups have begun to develop stronger antiracist views. Anthropologist Steve Selka found in questionnaires administered in the early 2000s that evangelicals in Bahia were as critical of racism as were nonevangelicals.[5]

Sales Augusto dos Santos notes that many of the black movement activists he interviewed in the 2000s developed their antiracist views inside of their churches (2011). André Cicalo, writing of students at the State University of Rio de Janeiro in the mid-2000s, reports that a "majority of activist black quota students . . . practiced Pentecostal (particularly neo-Pentecostal) faiths" (2012, 134). My own research has shown repeatedly that evangelical theology sustains the principles of antiracism (Burdick 1998a, 1998b, 1999, 2005). We clearly need more research into the interrelations between evangelical Protestantism and Brazil's racial politics. We need, for example, to understand better how practices of courtship and marriage inside of churches reshape attitudes about marriages between people of different phenotypes; whether and how practices of leadership formation in churches reinforce or challenge societywide race-exclusionary norms; whether and how evangelical practices of preaching have created new opportunities for the creation of black public authority; and whether and how evangelical musical practices affect racial attitudes. And we need to see how such practices translate into arenas of public action both inside and beyond the church. Claims about most of these arenas are currently based on conjecture, hearsay, and fragmentary evidence. The time is long past for matters of this importance to receive the sustained empirical scrutiny they deserve.

Complicating Blackness

Over a decade ago, Edmund Gordon and Mark Anderson argued that the time was ripe for

> an ethnography of diaspora, conceived not simply as the ethnography of various communities of African descent but, rather, as an ethnography of various forms of diasporic politics and identification. Such a project might begin with the following questions: How do particular individuals and groups imagine themselves as members of a Black community beyond the confines of national or regional communities? With what peoples, regions, and movements do these individuals or groups most closely identify or align themselves? What role does the figure of Africa itself play in these imaginings and attachments? What are the local conditions that help shape diasporic identifications as racial and cultural politics? (1999, 289–290)

These questions are as timely now as ever for Brazil, a continental society of nearly two hundred million people, with enormous internal variety. What are all the different ways of being *negro* in Brazil? In this book, I posed this question to a small group of Protestant evangelical musicians; to pursue these questions for evangelicals throughout Brazil will require taking into account factors about which I have only scratched the surface: region, denomination, generation, gender, class, and phenotype. Without going into great detail, let me comment on how each of these might make a difference in the construction of blackness.

It has long been recognized that in a country as vast and diverse as Brazil, it is hard to develop reliable national-level claims about ethnic identity (Lesser 1999; Nava and Lauerhass 2006). While nationalizing forces such as media soften the edges of Brazil's regions, Brazil remains a society of regions, in which variations in the demographic balance between *negros, morenos,* and *brancos* (among other categories) have consequences for differences in the meaning of such things as "blackness" (Blake 2011; Dent 2009). For too long, such differences have been acknowledged in theory but unexamined in practice, so that studies of *negros* consistently purport—imprudently—to be about an abstraction named "the Brazilian black" (e.g., Nascimento 2006; Caldwell 2007; Bailey 2009). It makes a great deal of difference whether we are looking at blacks in São Paulo or Rio de Janeiro or Salvador or Recife or São Luiz or Belo Horizonte or Porto Alegre (cf. Blake 2011; Alberto 2009; Linger 1992; Sansone 2003; Andrews 1991; P. Pinho 2010; Perry 2009; Smith 2009). From my own work over the years, it has become clear to me that being black in São Paulo, with its higher proportions of self-identified *negros* and vibrant history of black mobilization (Butler 1998; Andrews 1991; Hanchard 1999), means something quite different from being black in Rio, with its higher proportion of *morenos* and weaker tradition of black militancy (Goldstein 2003; Burdick 1998b). Future research needs to delve more deeply into this kind of variation.

I have referred in this book to "evangelicals," without much further specification. But how might black identity unfold differently inside historical, Pentecostal, or neo-Pentecostal churches? Historical churches, all things being equal, tend to be more "liberal" and more interested in engaging with the world; how do such tendencies interact with black identity? To what extent, and in what ways, do Pentecostal theologies of world renunciation relate to critiques of racism? What are some of the effects on racial identity among neo-Pentecostals of their religion's aggressive stance toward Afro-Brazilian spiritualities? While there is research on these questions in other societies (Beckford 2006; Toulis 1997; Austin-Broos 1997; Baer 2001), there still is surprisingly little of it in Brazil. Equally important, there is a need to question studies of "blacks" that assume blackness can be understood in isolation from other ethnoracial identities. In this book, I have focused on people who identify themselves as *negros*, in order to detect variation by musical scenes, but I did not examine what it meant to be *branco* or *moreno*. While 43% of Brazilians identified themselves on the 2010 census as belonging to a "mixed" ethnoracial category,[6] there is only a small handful of studies that engage seriously with what it means in Brazil to be *mestiço*, *mulato*, or *moreno* (Cantalice 2011; Ribeiro 2010; Pinho 2009; Pravaz 2012; Burdick 1998b). When these identities are referenced in the literature, it is frequently to say that they belong to people who have not yet realized that they are *negros* (e.g., Racusen 2009; Caldwell 2007); rarely are they given the more nuanced attention they deserve (a notable recent exception is Silva and Reis 2012). Similarly, though majorities of evangelicals often identify themselves as white, this whiteness remains unmarked and unanalyzed (but see Cardoso 2011). There is therefore a need to understand how such subjectivities are shaped and infused by evangelical ideas and practices. Only then will we be able to grasp the range of potentialities among evangelicals for effecting change in Brazil's dominant modes of ethnoracial discourse.

Refining Musical Analysis

I have focused in this book on three themes in musical practice that, I have suggested, endow collective identity with social density and weight: place, history, and the body. While there may be other themes in music that also contribute to the formation of collective identity, such as "culture," "tradition," or "custom," I chose to highlight place, history, and body because they possess, in my view, three important qualities. First, as analytical terms they are *versatile*: the "places" referred to may be real or imagined, near or far, huge or tiny; the "history" invoked may be long or short, national or regional, divine or mundane; and the "body" thematized may be sexual or sacred, hot or cold, alive or dead. Second, they are *concrete*: "place" evokes particular territories; "history" draws us into particular narratives of human action; "body" triggers associations with real corporeal experience. Finally, and most importantly, they are inextricably tied to *continuity* or *duration* over time. Philosopher Elizabeth Grosz has argued that visions of the future derive their appeal from being anchored in "three processes": "the forces and energies of bodies, . . . the pull or impetus of time, . . . and spaces of inhabitation" (2001, 137). She claims that these three elements endow utopic visions with social force because they give them the feel of durability through time. In a similar fashion, I argue that ideas and practices about place, time, and the body confer on ideas of collective identity the feeling of density, mass, solidity, momentum, and durability through time. These features of an idea are clearly important if one is expected to become dedicated to it. There is even, I want to suggest, a deep parallel between music-making and identity-formation. On the one hand, music-makers seek to endow their music with solidity, depth, transmissibility from generation to generation, and stable connections between the people who play it. On the other hand, these same goals are sought by identity-makers. Both groups, music-makers and identity-makers, find in ideas about the body, places, and history fundamental cognitive resources for making their respective cultural activities durable over time, socially sinewy, and transmissible. It thus is not surprising that these two fields of experience and endeavor overlap.

This idea is corroborated by research on the music-identity nexus. Reviewing scholarship that investigates this nexus, what emerges repeatedly is authors' reliance on generic, metaphorical statements that music "expresses" or is a "vehicle" for identity or that it "shapes" or "constructs" it. What is lacking is some sense of priority in the processes that link music and identity, that make one good to think the other with. Yet what is striking about the literature is that so central are the experiential drivers of place, body, and history in the logic of the music-identity nexus that in all of these analyses one invariably finds one, two, or all three of them present in a single study, even when the author does not highlight them.

Consider Chayantaka music in highland Bolivia. Here, a key component of ethnic identity is the social labor that Carnaval singing groups invest in defining their attachment to a particular region, by crisscrossing it physically, marking its boundaries, and referring to features of the landscape in song. In song battles, the logics of belonging, possession, and rivalry are articulated between specific stretches of territory and specific social collectivities, when youths from different communities declare themselves to be their landscapes and that theirs is more beautiful than the other (Solomon 2000). While these logics go a long way in rendering visible how music relates to identity- and subject-formation, our triadic model allows us to dig even deeper, to discover another layer in how the Chayantaka singing groups give tangible, solid, experiential substance to ethnic identity. Consider what we can see when we look for the logic of bodies here. Suddenly a whole dimension of the singing opens up, as we learn that Carnaval singers are unmarried youths who use their singing trips to meet and reinvigorate sexual relations with marriageable Chayantaka women. Upon closer inspection, the songs are about being Chayantaka not only because of the places they invoke but because of the sexual unions they are about to have, that promise in fact to propagate the next generation of Chayantaka bodies. That is why, I suggest, the language of the songs is so rich in sexual imagery and innuendo, from dancing over the luscious beauty of the fields to eating potatoes dug out of the earth with loving hands, to placing potatoes into "ovens made of earth." As for the dimension of time, the whole account is suffused with an awareness of chronological depth, as proof of continuity over the generations: every place-name carries with it narrative fragments of how these places originally became endowed with the features they have, invoking ancestral memories. Together, the invocation of place, fertile bodies, and ancestral depth communicate solidity and survivability of the ethnic group.[7]

But one need not push this hard to discover all three sources of identity-formation within a given music. In study after study, these axes of identity are frequently all in conversation with each other, without, however, the researcher theorizing or highlighting them. Consider Peter Manuel's splendid analysis of flamenco's relationship to Andalusian identity. What are the linkages? Manuel points to them all, without theorizing them as specific or central linkages. He draws our attention, first, to the role in flamenco of the body, in this case, the body-in-the-voice: "Valued in flamenco," he writes, "are stylistic features specifically associated with gypsies, such as raspy vocal timbre, sobbing-like falsetto breaks, and a generally strenuous, impassioned, and histrionic vocal style" (1989, 55). This group-music linkage via the body is reinforced through a particular reading of history, for the "cry of pain" implied in this raspiness is part and parcel of a narrative that flamenco enthusiasts keep alive, "of the persecuted gypsies, but in a more general sense, of Andalusians as a whole, whose post-reconquest history of poverty and exploitation has only been aggravated by the memory of their former glory under the Moors" (ibid., 52). Thus are we drawn into a tight ethnos-invigorating triad of body, history, and place: for the narrative of gypsies idealized by Romantic writers through the eighteenth and nineteenth centuries are, it turns out, closely associated with the cities of Andalusia (ibid.). Separately, vocal raspiness, historical persecution, and living in particular cities are all possible contributors to a sense of identity; together, they produce a dense, textured, sinewy ethnic sensibility (cf. Thompson 1991). It is to Manuel's credit that he documents all three of these dimensions of the music-identity nexus; hopefully, by rendering these more explicit, we can make public and useful a tool that allows other researchers to analyze how music works to generate or support ethnic identity.

Lest I seem to be arguing that practices of body, place, and history always sustain restrictive, narrow, bounded identities, I hasten to point out that no such logic is necessary. Musico-bodily practices can, for example, as readily weaken as reinforce ideologies of connection between specific types of music and specific ideas of collective bodies; indeed, in this book, I have argued that this is precisely what transpires in gospel rap. A similar example is provided by Lara Allen's analysis of vocal jive in 1950s apartheid South Africa. Allen attributes the working-class appeal of vocal jive to its tight embrace of local melodic traditions and lyrics that describe in detail immediate events and places familiar to its low-income listening audience. "Certainly," she writes, "the record-buying public enjoyed music that expressed a locally-rooted identity, for many numbers incorporating local melodies, current township argot, and topical subject matter became hits" (2003, 234). Yet by incorporating musical motifs of both European and African derivation in a hybrid mix, vocal jive became vivid, experience-near proof that apartheid's rigid biological theory of irreconcilable bodies was a lie. In Allen's analysis, musical hybridity becomes a declaration of the falsity of racial (bodily) separatism, an implicit claim that music transcended bodily difference to reveal what people had in common across the racial divide.

I could adduce more examples, but these should suffice to indicate the importance of the body-place-history triad in grasping the processes through which music generates, strengthens, and sometimes weakens ethnic identities. Yet I want also to suggest that the model is in need of further refinement, in at least three ways. First, as it currently stands, there is no gainsaying that it suffers from a whiff of arbitrariness. Why place, body, and time? Certainly these are important dimensions of human experience, but what privileges them in relation to music and identity? I have at several points suggested that these dimensions are particularly well suited to articulating and reinforcing belief in durability over time: places appear to survive beyond the fragile mobility of human volition and whim; bodies are the sites for the perpetuation of intergenerational continuities; and history is the public account of events and acts that reveal and invest "a people" with enduring moral agency, virtues, and qualities. These durabilities, I have suggested, are what we mean by identity. As a working hypothesis, this formulation is a reasonable one. Yet do places, bodies, and histories possess ideologically any more solidity-reinforcing features than, say, "culture"? Are all cultural practices—such as cuisine, sport, games, clothing—reducible to one or some of these three dimensions? If so, is there a level at which they may be redescribed as variants of something more encompassing, such as social labor, nature, human agency, or power? In order to push the model to the next level and to enrich its capacity to interface with broader theories of historical change, these questions will need to be addressed.

Second, the model, while useful in revealing certain aspects of musical/identity subjectivity, remains hamstrung in others. The triad is undoubtedly useful in focusing our attention on areas of music that are experience rich in ways that can be described in everyday, nontechnical language. Thus, the triad helps broach the linguistic wall surrounding musical experience, which is so often portrayed as insurmountable. How the musician feels about his or her music-making body (cf. Eidsheim 2011), how he or she feels about music-referenced places, how he or she feels when hearing a particular history of the genre—these can and should be brought into the ken of what we mean by "musical experience." Yet, when all is said and done, the model is better at drawing us ethnographically into the technically nonmusical than into the musical dimensions of music scenes. Our thesaurus of descriptors of musical experience still remains clumsy and limited. How often can we write phrases such as "explosive gusts of air" and hope that this corresponds even roughly to what it is like to belt? Are we destined as writers about music to what Simon Frith once described as the default mode, which is to beckon the reader to listen to the CD and be done with it?

Finally, like most models, this one remains refractory when confronted by the vicissitudes of agency, individuality, and conjunctural shifts in battles for power and dominance. How stable, for example, are the black gospel scene's problack attitudes? To what extent are these mainly the outcome of durable features of the genre (i.e., its vocal practices, its dedication to certain histories, its attraction to the North American black church), as I have argued; and to what extent are they the effects of the political views of the particularly influential black gospel musicians who just happen to espouse them? Obviously this is not an either/or; certainly it is desirable in any thorough analysis to take into account both the structure of the conjuncture and the structure of the structure. Thus, for example, in accounting for the decentering of "race" in the ideological project of gospel rap, it is useful to point out the rootedness of the genre in immediate locality (with its interracial implications) but also to point to shifts in conjunctural moments of social forces selecting for or against this centrality, issuing from the state and international media. The challenge is not to give in to the temptation of claiming that we have found the keys to the magic box. Conjuncture, history, and contingency always remain powerful shaping forces in determining what a current identity looks like and whether it will endure. The weakness of the triad model, then, is that it does not adequately incorporate awareness of this contingency and thus runs the risk of leading its users to overlook it. It would therefore be useful to work toward historicizing the model, rendering it sensitive to the volatile flows of power.

Ethnography and Strategy

Over the course of the past decade, I have been in close communication with leaders in the *movimento negro evangélico*, and as described in the introduction, my choices of topic and questions were influenced by the concerns and agenda of those leaders. Hernani da Silva, Luiz de Jesus, and Rolf da Souza have all encouraged me to pursue this project, invested as they are in understanding the political potential of building alliances with musicians on the black gospel scene. In reports I have made to them of my findings, I have suggested the value of an outreach strategy to artists who sing and direct black gospel music, rather than to those immersed in the worlds of gospel rap or gospel samba. This suggestion, after being met with some skepticism, is beginning to gain traction among MNE leaders. Hernani da Silva, one of the key organizers of the MNE, has published in response to my work a widely circulating article that suggests that black gospel music and the MNE are currently both part of the black movement but are "running along separate tracks" (Silva 2004). He has also recently appeared on national Brazilian television touting the view that there are potential intersections between the two movements. In his view, black gospel music operates mainly to attract blacks to the church, appealing to their sense of "attitude" and "pride." The music scene does not, however, in his view, generate much in the way of reflection or strategy. For that, one must turn to the MNE. Eventually, he says, "the two movements will converge, and we will walk the path and struggle together."[8]

Hernani's position reveals both the potentiality and limitations of activist ethnography. On the one hand, it suggests that careful ethnography, shared with stakeholders, advocates, and leaders, can have an effect on their thinking about hidden allies and possible new targeted constituencies. On the other, it suggests something of the discrepancy between the time lines of ethnography and social activism. Ethnography can reveal hidden, fragmentary, slow-moving dimensions of consciousness that can serve as hooks for reaching new audiences. Yet even such hooks come up against the limits of time, resources, and energy. How much energy should MNE activists expend in struggling to connect with and recruit musicians of black gospel? How much more energy should they dedicate to working with gospel rappers to persuade them to incorporate antiracism into their lyrics? MNE activists want to see results sooner rather than later in getting their churches to embrace the policy initiatives of the government about affirmative action and to begin to use the spaces of the church to educate a generation of young Christians about the importance of Africa in the Bible and fighting racism in the here and now. From this point of view, an ethnography of musicians may appear a luxury the movement can ill afford.

Yet I would argue the case the other way. The MNE began in the 1980s and is now sort of stuck, having added only a small handful of organizations to its roster since 2005. The movement is important but has been experiencing the same bottleneck that the secular black movement has long faced, that of identifying and connecting with a broader base of nonactivists. While the Internet has helped in this regard (the movement's main website, Afrokut, now has over five thousand members), the movement has not succeeded in transforming those numbers into consistent face-to-face meetings at which long-term strategic projects and decision-making can be undertaken. When we look at the roster of organizations of the MNE, they are quite top-heavy; that is, there are more regional and national "alliances" than local, grassroots organizations. (The locally based MNE organizations I described earlier are more the exception than the rule.) In this context, at the local level, a rich reservoir of evangelical leaders who seem to be thinking a good deal about race, blackness, history, and alternative strategic futures happen to be black gospel musicians. That, at least, is the claim of the present work. My ethnography has revealed, I submit, not just a world that is about "pride" but one that generates and sustains complex cognitive labor and reflection. As the MNE enters into its third decade, struggling to enlarge its base and to enrich its strategic thinking, I urge its leaders to take steps to visit, call, e-mail, and communicate with the directors and leaders of their city's gospel choirs. In that articulation, I further submit, lies a significant potential future of the movement.

A final suggestion: as indicated throughout this book, there are sites in Brazilian evangelical Protestantism which nurture complex thinking supportive of black ethnoracial identity, pride in African ancestry, enthusiasm for knowing more about African history, and antiracism. The sites I have examined here are music-making ones, but there are others as well. The MNE is growing and significant. Evangelical blacks are at the forefront of the students entering college supported by affirmative action. Evangelicals are growing in number, are not about to disappear, and far outnumber *candomblecistas*. The position of some churches, such as the Universal Church of the Kingdom of God, that it is acceptable to physically assault candomblé temples is a minority view; most evangelicals reject candomblé theologically but are not interested in attacking temples, since they regard the ultimate fate of non-Christian practitioners to be in the hands of God. Given all of this, it makes sense for secular black movement activists to reach out and strive to find common ground with the MNE and with other evangelicals who are sympathetic to the goals of the movement, such as musicians of black gospel. There is evidence that evangelicals who have found themselves on panels with *mães de santo* of candomblé have begun to see them in a different, more tolerant light. Encouraging more such panels, united under the banners of black identity and antiracism, could go a long way toward easing some of the tensions that currently exist.

But of course, we ethnographers must be wary of making recommendations to anyone. Our strength is our ability to illumine darkened places, to lift shadows, to help the socially unseen, unheard, or misunderstood be seen, heard, and better understood. If this work has done any of these things, it has achieved its purpose.

NOTES

NOTES TO THE INTRODUCTION

1. In Brazil's ethnoracial lexicon, *morena* is translated as "brown." Widely considered a "positive" term, it has been deployed since the 1930a as a diplomatic way to refer to African ancestry. In contrast, between the 1890s and the 1980s, the term *negra*, often translated as "black," carried a negative connotation. Since the 1990s, *negra* caught on as a term of pride and self-respect. Still, today fewer people with African heritage identify themselves as *negros* than as *moreno*, *mestiço* (mixed), or *mulato* (mulatto). In the 2010 census, 7.6% of all Brazilians identified themselves as *negros*, while 43.1% identified themselves as *pardo*—an artificial census category that no one uses in everyday life but that corresponds for the purpose of the census to all "mixed-race" terms of reference; 47.7% of Brazilians told census takers in 2010 that they were *branco* (white). For recent, high-quality analyses of Brazil's still-evolving racial terminological system, see Bailey 2009 and Silva and Reis 2011.

2. While there has been no large-scale survey of differential treatment of siblings by color in Brazil, qualitative evidence suggests a pattern of inequality between sisters of different degrees of darkness. See Sheriff 2001, Burdick 1998b, and P. Pinho 2009.

3. Given the expectation that families should be places of love and acceptance, disapproval of one's phenotype by close family members is particularly devastating in Brazil. For a broader discussion of intrakin racism, see Wade 2009, 156–160.

4. I use the term *racism*, for Brazil, to refer to patterned differential treatment and attitudes, supported by powerful institutions, that favor people of European and disfavor people of African and/or indigenous descent. These attitudes and treatment favor people with phenotypes closer to a European "white" ideal and disfavor those whose phenotype reveals African or indigenous descent. See Winant 2001, 317. The terms *race*, *racism*, and *racial* are not at all foreign to Brazilian culture, having been current there since the abolition of slavery. See Dávila 2003, Stepan 1996, and Schwarcz 1999.

5. "Zumbi" is the name normally used to refer to the leader of the major runaway-slave community in Pernambuco known in the late seventeenth century as Palmares. In 1693, this leader defended the community against a concerted assault by the massed Portuguese-Dutch military and lost. Legend has it that Zumbi fought a heroic last stand and that after his defeat the conquering Europeans

placed his head on a stake and paraded it through the countryside. The black movement in Brazil has long advocated for the establishment of the date marking the death of Zumbi—November 20—as a national holiday. See Hanchard 2008.

6. Whites in São Paulo in 2005 registered a 3.4% illiteracy rate, while *negros* and *pardos* had a 6.5% rate. (Nationally the contrast was 7% for white versus 15% for *negros* and *pardos*.) IBGE 2006, 249. Meanwhile, in São Paulo, whites registered a 10.7% functional illiteracy rate, and *negros* and *pardos*, an 18% rate. See ibid.

7. In 2006, the literacy rate by race/color and gender was the following in Brazil: white males, 93.7%; white females, 93.3%; black males (black and brown), 85.9%; black females (black and brown), 84.9% (Paixão and Carvano, 2008, 68). See also Jaccoud and Theodoro 2007. Cicalo reports, "Although differences seem smaller in relation to the *ensino fundamental* (schooling of people between seven and 14 years old), white people over 15 years old in 2006 studied for an average of 8.0 years, whereas their 'black' counterparts (brown + black people) studied for just 6.2 years" (2012, 8).

8. According to Brazil's Pesquisa Nacional de Amostragem de Domicílio (2006), in 2005, three-quarters of the poorest quintile of Brazil's population was still made up of nonwhites. Nonwhites were 67.9% of the population among the poorest 10%; their monthly income averaged 500 reais, while whites' monthly income averaged 986 reais; in São Paulo, nonwhites earned an average of 3.98 reais per hour, while whites earned an average of 7.33 reais per hour; of the eight million people living in favelas, 66% were headed by nonwhites, 33% by whites. Whites earned an average of 5 times the minimum wage in São Paulo, while *pretos* and *pardos* earned only an average of 2.5 times the minimum wage.

9. That is, 115 deaths per 100,000 versus 54 per 100,000. See Chor and Risso de Araujo 2005, 1589.

10. That is, 275 per 100,000 versus 43 per 100,000. Ibid., 1588; see also F. Oliveira 2002.

11. See also IBGE 2010.

12. In 2006, 14.5% of *brancos* fell below the poverty line, while over 33% of *pretos* did so.

13. Marco Davi Oliveira, personal communication, March 2011.

14. Datafolha 2007.

15. Franco 2010.

16. Madambashi 2011.

17. In the 2010 presidential election, all the major candidates actively courted evangelicals. See Franco 2010.

18. The term *pardo* is rarely used in everyday speech. It is a census term that covers, broadly, all people who identify themselves to census takers according to one of the "mixed race" terms, such as *moreno*, *mulato*, and *mestiço*.

19. n a similar spirit, leaders of the Igreja Universal do Reino de Deus in Salvador refused to allow anthropologist Steve Selka to conduct interviews with congregants when they discovered that he intended to broach the topic of race. See Selka 2007, 105.

20. The Brazil-based social networking site Orkut currently hosts dozens of virtual communities that identify themselves as having to do with being *negro* and *evangélico*, such as Negros Evangélicos, Movimento Negro Evangélico, and 100% Negros Evangélicos.

21. In a recent analysis of affirmative action at the State University of Rio de Janeiro, for example, anthropologist André Cicalo found that many of the black militants he came to meet were evangelical Protestants. See Cicalo 2012.

22. More generally, bodily movement may be regarded as the occasion for the public display of "sexiness," which indexes, in part, the ability of a group to maintain continuity over generations (i.e., through procreation). Tamara Johnson, for example, suggests that talk about the "naturalness" and "untrained" quality of the On-1 dancers (in contrast to the trained, methodical qualities of the On-2 dancers) moves quickly into talk about the "sexiness" of the former. The idea of "sexiness" evokes ideas of inherency, innateness, inner substances and properties transmissible through procreation. Sexiness is something one can enhance and work on, but it is, ultimately, a feature rather than an achievement of the self. The ethnic-identity dimension of this emerges because the majority of On-1 dancers (the "sexy" ones) are Latinos, while the majority of the On-2 dancers are not. This contrast reinforces the association of Latino descent (ultimately, blood) with certain "natural," inborn properties that cannot be taught or acquired through training or in the classroom—of swing, spontaneity, "cool," and sexiness. See Johnson 2011, 109.

NOTES TO CHAPTER 1

1. A key force in this trend was the enormously innovative rap group Racionais MCs. One of the most striking patterns I found in all of my interviews was the near-universal acclaim heaped on the Racionais, especially Mano Brown (the lead MC of the group), who was regarded as someone who had stood for a vision—that of speaking truth to power, of seeking to represent the voices and reality of black people. The respect felt toward the group was palpable. Every rapper I interviewed recounted one version or another of what they were doing when they heard the iconic albums *Holocausto Urbano*, *Escolha o Seu Caminho*, and *Sobrevivendo no Inferno*. Listen to Dexter, describing the moment he heard "Panico na Zona Sul" for the first time, in 1990: "So a friend put on a song called 'Panico na Zona Sul,' by a group called Racionais MCs. Man, I started to listen to that song, and I had to sit down on my bed. So I sat down on the bed, and I said, 'Man, what is this?' I sat there listening, and I said, 'My God, what is this?' That thing spoke to me immediately—the beat,

the lyric—spoke to me immediately, and I said, 'Geez, God, that's it exactly. That is what I want to do.'"

2. Derek Pardue has noted that on the tracks of the Racionais' 1997 album, "the term 'negro' disappears and 'preto' is reduced to solely its assumed impoverished banality" (2008, 111).

3. As Derek Pardue has argued, these NGOs were "general in focus." They were "faced with fundamental problems of violence (police and drug traffickers), shortage of basic public services (sanitation, water, health, education, pavement, transportation), and general social stigma. . . . Organizations such as Projeto Monte Azul, CEDECA (Center for the Defense of Children and Adolescents), Aldeia de Futuro, and Ação Educativa have been instrumental in providing financial support for hip-hop culture as part of neighborhood life on an everyday basis" (Pardue 2008, 55).

4. It is also pertinent to note that in 1993, one of the Racionais MCs' white crew members was murdered, an event that seems to have impressed on the group the fact that the tough streets of São Paulo did not discriminate by race. Many observers have noted that in that year their lyrics shifted from utopian preaching to the stark realism of the song "X-Ray of Brazil."

5. Projeto Vida Nova, "Evangelismo estratégico de Carnaval: Bloco Cara de Leão," http://www.projetovidanova.com.br/galeriaEvangCarnaval/galeria.htm (accessed 5/11/12).

6. GustavoXimenes, "Ala Ilusão—Bloco Car de Leão 2007," YouTube, September 20, 2007, http://www.youtube.com/watch?v=AhpodqPCigY&feature=related. None of this went unopposed inside the church. "There were some who called the minister 'Rei Momo gospel' [a derogatory way to refer to a sambista]," explained Projeto Nova Vida's musical director. "Someone threw stones at the church. We found an improvised bomb inside. . . . Someone even threw a big concrete block at the car of the brothers who were active in the *bloco*." See "Estratégia ou inovação? Igrejas Criam Estratégias para o Carnaval," *Diones Brito* (blog), January 29, 2009, http://dionesbrito.blogspot.com/2009/01/29012009002547-igrejas-criam.html.

7. GustavoXimenes, "Bateria do Bloco Cara de Leão 2007," YouTube, September 28, 2007, http://www.youtube.com/watch?v=6a9TWx3yDdw.

8. The term *crentes*, which means "believers," went through a period of decline in everyday use in the 1990s and early 2000s, but by 2005, it was back in style, as a term of ironic self-designation.

9. Bicudo's widow, interviews by Rolf da Souza, 2006–2007.

10. 10. Josué and Josias, directors of Kadoshi, interview with the author, November 2005. See also Alberto 2009.

11. This musical movement laced rock and roll with samba and bossa nova. See Dunn 2001, 58–61.

12. This argument received a boost during this period from the Victors for Christ (VPC) mission, which famously promoted rock and roll in the name of Jesus.

In-house history of VPC available at http://www.vpc.com.br/website/ (accessed 6/30/08).

13. I have assembled this history from several long interviews with Isabêh, one of the major chroniclers of the movement, as well as with members of Kadoshi, the heirs of Os Redimidos and Atos II. A good on-line account of this musical period may be found at the UniversoMusical website: http://www.universomusical.com.br/materia.asp?mt=sim&id=165&cod=go (accessed 7/18/05).

14. Throughout my gathering of narratives for this chapter, the identification of Pedra Viva as a Brazilian Apollo Theater was constant. In particular, Robson Nascimento and Isabêh insisted on this point. Their knowledge of the Apollo Theater came via cinema and the recordings of R&B artists. Pregador Luo, an unorthodox gospel rapper, was also a fount of information on this point. In addition to my interviews with him, see his published interviews at http://www.7tacas.com.br (accessed 5/3/06).

15. The members of Kadoshi insisted repeatedly on this point. They were inspired, they said, by the Holy Spirit to bring the word of God in the most convincing, effective way they knew how to new, young audiences. The agenda of racial pride emerged secondarily, after they had committed to the musical style and found themselves asked and expected to take a public stand on racial issues. Pregador Luo makes this point in his interviews at http://www.7tacas.com.br (accessed 5/2/06).

16. The number is an estimate based on interviews with gospel music recording producers and the encyclopedically minded Isabêh, as well as my own informal count based on extensive searching for groups between 2003 to 2005.

17. By the early 1990s, for example, Renascer em Cristo, São Paulo's second-largest neo-Pentecostal church, was hosting the largest annual Christian music festival in Latin America and running Gospel Records, the biggest Christian music label in the country. At the very same time, in Rio de Janeiro, in response to the explosion of funk dances, widely seen as hotbeds of crime and violence, several large neo-Pentecostal churches began to experiment with evangelical funk music, as a way to steal souls back from the devil. See Pinheiro 2003.

18. Images of black choirs had been around for a while in Brazil; it is just that they had not yet been disseminated so widely as in the 1990s. Images of black choirs arrived in Brazil in the early 1960s via the film *Imitation of Life* (1959) and television reports on the civil rights struggle, but it was not until the 1990s that Brazilians could rent and buy videotapes of black choirs or of films with choir scenes such as *Blues Brothers* (1980), *The Color Purple* (1985), *Go Tell It on the Mountain* (1985), *Mississippi Burning* (1988), and *Driving Miss Daisy* (1989). One of my informants reported having rented the video of *Imitation of Life* fifty times just to watch the finale. On the representation of black choirs in US film, see Lindvall, Terry, and Williams 1996.

NOTES TO CHAPTER 2

1.
> A luz vai brilhar na periferia,
> a luz vai brilhar trazendo amor e alegria
> Periferia, favela, viela, parceiro morto, mano na cela
> Revolta que cega, acorda limpa a remela
> Lava esse rosto, Cristo te espera
> Te chama, por ti ele clama, saia da lama
> esqueça da fama, esqueça da grana
> Algo melhor ele tem pra ti
> mais é você que vai decidir
> não siga o diabo e não siga a mim
> Somente pra Cristo tem que dizer sim

2. Here are the percentages of people in these neighborhoods who identify as *branco*: Marsilac, 59%; Iguatemi, 63%; Cidade Tiradentes, 50% ; Brasilândia, 58%; Cidade Ademar, 56%; Guaianazes, 52%. These numbers are reported by Vargas and Alves 2010.

3. There is one exception: the accent of the *preto velho*. A variety of linguistic markers set aside this accent, associated in Brazilian popular culture with the nineteenth-century black slave and embodied in the figure of the *preto velho*, a spirit in the Afro-Brazilian religion of umbanda. However, this accent is restricted to the world of umbanda and has not penetrated everyday social life to be used by any living population of Brazilians.

4. A. H. Chapman, comment on "My century . . . the story of the twentieth century—told by those who made it," BBC World Service website, http://www.bbc.co.uk/worldservice/people/features/mycentury/living.shtml (accessed 6/26/10).

5. Carlos69, comment on "Ebonics in Brazil?," *Thorn Tree Travel Forum*, Lonely Planet, December 12, 2009, http://www.lonelyplanet.com/thorntree/thread.jspa?threadID=1853865 (accessed 6/26/10).

6. Jimeluiz, comment on ibid

NOTES TO CHAPTER 3

1. 505damush, "Nelson Cavaquinho—Vou Partir," YouTube, July 3, 2008, http://www.youtube.com/watch?v=BtEhO4hYKbg.

2. Nandabroering, "Dori Caymmi—O bem do mar," YouTube, December 24, 2008, http://www.youtube.com/watch?v=OtzCx9lFxf8.

3. Emersonpantuzzo, "Cartola—Peito Vazio," YouTube, October 5, 2010, http://www.youtube.com/watch?v=6sHyXB3e89M&feature=fvsr.

4. Scavenger100, "Paulo César Pinheiro—Poema Capitão," YouTube, April 8, 2008, http://www.youtube.com/watch?v=HdLDZuoqucQ&feature=related.

5. 5. Juliano Coelho, comment on Murilo Mendes, "Pra cantar samba se precisa muito mais . . . ," *Vermute com Amendoim* (blog), October 25, 2007, http://www.vermutecomamendoim.com/2007/10/pra-cantar-samba-se-precisa-muito-mais.html.

6. Mendes, "Pra cantar samba se precisa muito mais . . ."
7. Valéria n.d.
8. baixo2356, "Samba Gospel—Divina Unção," YouTube, December 18, 2007, http://www.youtube.com/watch?v=1YAemdLbvhg&feature=related.
9. baixo2356, "Samba Gospel Brasil," YouTube, June 30, 2008, http://www.youtube.com/watch?v=FjNBMQTsblM.

10.

Brasil, meu brasileiro toque o pandeiro de norte a sul
Brasil, meu brasileiro mostre ao estrangeiro quem é Jesus
Verde amarelo branco azul da cor de anil
Este é o colorido da bandeira do Brasil
Nela esperança a riqueza céu de paz
Pois Jesus comanda este país de terra e mar
Brasil, meu brasileiro toque o pandeiro de norte a sul
Brasil, meu brasileiro mostre ao estrangeiro quem é Jesus
Cuíca, berimbau, chocalho, dá uma geral
Cavaco, pandeiro, surdo, Sou brasileiro
Samba sem fronteira e Jesus Cristo na nossa bandeira
País que é um gigante e acordou pro mundo inteiro
Pode alimentar muitas nações com seu celeiro
Nele há um pão vivo que sustenta e satisfaz
Quem dele comer nunca mais fome sentirá
Brasil meu brasileiro toque o pandeiro de norte a sul
Brasil meu brasileiro mostre ao estrangeiro quem é Jesus
Jesus campeão o Rei da salvação
No jogo da vida a única saída
Só ele ressuscitou e este samba é pro meu Senhor
Brasil meu brasileiro toque o pandeiro de norte a sul
Brasil meu brasileiro mostre ao estrangeiro quem é Jesus

11.

Brasil, meu Brasil brasileiro,
Meu mulato inzoneiro,
Vou a cantar-te nos meus versos.
Ô Brasil, samba que dá
Bamboleio que faz gingá.
Ô Brasil do meu amor,
Terra do Nosso Señor,
Brasil, Brasil, prá mim, prá mim!
Ô abre a cortina do passado.
Tira a mae preta do cerrado.
Bota o rei congo no congado.
Brasil, Brasil, prá mim, prá mim!
Deixa cantar de novo o trovador

Á merencória luz da lua
Toda canção de meu amor.
Quero ver a Sà Dona caminando
Pelos saloes arrastrando
O seu vestido rendado.
Brasil, Brasil, prá mim, prá mim!
Brasil, terra boa e gostosa,
Da moreninha sestrosa,
De olhar indiferente.
Ô Brasil, verde que dá
Para o mundo admirá.
Ô Brasil do meu amor,
Terra do Nosso Señor,
Brasil, Brasil, prá mim, prá mim!
Ô, esse coqueiro que dá coco,
Oi onde amarro a minha rede
Nas noites claras de luar.
Brasil, Brasil.
Ô oi estas fontes murmurantes,
Oi onde eu mato a minha sede
E onde a lua vem brincá.
Oi, esse Brasil lindo e trigueiro
É o meu Brasil brasileiro,
Terra de samba e pandeiro.
Brasil, Brasil, prá mim, prá mim

12. Brazilian Ministry of Culture, "Dia nacional do samba," November 30, 2007, http://www.cultura.gov.br/site/2007/11/30/aviso-de-pauta-8/.

13. Delcio Luiz, interview by Lila Arajo, Sambando website, http://sambando.com/entrevista_delcioluiz.html (accessed 6/3/09).

14. Rogério, a sambista who introduced samba into his Assembly of God church, said that showing the flag tapped into the tradition of evangelical obedience to the state. "The colors of the flag calm people down," Rogério explained. "They look up at the front, see the colors, and say, 'Oh, this can't be so bad, because the government has approved it.'"

NOTES TO CHAPTER 4

1. For a general analysis of the spiritual conceptualization of voice in Brazilian gospel, see Penteado, Silva, and Pereira 2008.

2. Mark Baxter, "FAQ's Vocal Damage," VoiceLesson.com, http://www.voicelesson.com/html/faq/faq_03.htm (accessed 5/27/12).

3. A separate analysis could be undertaken on racial ideology in Brazilian scientific research. Journals in *fonoaudiologia*, for example, routinely consider the physiology of "*negro* vocal timbre" (Camargo and Andrada e Silva 2006; Coelho

2006). A review of research in *fonoaudiologia* sought "to clarify the causes of the vocal differentiation of singers of a race distinguished by the extreme beauty of their voices" (S. Pinho 2001, 89). *Fonoaudiologistas* integrate into their courses the idea that the difference between *negro* and white singing is due to a difference in cranial and laryngeal structures. See "Timbre???," discussion on "Canto" forum of fórum.cifraclub.com.br, February 23, 2005, http://forum.cifraclub. terra.com.br/forum/1/79194/; and Patricia Valeriano Nolli, "A busca do equilíbrio através do canto," *Revelação Online*, http://www.revelacaoonline.uniube.br/ a2002/campus/semi15.html (accessed 5/11/12). In the United States, voice science rejects racial explanations of vocal performance or capacity (Corey et al. 1998; An Xue and Hao 2006; Miller 2004, 220). Julianna Sabol, professor of voice at Syracuse University, notes that in the United States there is no research on the role of racial difference to explain singing voice qualities because it would be impossible to get such research funded.

4. The handout also argued, incidentally, that in the British colonies the intact slave family provided the foundation for Christianity. The notion of strong slave family life is based on the old idea that US slave owners supported the slave family. "The important factor that differentiated the United States from Brazil," Michael's handout declared, "was that generally in the sale of slaves families were sold together, and in Brazil they were sold separately." The tone here was remarkably tough-minded. "The British understood that if slaves were sold together their productivity would be greater." For historical evidence on this issue, see Degler 1970.

NOTES TO CHAPTER 5

1. See the church's website: http://www.azusa.com.br/.
2. "Reverendo Sérgio Melo—Superintendente da Azusa," *Guiame*, December 12, 2008, http://www.guiame.com.br/m5_imprime. asp?cod_noticia=11807&cod_pagina=1691.
3. "Coral Kadmiel," *Gospel Inside*, September 26, 2007, http://gospelinside.word-press.com/2007/09/26/coral-kadmiel/.
4. studiotaka, "HSBC—Cor&Acao," YouTube, January 20, 2010, http://www. youtube.com/watch?v=CLApjxof4Ew; "Grupo gospel faz apresentação gratuita," Portal da Cultura na RMC, December 23, 2009, http://www.portalculturarmc. agemcamp.sp.gov.br/index.php?option=com_content&view=article&id=480%3 Agrupo-gospel-faz-apresentacao-gratuita-231209&lang=es.
5. Por um Brasil sem racismo, Movimento propõe lotar Paulista," *AfroPress*, March 11, 2007, http://www.afropress.com/noticiasLer.asp?id=1385.
6. Ibid.
7. "Racismo na igreja: Sob as máscaras do amor ao próximo," Afrokut, November 20, 2009, http://negrosnegrascristaos.ning.com/forum/topics/ racismo-na-igreja-sob-as.
8. See, for example, the Bayah blog: http://cnncba.blogspot.com.

NOTES TO THE CONCLUSION

1. In 2000, 6.2% of Brazil's population (or about 10.5 million people) declared themselves to census takers to be *negros* or *pretos*; in 2010, that percentage had increased to 7.6%, or about 14.5 million people.
2. The study of racial identity and Christianity has of course long been embraced in US scholarship. Recent examples include Shelton and Emerson 2012; Yong and Alexander 2011; Gates 2011.
3. Mission Quilombo, "Pastoral da Negritude da Igreja Batista do Pinheiro," Afrokut, http://negrosnegrascristaos.ning.com/group/pastoraldanegritudedaibp (accessed 5/11/12).
4. Centro de Estudos Prospectivos de Educação e Cultura, Campinas, São Paulo, "Caçadas de pedrinho e o CNE, a falsa polêmica," November 3, 2010, http:// blog.centrodestudos.com.br/2010/11/03/cacadas-de-pedrinho-e-o-cne/.
5. Stephen Selka, personal communication, June 2011.
6. Luciana Nunes Leal, "IBGE aponta aumento de brasileiro que se declaram pardos ou pretos," O. Estado de S. Paul, July 22, 2011, http://www.estadao.com.br/ noticias/cidades,ibge-aponta-aumento-de-brasileiros-que-se-declaram-pardos-ou-pretos,748620,0.htm.
7. A similar dynamic is at work in David Harnish's analysis of music in Bali. In his examination of how Balinese village communities use dance to reinforce group identity, Harnish is interested in the role of place in dancers' narratives "that explain the founding of Lingsar and the group's special connection to it" (2005, 4). But identity is forged not just through attachment to place; tied closely with places are bodily substances, ensured by temple-based dancing that transmits fertility to the women associated with the group that attends the temple (ibid.).
8. Hernaniquilombo, "Entrevista Hernani Francisco da Silva—Análise direta—o movimento negro," YouTube, December 19, 2009, http://www.youtube.com/ watch?v=r328hZCZLBo.

Adelt, Ulrich. 2007. "Black, white and blue: Racial politics of blues music in the 1960s." PhD dissertation, American Studies, University of Iowa.

Alberto, Paulina. 2009. "When Rio was *black*: Soul music, national culture, and the politics of racial comparison in 1970s Brazil." *Hispanic American Historical Review* 89/1: 3–39

Allen, Lara. 2003. "Commerce, politics, and musical hybridity: Vocalizing urban black South African identity during the 1950s." *Ethnomusicology* 47/2: 228–249.

Alvez, Kelly Regina, Claudio de Souza, and Daniel Hilario. 2005. "Define-se." Kinoforum. http://www.kinoforum.org/oficinas (accessed 5/15/07).

André, Maria da Consolação. 2008. *O Ser negro: A construção da subjetividade em afrobrasileiros*. Brasília: LGE Editora.

Andrews, George Reid. 1991. *Blacks and whites in São Paulo, Brazil, 1888–1988*. Madison: University of Wisconsin Press.

An Xue, Steve, and Jianping G. Hao. 2006. "Normative standards for vocal tract dimensions by race as measured by acoustic pharyngometry (differences in vocal tract diameters)." *Journal of Voice* 20/2: 391–401.

Aparicio, Frances. 2000. "Ethnifying rhythms, feminizing cultures." In Philip Vilas Bohlman and Ronald Radano, eds., *Music and the racial imagination*, 95–112. Chicago: University of Chicago Press.

Aquino, Rosa Maria de. 2007. "Relações raciais no protestantismo recifense—O caso da Igreja Internacional da Graça de Deus." Dissertação de mestrado, Universidade Federal de Pernambuco.

Assef, Claudia. 2003. *Todo DJ já sambou: A história do disc-jóquei no Brasil*. São Paulo: Conrad Editora do Brasil.

Austin-Broos, Diane J. 1997. *Jamaica genesis: Religion and the politics of moral orders*. Chicago: University of Chicago Press.

Avelar, Idelber, Christopher Dunn, and Adalberto Paranhos. 2011. *Brazilian popular music and citizenship*. Durham: Duke University Press.

Baer, Hans. 2001. *The black spiritual movement: A religious response to racism*. 2nd ed. Knoxville: University of Tennessee Press.

Bailey, Stanley. 2009. *Legacies of race: Identities, attitudes, and politics in Brazil*. Stanford: Stanford University Press.

Bairros, Luiza. 2008. "A community of destiny: New configurations of racial politics in Brazil." *Souls* 10/1: 50–53.

———. 2002. "III Conferência mundial contra o racismo." *Revista estudos feministas* 10/1: 169–170.

Baker-Fletcher, Garth Kasimu. 2003. "African American Christian rap: Facing truth and resisting it." In Anthony B. Pinn, ed., *Noise and spirit: The religious and spiritual sensibilities of rap music*, 29–48. New York: NYU Press.

Balbino, Jéssica. 2010. "Abolição ou senzala moderna?" Jéssica Balbino's blog, May. http://jessicabalbino.blogspot.com/2010/05/abolicao-ou-senzala-moderna.html.

Bastos, Rafael Jose de Menezes. 1999. "The 'origin of samba' as the invention of Brazil (why do songs have music?)." *British Journal of Ethnomusicology* 8: 67–96.

Batista, Luiz Eduardo. 2002. "Mulheres e homens negros: Saúde, doença e morte." PhD dissertation, Universidade Estadual Paulista.

Batista, Luís Eduardo, and Suzana Kalckmann, eds. 2005. *Seminário saúde da população negra estado de São Paulo 2004*. São Paulo: Instituto de Saúde.

Beckford, Robert. 2006. *Jesus dub: Theology, music and social change*. New York: Routledge.

Behague, Gerard. 2006. "Rap, reggae, rock, or samba: The local and the global in Brazilian popular music (1985–95)." *Latin American Music Review* 27/1: 79–90.

Bell, Allan. 1999. "Styling the other to define the self: A study in New Zealand identity making." *Journal of Sociolinguistics* 3/4: 523–541.

Bennett, Andy. 2004. "Consolidating the music scene's perspective." *Poetics* 32: 223–234.

Bennett, Andy, and Richard A. Peterson, eds. 2004. *Music scenes: Local, translocal and virtual*. Nashville: Vanderbilt University Press.

Bento, Maria Aparecida da Silva. 2005. "A implementação do quesito cor na área da saúde: O caso da Prefeitura de São Paulo." In Luís Eduardo Batista and Suzana Kalckmann, eds., *Seminário Saúde da População Negra: Estado de São Paulo 2004*, 133–154. São Paulo: Instituto de Saúde.

Berger, Harris. 1999. *Metal, rock, and jazz*. Middletown, CT: Wesleyan University Press.

Bevilaqua, Ciméa Barbato. 2005. "Entre o previsível e o contingente: Etnografia do processo de decisão sobre uma política de ação afirmativa." *Revista de Antropologia* 48/1: 167–225.

Birman, Patricia. 2006. "Future in the mirror: Media, evangelicals, and politics in Rio de Janeiro." In Birgit Meyer and Annelies Moors, eds., *Religion, media, and the public sphere*, 52–72. Bloomington: Indiana University Press.

———. 1997. "Males e malefícios no discurso neopentecostal." In Patricia Birman, Rehina Novaes, and Samira Crespo, eds., *O mal á brasileira*, 62–97. Rio de Janeiro: Editora UERJ.

Blacking, John. 1995. *Music, culture, and experience: Selected papers of John Blacking*. Ed. Reginald Byron. Chicago: University of Chicago Press.

Blackman, Alma Montgomery. 1996. "Black Seventh-Day Adventists and church music." In Calvin B. Rock, ed., *Perspectives: Black Seventh-Day Adventists face the twenty-first century*. Hagerstown, MD: Review and Herald.

Blake, Stanley. 2011. *The vigorous core of our nationality: Race and regional identity in northeast Brazil*. Pittsburgh: University of Pittsburgh Press.

Bousquat, Aylene, and Amelia Cohn. 2003. "A construção do mapa da juvenude de São Paulo." *Lua nova* 60: 81–96.

Bowen, Dawn S. 1997. "Lookin' for Margaritaville: Place and imagination in Jimmy Buffett's songs" *Journal of Cultural Geography* 16/2: 99–108.

Bradford, Charles. 1996. "Black Seventh-Day Adventists and church loyalty." In Calvin B. Rock, ed., *Black Seventh-Day Adventists face the twenty-first century*, 11–19. Hagerstown, MD: Review and Herald.

Branchini, Diná da Silva, and Selenir Corrêa Gonçalves Kronbauer. 2011. "Encontros afro-cristãos: Histórico e memórias." *Identidade!* 16/1: 94–104.

Brooker, Will, and Deborah Jermyn, eds. 2002. *The audience studies reader*. New York: Routledge.

Broughton, Viv. 1996. *Too close to heaven*. London: Midnight Books.

Brubaker, Rogers. 2004. *Ethnicity without groups*. Cambridge: Harvard University Press.

Burdick, John. 2009a. "Collective identity and racial thought on São Paulo's black gospel music scene." *Music and Arts in Action* 1/2: 16–29.

———. 2009b. "The singing voice and racial politics on the Brazilian evangelical music scene." *Latin American Music Review* 30: 1: 25–55.

———. 2008. "Class, place and blackness in São Paulo's gospel music scene," *Latin American and Caribbean Ethnic and Racial Studies* 3/2 (July): 149–169.

———. 2005. "Why is the evangelical black movement growing in Brazil?" *Journal of Latin American Studies* 37/2 (May): 311–332.

———. 1999. "What is the color of the holy spirit? Pentecostalism and black identity in Brazil. " *Latin American Research Review* 34/2: 109–131.

———. 1998a. *Blessed Anastácia: Women, race, and popular Christianity in Brazil*. New York: Routledge.

———. 1998b. "The lost constituency of Brazil's black consciousness movements." *Latin American Perspectives* 98/2 (January): 136–155.

———. 1995. "Uniting theory and practice in the study of social movements: Notes toward a hopeful realism." *Dialectical Anthropology* 20: 361–385.

Butler, Kim D. 1998. *Freedoms given, freedoms won: Afro-Brazilians in post-abolition São Paulo and Salvador*. New Brunswick: Rutgers University Press.

Caldwell, Kia Lilly. 2007. *Negras in Brazil: Re-envisioning black women, citizenship, and the politics of identity*. New Brunswick: Rutgers University Press.

Camargo, Patricia de Castro, and Marta Assumpção Andrada e Silva. 2007. "Cantores negros e brancos; Comparação entre tipologia fácil, ajustes do trato vocal e a voz." In *Anais da 6a mostra de estudos e pesquisas sobre voz da PUC-SP*.

Cantalice, Tiago. 2011. "O melhor do Brasil é brasileiro! Corpo, identidade, desejo e poder." *Sexualidad, Salud y Sociedad: Revista Latinoamericana* 7: 69–102.

Capone, Stefania. 2010. *Searching for Africa in Brazil: Power and tradition in candomblé*. Durham: Duke University Press.

Cardoso, Lourenço. 2011. "O branco-objeto: O movimento negro situando a branquitude." *Instrumento: Revista de Estudo e Pesquisa na Educação Juiz de Fora* 13/1: 81–93.

Carneiro, Sueli. 2002. "A batalha de Durban." *Estudos feministas* 10/1: 209–214.

Carril, Lourdes de Fatima Bezerra. 2004. "Quilombo, favela e periferia: A longa busca da cidadania." PhD dissertation, Universidade de São Paulo.

Carvalho, José Jorge. 2006. "As artes sagradas afro-brasileiras." Available at http:// arifsite.org/book/book.php?wapedewe=mobile/doc/5369679 (accessed 5/11/12).

Chasteen, John Charles. 1996. "The prehistory of samba: Carnival dancing in Rio de Janeiro, 1840–1917." *Journal of Latin American Studies* 28: 29–47.

Chitando, Ezra. 2002. *Singing culture: A study of gospel music in Zimbabwe.* Uppsala, Sweden: Nordiska Afrikainstitutet.

Chor, Dóra, and Lima Claudia Risso de Araujo. 2005. "Aspectos epidemiológicos das desigualdades raciais em saúde no Brasil." *Cadernos da Saúde Pública* 21/5: 1586–1594.

Cicalo, André. 2012. *Urban encounters: Affirmative action and black identities in Brazil.* New York: Palgrave Macmillan.

Coelho, Jade. 2005. "Expressões da voz do negro na musicalidade." In *4a mostra de estudos e pesquisas sobre a voz da PUC-SP.* http://www.pucsp.br/laborvox/eventos/ downloads/IV_MOSTRA.pdf.

Cohen, Sarah. 1995. "Sounding out the city: Music and the sensuous production of place." *Transactions of the Institute of British Geographers* 20/4: 434–446.

Collins, John. 2005. "'But what if I should need to defecate in your neighborhood, madame?': Empire, redemption, and the 'tradition of the oppressed' in a Brazilian world heritage site." *Cultural Anthropology* 23/2: 279–328.

———. 2004. "'X marks the future of Brazil': Protestant ethics and bedeviling mixtures in a Brazilian cultural heritage center." In Andrew Shryock, ed., *Off stage/on display: Intimacy and ethnography in the age of public culture,* 191–224. Stanford: Stanford University Press.

Contins, Marcia. 2008. "Religião, etnicidade e globalização: Uma comparação entre grupos religiosos nos contextos brasileiro e norte-americano." *Revista de Antropologia* 51/1: 67–106.

Corbitt, J. Nathan. 1998. *The sound of the harvest.* Grand Rapids, MI: Baker.

Corey, J. P., A. Gungor, R. Nelson, X. Liu, and J. Fredberg. 1998. "Normative standards for nasal cross-sectional areas by race as measured by acoustic rhinometry." *Otolaryngology—Head & Neck Surgery* 119: 389–393.

Corten, Andrew, and Angelica Marshall-Fratani, eds. 2001. *Between Babel and Pentecost: Transnational Pentecostalism in Africa and Latin America.* Bloomington: Indiana University Press.

Côrtes, Cristiane Felipe Ribeiro de Araújo, and Maria do Socorro Vieira Coelho. 2008. "Conceição Evaristo: literatura e vida." In Constância Lima Duarte, ed., *Escritoras mineiras: Poesia, ficção, memória,* 111–116. Belo Horizonte, Brazil: Viva Voz.

Courlander, Harold. 1963. *Negro folk music.* New York: Columbia University Press.

Covin, David. 2006. *The unified black movement in Brazil, 1978–2002.* Jefferson, NC: McFarland.

Cruz, Isabel Cristina Fonseca da. 2004. "A sexualidade, a saúde reprodutiva e a violência contra a mulher negra: Aspectos de interesse para assistência de enfermagem."
Revista da Escola de Enfermagem da Universiade de São Paulo 38/4: 448–457.

Cumming, Naomi. 2000. *The sonic self*. Bloomington: Indiana University Press.

Cunha, Magali do Nascimento. 2007. *Explosão gospel: Um olhar das ciências humanas
sobre o cenário*. Rio de Janeiro: Mauad.

Damasceno, Caetana, Sonia Giacomini, and M. Santos, eds. 1988. "Catálogo de enti-
dades do movimento Negro." *Comunicações do ISER* 29: 1–89.

Daniels, G. Reginald. 2006. *Race and multiraciality in Brazil and the United States:
Converging paths?* College Park: Pennsylvania State University Press.

Darden, Robert. 2006. *People get ready: A new history of black gospel music*. New York:
Continuum.

Datafolha. 2007. "64% dos brasileiros se declaram católicos." May 5. http://datafolha.
folha.uol.com.br/po/ver_po.php?session=447.

Dávila, Jerry. 2003. *Diploma of whiteness: Race and social policy in Brazil, 1917–1945*.
Durham: Duke University Press.

Dawe, Kevin, and Andy Bennett. 2001. "Introduction: Guitars, culture, people and
places." In Kevin Dawe and Andy Bennett, eds., *Guitar cultures*. New York: Berg.

Dawson, Alan Charles. 2008. "In light of Africa: Globalising blackness in northeast
Brazil." PhD dissertation, Anthropology, McGill University.

Daynes, Sarah. 2005. "The musical construction of diaspora: The case of reggae and
Rastafari." In Sheila Whiteley, Andy Bennett, and Stan Hawkins, eds., *Music, space,
and place: Popular music and cultural identity*, 25–41. Burlington, VT: Ashgate.

Degler, Carl. 1970. "Slavery in Brazil and the United States: An essay in comparative
history." *American Historical Review* 75/4: 1004–1028.

DeNora, Tia. 2000. *Music in everyday life*. Cambridge: Cambridge University Press.

Dent, Alexander Sebastian. 2009. *River of tears: Country music, memory, and modernity in Brazil*. Durham: Duke University Press.

Dimitriadis, Greg. 2001. *Performing identity/performing culture: Hip hop as text, pedagogy, and lived practice*. New York: Peter Lang.

DJ TR. 2007. *Acorda hip-hop! Despertando um movimento em traformação*. Rio de
Janeiro: Aeroplano.

Domingues, Petrônio. 2007. "Movimento Negro brasileiro: Alguns apontamentos
históricos." *Tempo* 12/23: 100–122.

Dunn, Christopher. 2001. *Brutality garden: Tropicália and the emergence of a Brazilian
counterculture*. Chapel Hill: University of North Carolina Press.

Dunsby, Jonathan. 2009. "Roland Barthes and the grain of Panzéra's voice." *Journal of
the Royal Musical Association* 134/1: 113–132.

Eidsheim, Nina Sun. Forthcoming. "Racialization and the aesthetics of vocal timbre."
In Olivia Bloechl, Jeffrey Kallberg, and Melanie Lowe, eds.,*Rethinking Difference in
Music Scholarship*. Cambridge: Cambridge University Press.

———. 2011. "Sensing voice: Materiality and presence in singing and listening." *Senses
and Society* 6 /1.

————. 2009. "Synthesizing race: Towards an analysis of the performativity of vocal timbre." *TRANS—Transcultural Music Review* 13/7.

————. 2006. "Constructing difference: Vocal pedagogy and timbre." Unpublished paper.

Estill, Jo. 1988. "Belting and classic voice quality: Some physiological differences." *Medical Problems of Performing Artists* 3/1: 37–43.

Felix, João Batista de Jesus. 2000. "Chic Show e Zimbabwe: A construção da identidade nos bailes black paulistanos." PhD dissertation, Universidade de São Paulo.

Finnegan, Ruth. 1989. *The hidden musicians: Music-making in an English town.* Cambridge: Cambridge University Press.

Floyd, Samuel A. 1995. *The power of Negro music.* New York: Oxford University Press.

Fonseca, Alexandre Brasil . 2008. "Muito além do sábado: O pioneirismo adventista na mídia eletrônica religiosa." *Revista de Estudos da Religião* 8/3: 89–100.

Forman, Murray. 2002. *The 'hood comes first: Race, space, and place in rap and hip hop.* Middletown, CT: Wesleyan University Press.

Fox, Aaron. 2004. *Real country: Music and language in working-class culture.* Durham: Duke University Press.

Franco, Bernardo Mello. 2010. "Presidenciáveis disputam voto evangélico." *Folha de São Paulo*, April 26.

Freston, Paul, ed. 2008. *Evangelical Christianity and democracy in Latin America.* Oxford: Oxford University Press.

————. 2004. *Evangelicals and politics in Asia, Africa, and Latin America.* Cambridge: Cambridge University Press.

————. 1998. "Pentecostalism in Latin America: Characteristics and controversies." *Social Compass* 45/3: 335–358.

Frith, Simon. 1996a. "Music and identity." In Stuart Hall and Paul de Gay, eds., *Questions of cultural identity*, 108–127. London: Sage.

————. 1996b. *Performing rites.* Cambridge: Harvard University Press.

Gates, Henry Louis. 2011. *Black in Latin America.* New York: NYU Press.

Gilbert, Jeremy, and Ewan Pearson. 1999. *Discographies: Dance music, culture and the politics of sound.* New York: Routledge.

Gilroy, Paul. 1993. *The black Atlantic.* Cambridge: Harvard University Press.

————. 1991. "Sounds authentic: Black music, ethnicity, and the challenge of a 'changing' same." *Black Music Research Journal* 11/2: 111–136.

Giumbelli, Emerson. 2007. "Um projecto de cristianismo hegemônico." In Vagner Gonçalves da Silva, ed., *Intolerância religiosa: Impactos do neopentecostalismo no campo religioso afro-brasileiro*, 149–169. São Paulo: EDUSP.

Goldstein, Donna. 2003. *Laughter out of place: Race, class, violence, and sexuality in a Rio shantytown.* Berkeley: University of California Press.

Gomes, Marcus Vinicius Peinado. 2009. "O movimento negro e a secretaria especial de promoção da igualdade racial: Uma análise sob a perspectiva da teoria de movimentos raciais." Dissertação de mestrado, Fundação Getúlio Vargas.

Gomes, Nilma Lina. 2011. "Movimento negro, saberes e a tensão regulação-emancipação do corpo e da corporeidade negra." *Contemporânea* 2: 37–60.

Gonçalves da Silva, Vagner. 2007. "Neo-Pentecostalism and Afro-Brazilian religions: Explaining the attacks on symbols of the African religious heritage in contemporary Brazil." *Mana* 13/1: 207–236.

Gordon, Edmund T., and Mark Anderson. 1999. "The African diaspora: Toward an ethnography of diasporic identification." *Journal of American Folklore* 112/445: 282–296.

Goss, Karine Pereira. 2009. "Retóricas em disputa: O debate intelectual sobre as políticas de ação afirmativa para estudantes negros no Brasil." *Ciências sociais Unisinos* 45/2: 114–124.

Grosz, Elizabeth. 2001. *Architecture from the outside: Essays on virtual and real space.* Cambridge: MIT Press.

———. 1994. *Volatile bodies: Toward a corporeal feminism.* Bloomington: Indiana University Press.

Hale, Charles. 2006. "Activist research v. cultural critique: Indigenous land rights and the contradictions of politically engaged anthropology." *Cultural Anthropology* 21/1: 96–120.

Hanchard, Michael. 2008. "Black memory versus state memory: Notes toward a method." *Small Axe* 12/2: 45–62.

———. 1999. "Afro-modernity: Temporality, politics and the African diaspora." *Public Culture* 11/1: 245–268.

———. 1994. *Orpheus and power: The movimento negro of Rio de Janeiro and São Paulo, Brazil, 1945–1988.* Princeton: Princeton University Press.

Hansen, Karen Tranberg, and Anne Line Dalsgaard. 2008. *Youth and the city in the Global South.* Bloomington: Indiana University Press.

Harding, Rachel. 2003. *A refuge of thunder: Candomblé and alternative spaces of blackness.* Bloomington: University of Indiana Press.

Harnish, David. 2005. "'Isn't this nice? It's just like being in Bali': Constructing Balinese music culture in Lombok." *Ethnomusicology Forum* 14/1: 3–24.

Harris, Michael. 1992. *The rise of gospel blues.* Oxford: Oxford University Press.

Heringer, Rosana, and Renato Ferreira. 2009. "Análisis das principais políticas de inclusão de estudantes negros no ensino superior no Brasil no período 2001–2008." In Marilena de Paula and Rosana Heringer, eds., *Caminhos convergentes.* Rio de Janeiro: Fundação Heinrich Boll.

Hinson, Glenn. 2000. *Fire in my bones: Transcendence and the holy spirit in African American gospel.* Philadelphia: University of Pennsylvania Press.

Htun, Mala. 2005. "From 'racial democracy' to affirmative action: Changing state policy on race in Brazil." *Latin American Research Review* 39/1: 60–89.

IBGE. 2010. "Diminuição da desigualdade racial é lenta, alertam especialistas: Mesmo com mudanças, brancos vivem com o dobro da renda da população negra." *Notícias*, November 20. http://noticias.r7.com/brasil/noticias/diminuicao-da-desigualdade-racial-e-lenta-e-pode-se-esgotar-alertam-especialistas-20101120.html.

———. 2006. *Síntese de indicadores socias*. Rio de Janeiro: IBGE. http://www.ibge.gov. br/home/estatistica/populacao/condicaodevida/indicadoresminimos/sinteseindic-sociais2006/indic_sociais2006.pdf.

Jaccoud, Luciana, and Mario Theodoro. 2007. "Raça e Educação: Os limites das políticas universalistas." In Sales Augusto dos Santos, ed., *Ações afirmativas e combate ao racismo nas Américas*, 106–163. Brasilia: Edições MEC/Unesco.

Jackson, Jerma A. 2004. *Singing in my soul: Black gospel music in a secular age*. Chapel Hill: University of North Carolina Press.

Jackson, John L. 2005. *Real black: Adventures in racial sincerity*. Chicago: University of Chicago Press.

Johnson, Tamara. 2011. "Salsa politics." *Aether* 7: 97–118.

Jungr, Barbara. 2002. "Vocal expression in the blues and gospel." In Allen F. Moore, ed., *The Cambridge companion to blues and gospel music*, 102–115. Cambridge: Cambridge University Press.

Kaemmer, John. 1993. *Music in human life: Anthropological perspectives on music*. Austin: University of Texas Press.

Kalckmann, Suzana, Claudete Gomes dos Santos, Luís Eduardo Batista, and Vanessa Martins da Cruz. 2007. "Racismo institucional: Um desafio para a eqüidade no SUS?" *Saude e Sociedade* 16/2: 146–155.

Kayes, Gilyeanne. 2004. *Singing and the actor*. New York: Routledge.

Keil, Charles. 1966. *Urban blues*. Chicago: University of Chicago Press.

Kelly, Cristina. 2010. "Religião e negritude: Discursos e práticas no protestantismo e nos movimentos pentecostais." *Correlatio* 9/18: 95–113.

Krims, Adam. 2000. *Rap music and the poetics of identity*. Cambridge: Cambridge University Press.

Lavalle, Adrian, and Bruno Komatso. 2008. "Associativismo e redes sociais— Condições e determinantes de acesso á políticas sociais pela população de baixa renda." In CEBRAP, *Desenvolvimento regional de desigualdades sócioprodutivas: Tendências recentes, redefinições conceituais e desdobramento em termos de políticas públicas*. Relatório final.

Layshon, Andrew, David Matless, and George Revill, eds. 1998. *The place of music*. New York: Guilford.

Leal, Sandra Maria Cezar, and Marta Júlia Marques Lopes. 2005. "A violência como objeto da assistência em um hospital de trauma: 'O olhar' da enfermagem." *Ciências da Saúde Coletiva* 10/2: 419–431.

Lesser, Jeffrey. 1999. *Negotiating national identity: Immigrants, minorities, and the struggle for ethnicity in Brazil*. Durham: Duke University Press.

Lima, Márcia. 2009. "'Race' and class dynamics in metropolitan contexts." Paper presented at Metropolis and Inequalities Seminar, São Paulo.

Lindvall, Terry, Arte Terry, and Wally Williams. 1996. "Spectacular transcendence: Abundant means in the cinematic representation of African-American Christianity." *Howard Journal of Communication* 7: 205–220.

Linger, Daniel T. 1992. *Dangerous encounters*. Stanford: Stanford University Press.

Lopes, Fernanda. 2005. "Para além da barreira dos números: Desigualdades raciais e saúde." *Cadernos da Saúde Pública* 21/5: 1595–1601.

Loureiro, Monique M., and Suely Rozenfeld. 2005. "Epidemiology of sickle cell disease hospital admissions in Brazil." *Revista da Saúde Pública* 39: 943–949.

Lovell, Peggy. 2006. "Race, gender, and work in São Paulo, Brazil, 1960–2000." *Latin American Research Review* 41/3: 63–87.

Lucena, Francisco Carlos de, and Jorge dos Santos Lima. 2009. "Ser negro: Um estudo de caso." *Saberes* 1/2: 33–51.

Macedo, Suzana. 2003. *DJ Marlboro na terra do funk*. Rio de Janeiro: Dantes.

Madambashi, Andrea Marcela. 2011. "Half of Brazil's Population to Be Evangelical Christian by 2020." *Christian Post*, February 21. http://www.christianpost.com/news/half-of-brazils-population-to-be-evangelical-christian-by-2020-49071/.

Magowan, Fiona. 1997. "'The land is our märr (essence), it stays forever': The Yothu-Yindi relationship in Australian aboriginal traditional and popular musics." In Martin Stokes, ed., *Ethnicity, identity and music: The musical construction of place*, 135–156. New York: Berg.

Manuel, Peter. 1989. "Andalusian, gypsy, and class identity in the contemporary flamenco complex." *Ethnomusicology* 33/1: 47–65.

Martins, Sérgio, Carlos Alberto Medeiros, and Elise Larkin Nascimento. 2004. "Paving paradise: The road from 'racial democracy' to affirmative action in Brazil." *Journal of Black Studies* 34/6: 787–816.

McCann, Bryan. 2004. *Hello, hello Brazil: Popular music in the making of modern Brazil*. Durham: Duke University Press.

McClary, Susan. 1994. "Construction of subjectivity in Schubert's music." In Philip Brett, ed., *Queering the pitch: The new gay and lesbian musicology*, 205–234. New York: Routledge.

McGann, Mary E. 2004. *A precious fountain: Music in the worship of an African-American Catholic community*. Collegeville, MN: Liturgical.

McGowan, Chris, and Ricardo Pessanha. 1998. *The Brazilian sound: Samba, bossa nova, and the popular music of Brazil*. Philadelphia: Temple University Press.

Mendes, Ana, Howard B. Rothman, Christine Sapienza, and W. S. Brown, Jr. 2003. "Effects of vocal training on the acoustic parameters of the singing voice." *Journal of Voice* 17/4: 529–543.

Middleton, Richard. 2006. *Voicing the popular*. New York: Routledge.

Miller, Richard. 2004. *Solutions for singers*. New York: Oxford University Press.

Mohanty, Satya P. 2000. "The epistemic status of cultural identity." In Paula M. L. Moya and Michael R. Hames-García, eds., *Reclaiming identity: Realist theory and the predicament of the postmodern*, 29–66. Berkeley: University of California Press.

———. 1997. *Literary theory and the claims of history: Postmodernism, objectivity, multicultural politics*. Ithaca: Cornell University Press.

Monks, Susan. 2003. "Adolescent singers and perceptions of vocal identity." *British Journal of Music Education* 20: 243–256.

Monson, Ingrid. 1996. *Saying something*. Chicago: University of Chicago Press.

Moore, Zelbert. 1989. "Out of the shadows: Black and brown struggles for recognition and dignity in Brazil, 1964–1985." *Journal of Black Studies* 19/4: 394–410.

Motta, Roberto. 2009. "Enchantment, identity, community and conversion." In Giuseppe Giordan, ed., *Conversion in the age of pluralism*, 163–188. Leiden, Netherlands: Brill.

Moya, Paula M. L. 2006. "What's identity got to do with it? Mobilizing identities in the multicultural classroom." In Linda Alcoff, ed., *Identity politics reconsidered*, 96–117. New York: Palgrave.

Murphy, John P. 2006. *Music in Brazil: Experiencing music, expressing culture*. New York: Oxford University Press.

Nascimento, Elisa Larkin. 2006. *The sorcery of color: Identity, race, and gender in Brazil*. Philadelphia: Temple University Press.

Nava, Carmen, and Ludwig Lauerhass, eds. 2006. *Brazil in the making: Facets of national identity*. Lanham, MD: Rowman and Littlefield.

Naveda, Luiz, and Marc Leman. 2009. "Accessing structure of samba rhythms through cultural practices of vocal percussion." Paper presented at Sound and Music Conference, Porto, Portugal.

Nogueira, João Carlos. 2004. "Movimento Negro: Das denúncias do racismo á prática de políticas públicas." *Política e Sociedade* 5: 89–99.

Novaes, Regina. 1985. *O negro evangélico*. Rio de Janeiro: Instituto de Estudos da Religião.

Oliveira, Fátima. 2002. *Saúde da população negra: Brasil ano 2001*. Brasília, DF: Organização Pan-Americana da Saúde.

Oliveira, Marco David de. 2004. *A religião mais negra do Brasil*. São Paulo: Editora Mundo Cristão.

Oliver, Paul. 1984. *Songsters and saints: Vocal traditions on race records*. Cambridge: Cambridge University Press.

Oosterbaan, Martijn. 2008. "Spiritual attunement: Pentecostal radio in the soundscape of a favela in Rio de Janeiro." *Social Text* 26/3: 123–145

Oro, Pedro. 1997. "Neopentecostais e afro-brasileiros: Quem vencerá esta guerra?" *Debates do NER* 1/1: 10–36.

Paixão, Marcelo, and Luiz M. Carvano. 2008. *Relatório anual das desigualdades raciais no Brasil, 2007–2008*. Rio de Janeiro: Garamond.

Paranhos, Adalberto. 2005. "A ordem disciplinar e seu avesso: Música popular e relações de gênero no 'Estado Novo.'" *Lutas Sociais* 13/14: 80–89.

Pardue, Derek. 2011. "'Conquisantdo espaço': Hip-hop occupations of São Paulo." In Idelber Avelar and Christopher Dunn, eds., *Brazilian popular music and citizenship*, 205–222. Durham: Duke University Press.

———. 2008. *Ideologies of marginality in Brazilian hip hop*. New York: Palgrave Macmillan.

———. 2005. "CD cover art as cultural literacy and hip-hop design in Brazil." *Education, Communication and Information* 5/1: 61–81.

———. 2004a. "Putting *mano* to music: The mediation of blackness in Brazilian rap." *Ethnomusicology Forum* 13/1: 253–286.

———. 2004b. "'Writing in the margins': Brazilian hip-hop as an educational project." *Anthropology and Education Quarterly* 35/4: 411–432.

Parker, Richard G. 1992. *Bodies, pleasures, and passions: Sexual culture in contemporary Brazil.* Boston: Beacon.

Parkes, Peter. 1997. "Personal and collective identity in Kalasha song performance: The significance of music-making in a minority enclave." In Martin Stokes, ed., *Ethnicity, identity and music*, 157–188. New York: Berg.

Pasternak, Suzana. 2005. "A favela que virou cidade." Unpublished presentation, World Bank Group, Urban Research Symposium.

Pedde, Valdir. 2002. "Etnia, religião e política: Relações e deslocamento de fronteiras." *Noticias de Antropología y Arqueología (NAYA).* http://www.naya.org.ar/congreso2002/ponencias/valdir_pedde.htm (accessed 5/11/12).

Peddie, Ian. 2006. "The bleak country? The black country and the rhetoric of escape." In Ian Peddie, ed., *The resisting muse*, 132–147. Burlington, VT: Ashgate.

Penteado, Regina Zanella, Cibelle Brito da Silva, and Priscila Fabiana Agostinho Pereira. 2008. "Aspectos de religiosidade na saúde vocal de cantores de grupos de louvor." *Revista CEFAC* 10/3: 359–368.

Pereira, Amilcar Araujo, and Verena Alberti. 2007. "Qual África? Significados da África para o movimento Negro no Brasil." *Revista Estudos Históricos* 1/39: 25–56.

Perrone, Charles A., and Christopher Dunn, eds. 2001. *Brazilian popular music and globalization.* New York: Routledge.

Perry, Keisha Khan. 2009. "Racialized history and urban politics: Black women's wisdom in grassroots struggles." In Bernd Reiter and Gladys L. Mitchell, eds., *Brazil's new racial politics*, 141–164. Boulder, CO: Lynne Rienner.

Pesquisa Nacional de Amostragem de Domicílio. 2006. "Síntese de Indicadores Sociais 2006." http://www.ibge.gov.br/home/estatistica/populacao/condicaodevida/indicadoresminimos/sinteseindicsociais2006/default.shtm.

Phelan, Helen. 2008. "Practice, ritual and community music: Doing as identity." *International Journal of Community Music* 1/2: 143–158.

Pierucci, Flavio. 2006. "Religião como solvente." *Novos estudos CEBRAP* 75: 111–127.

Pinheiro, Marcia. 2009. "Dinâmicas da religiosidade: Experiências musicais, cor e noção de sagrado." *Stockholm Review of Latin American Studies* 4: 61–72.

———. 2004. "Produção musical: A periferia do meio evangélico." *Anais do V Congresso Latinoamericano da Associação Internacional para o Estudo da Música Popular.*

———. 2003. "Experiências sonoras e inovações religiosas." Paper presented at symposium "Cultos religiosos populares na America Latina," Ica, Chile.

———. 1998. "O proselitismo evangélico: Musicalidade e imagem." *Cadernos de Antropologia e Imagem* 7/2: 57–67.

Pinho, Patricia de Santana. 2010. *Mama Africa: Reinventing blackness in Bahia.* Durham: Duke University Press.

———. 2009. "White but not quite: Tones and overtones of whiteness in Brazil." *Small Axe: A Caribbean Journal of Criticism* 13/1: 39–56.

Pinho, Silvia Maria Rebelo. 2001. "A voz do negro." In Silvia Maria Rebelo Pinho, ed., *Tópicos em voz*, 89–96. Rio de Janeiro: Guanabara.

Prandi, Reginaldo. 2004. "O Brasil com axé: Candomblé e umbanda no mercado religioso." *Estudos Avançados* 18/52: 223–238.

Pravaz, Natasha. 2012. "Performing *mulata*-ness: The politics of cultural authenticity and sexuality among carioca samba dancers." *Latin American Perspectives* 39/2: 113–133.

———. 2008. "Where is the carnivalesque in Rio's Carnaval? Samba, *mulatas* and modernity." *Visual Anthropology* 21/2: 95–111.

———. 2003. "Brazilian *mulatice*: Performing race, gender, and the nation." *Journal of Latin American Anthropology* 8/1: 116–146.

Purnell, Thomas, William Idsardi, and John Baugh. 1999. "Perceptual and phonetic experiments on American English dialect identification." *Journal of Language and Social Psychology* 18/1: 10–30.

Racusen, Seth. 2009. "Affirmative action and identity." In Bernd Reiter and Gladys L. Mitchell, eds., *Brazil's new racial politics*, 89–122. London: Lynne Rienner.

Radano, Ronald M. 2003. *Lying up a nation: Race and black music*. Chicago: University of Chicago Press.

Ramsey, Guthrie P. 2004. *Race music: Black cultures from bebop to hip-hop*. Berkeley: University of California Press.

Reagon, Bernice Johnson. 2001. *If you don't go, don't hinder me: The African American sacred song tradition*. Lincoln: University of Nebraska Press.

Reily, Suzel. 1994. "Macunaíma's music: National identity and ethnomusicological research in Brazil." In Martin Stokes, ed., *Ethnicity, identity and music: The musical construction of place*, 71–96. Oxford, UK: Berg.

Reinhardt, Bruno. 2007. "'Guerra santa': Encarando o espelho neopentecostal: O movimento contra a intolerância religiosa como uma nova reflexividade política do candomblé de Salvador." Paper presented at VII Reunião Antropológica do Mercosul.

Reiter, Bernd. 2008. *Negotiating democracy in Brazil: The politics of exclusion*. London: Lynne Rienner.

Reiter, Bernd, and Gladys L. Mitchell, eds. 2009. *Brazil's new racial politics*. London: Lynne Rienner.

Ribeiro, Alan Augusto Moraes. 2010. "'No meio e misturado': O moreno como identificação de cor entre estudantes de uma escola pública." *Conjectura: Filosofia e Educação* 15/1: 67–77.

Rocha, Janaina, M. Domenich, and P. Casseano. 2001. *Hip hop: A periferia grita*. São Paulo: Fundação Perseu Abramo.

Rose, Tricia, and Susan McClary. 1994. *Black noise: Rap music and black culture in contemporary America*. Middletown, CT: Wesleyan University Press.

Roth-Gordon, Jennifer. 2008. "Conversational sampling, race trafficking, and the invocation of the *gueto* in Brazilian hip hop." In Samy Alim, Awad Ibrahim, and Alastair Pennycook, eds., *Global linguistic flows: Hip hop cultures, youth identities, and the politics of language*, 63–77. New York: Routledge.

Saldanha, Arun. 2002. "Music, space, identity: Geographies of youth culture in Bangalore." *Cultural Studies* 16/3: 337–350.

Sancar, Fahriye Hazer. 2003. "City, music and place attachment: Beloved Istanbul." *Journal of Urban Design* 8/3: 269–291.

Sansi, Roger. 2009. *Fetishes and monuments: Afro-Brazilian art and culture in the 20th-century Brazil.* New York: Berghahn Books.

Sansone, Livio. 2003. *Blackness without ethnicity: Constructing race in Brazil.* New York: Palgrave Macmillan.

———. 2000. "Os objetos da identidade negra: Consumo, mercantilização, globalização e a criação de culturas negras no Brasil." *Mana* 6/1: 87–119.

Santos, Sales Augusto dos. 2011. "The metamorphosis of black movement activists into black organic intellectuals." *Latin American Perspectives* 38/3: 124–135.

Schor, Silvia Maria, and Renaldo Artes. 2001. "Primeiro censo dos moradores de rua da cidade de São Paulo: Procedimentos metodológicos e resultados." *Revista de Economia Aplicada* 5/4: 861–883.

Schünemann, Haller Elinar Stach. 2009. "O papel das imigrações no crescimento da Igreja Adventista do Sétimo Dia." *Estudos de Religião* 23/37: 146–170.

Schwarcz, Lilia Moritz. 1999. *The spectacle of the races: Scientists, institutions, and the race question in Brazil, 1870–1930.* New York: Hill and Wang.

Scott, Joan W. 1991. "The evidence of experience." *Critical Inquiry* 17: 773–797.

Selka, Stephen. 2010. "Morality in the religious marketplace: Evangelical Christianity, candomblé, and the struggle for moral distinction in Brazil." *American Ethnologist* 37/2: 291–307.

———. 2007. *Religion and the politics of ethnic identity in Bahia, Brazil.* Gainesville: University Press of Florida.

———. 2005. "Ethnoreligious identity politics in Bahia, Brazil." *Latin American Perspectives* 32/1: 72–94.

Shaw, Lisa. 2002. "Samba and 'brasilidade': Notions of national identity in the lyrics of Noel Rosa (1910–1937)." *Lusotopie* 2: 81–96.

———. 1999. *The Social history of the Brazilian samba.* Aldershot, UK: Ashgate.

Shaw, Lisa, and Stephanie Dennison. 2007. *Brazilian national cinema.* New York: Routledge.

Shelton, Jason, and Michael O. Emerson. 2012. *Blacks and whites in Christian America: How racial discrimination shapes religious convictions.* New York: NYU Press.

Sheriff, Robin. 2001. *Dreaming equality: Color, race, and racism in urban Brazil.* New Brunswick: Rutgers University Press.

———. 1999. "The theft of Carnaval: National spectacle and racial politics in Rio de Janeiro." *Cultural Anthropology* 14/1: 3–28.

Silva, Graziella Moraes da, and Elisa P. Reis. 2012. "The multiple dimensions of racial mixture in Rio de Janeiro, Brazil: From whitening to Brazilian negritude." *Ethnic and Racial Studies* 35/3: 382–399.

Silva, Hernani da. 2004. "As Igrejas Evangélicas Neopentecostais e os afrodescendentes." *Negros e Politicas Publicas* (Yahoo Group). http://br.groups.yahoo.com/group/negrosepoliticaspublicas/message/2207 (accessed 5/11/12).

Silva, Tarcia Regina. 2010. "A construção da identidade negra em teritórios de maioria afrodescendente." *Revista Africa e Africanidades* 3/11.

Skidmore, Thomas. 1993. *Black into white: Race and nationality in Brazilian thought.* Durham: Duke University Press.

Smith, Christen. 2009. "Scenarios of racial contact: Police violence and the politics of performance and racial formation in Brazil." *E-Misférica* 5/2: 1–23. http://hemi.nyu. edu/hemi/en/e-misferica-52/smith (accessed 5/11/12).

Snow, David A., and Robert D. Benford, 1988. "Ideology, Frame Resonance and Participant Mobilization." *International Social Movement Research* 1: 197–217.

Snow, David A., E. Burke Rochford, Jr., Steven K. Worden, and Robert D. Benford. 1986. "Frame alignment processes: Micromobilization and movement participation." *American Sociological Review* 51: 464–481.

Solomon, Thomas. 2000. "Dueling landscapes: Singing places and identities in highland Bolivia." *Ethnomusicology* 44/2: 257–280.

Speed, Shannon. 2006. "At the crossroads of human rights and anthropology: Toward a critically engaged activist research." *American Anthropologist* 108/1: 66–76.

Stam, Robert. 1997. *Tropical multiculturalism: A comparative history of race in Brazilian cinema and culture.* Durham: Duke University Press.

Stepan, Nancy. 1996. *The hour of eugenics: Race, gender, and nation in Latin America.* Ithaca: Cornell University Press.

Stokes, Martin, ed. 1997. *Ethnicity, identity and music: The musical construction of place.* Oxford, UK: Berg.

Stone-Mediatore, Shari. 2003. *Reading across borders: Storytelling and knowledges of resistance.* New York: Palgrave Macmillan.

Telles, Edward. 2004. *Race in another America: The significance of skin color in Brazil.* Princeton: Princeton University Press.

———. 1995. "Race, class, and space in Brazilian cities." *International Journal of Urban and Regional Research* 19: 395–406.

Thompson, Gordon. 1991. "The Carans of Gujarat: Caste identity, music and cultural change." *Ethnomusicology* 35/3: 381–391.

Toulis, Nicole. 1997. *Believing identity: Pentecostalism and the mediation of Jamaican ethnicity and gender in England.* New York: Berg.

Turino, Thomas. 2008. *Music as social life: The politics of participation.* Chicago: University of Chicago Press.

Valente, Ana Lúcia. 2005. "Ação afirmativa, relações raciais e educação básica." *Revista Brasileira de Educação* 28: 62–76.

Valéria, Nilza. n.d. "Quem tem medo de ritmos africanos?" *Revista Enfoque.* http:// www.revistaenfoque.com.br/index.php?edicao=64&materia=590.

Vargas, João Costa, and Jaime Amparo Alves. 2010. "Geographies of death: An intersectional analysis of police lethality and the racialized regimes of citizenship in São Paulo." *Ethnic and Racial Studies* 33/4: 611–636.

Vaz, Sérgio. 2006. "Cooperifa, uma história de amor à periferia." *Revista Fórum*. http://
www.revistaforum.com.br/conteudo/detalhe_materia.php?codMateria=7696/
(accessed 5/11/12).

Veja Online. 2001. "Diário da periferia." November 13. http://veja.abril.com.
br/131102/p_146.html.

Vianna, Hermano. 1999. *The mystery of samba: Popular music and national identity in
Brazil*. Chapel Hill: University of North Carolina Press.

Wade, Peter. 2009. *Race and sex in Latin America*. London: Pluto.

———. 2002. *Race, nature and culture: An anthropological approach*. London: Pluto.

———. 2000. *Music, race, and nation: Música tropical in Colombia*. Chicago: University of Chicago Press.

Walser, Robert. 1994. "Rhythm, rhyme and rhetoric in the music of Public Enemy."
Ethnomusicology 39: 193–217.

Weller, Wivian, and Marco Aurélio Paz Tella. 2011. "Hip-hop in São Paulo: Identity,
community formation, and social action." In Idelber Avelar and Christopher Dunn,
eds., *Brazilian popular music and citizenship*, 188–204. Durham: Duke University
Press.

Whiteley, Sheila, Andy Bennett, and Stan Hawkins, eds. 2005. *Music, space and place:
Popular music and cultural identity*. Aldershot, UK: Ashgate.

Wiehl, Lis. 2002. "Sounding Negro in the courtroom." *Harvard Negro Letter Law Journal* 18: 185–210.

Willeman, Estela Martini, and Guiomar Rodrigues de Lima. 2010. "O preconceito e a
discriminação racial nas religiões de matriz africana no Brasil." *Revista Uniabeu* 3/5:
70–94.

Williams-Jones, Pearl. 1975. "Afro-American gospel music: A crystallization of the
Negro aesthetic." *Ethnomusicology* 19/3: 373–385.

Winant, Howard. 2001. *The world is a ghetto: Race and democracy since World War II*.
New York: Perseus.

Wong, Deborah. 2000. "The Asian American body in performance." In Ronald Radano
and Philip Bohlman, eds., *Music and the racial imagination*, 57–94. Chicago: University of Chicago Press.

Yong, Amos, and Estrelda Alexander, eds. 2011. *Afro-Pentecostalism: Black Pentecostal
and charismatic Christianity in history and culture*. New York: NYU Press.

INDEX

Aborigines, 20
Abreu, Fernanda, 123
Accents (Brazilian), 87–91
Adam, 93–94
Adams, Yolanda, 132
Adimilson, 65, 86
Advertising, 15
Affirmative action, race and, 176
Africans: in Bible, 160, 163, 165, 172, 173,
    177, 186; in Bible, Isabêh on, 172; in Bra-
    zil, heritage of, 6; samba and ancestry
    of, 108–9, 115–16; vocal rhythm of, 109;
    voice and ancestry of, 137, 143
Afrobrás, 173
Afro-Brazilians: churches, 165–74; culture
    of, 6; media and, 6
AIDS, 33
Alerta Vermelha, 89
Alex, 32
Aliados de Cristo (Allies in Christ), 64–65,
    67
Aliança de Negras e Negros Evangélicos do
    Brasil, 177
Alibi, 34
Allen, Lara, 183
Allen, Rance, 1–2
Allies in Christ. See Aliados de Cristo
Alpiste, DJ, 31, 33–34, 89, 94
Alternativa C, 34
Ancestry: of African and samba, 108–9,
    115–16; of Africans and voice, 137, 143;
    black identity and Brazilian, 168–69,
    178–80
Andalusia, 182–83
Anderson, 89, 94
Anderson, Mark, 178
The Anointing, 56–57, 155, 158

Antiessentialism: in gospel rap, 81–87; in
    gospel samba, 127–29
Antiracist activism, 4–5
Ao Cubo, 34
Apartheid, 183
Apocalipse 16, 34
"Aquarela do Brasil," 121
Armenian singers, 20
Artists, 26
Asfalto (lower-middle and working class),
    14
Assembléia de Deus (Assemblies of God),
    8
Assemblies of God. See Assembléia de
    Deus
Atalaia, Lito, 34, 161–62, 163
Atlanta Gospel Choir, 132
Atos II, 50
Atualidade Negra (Black Reality), 32
Avenida Presidente Vargas, 122
Azusa church, 145

Back Spin, 30
Bailes nostalgia (nostalgia dances), 30
Bailes soul (soul dances), 30
Balbino, Jessica, 78
Banda Azusa, 16
Banda Rara, 49
Barroso, Ary, 121
Bars, 71
Beat-boxing, 85
Beat Street, 30
Beauty, perception of, 3–4
Beloved Amada. See "Periferia Amada"
Belting (singing technique), 134; feeling of,
    139; science of, 138
Ben, Jorge, 30, 48

ABOUT THE AUTHOR

John Burdick is Professor of Anthropology at Syracuse University. He is the author of *Legacies of Liberation* (2004), *Blessed Anastácia* (1998), *Looking for God in Brazil* (1993), and numerous articles about religion, race, and social movements in Brazil.